Clown Prince

of

Hollywood

ALSO BY BOB THOMAS

BIOGRAPHY

King Cohn
Thalberg
Selznick
Winchell
Marlon: Portrait of the Rebel as an Artist
Walt Disney: An American Original
Bud & Lou: The Abbott and Costello Story
The One and Only Bing
Joan Crawford
Golden Boy: The Untold Story of William Holden
Astaire: The Man, The Dancer
I Got Rhythm: The Ethel Merman Story
Liberace

GENERAL

If I Knew Then (with Debbie Reynolds)
The Art of Animation
The Massie Case (with Peter Packer)
The Secret Boss of California (with Arthur H. Samish)
The Heart of Hollywood
Howard, The Amazing Mr. Hughes (with Noah Dietrich)
The Road to Hollywood (with Bob Hope)
Reflections in Two Worlds (with Ricardo Montalban)

FICTION

The Flesh Merchants
Weekend 33

FOR CHILDREN

Walt Disney: Magician of the Movies
Donna DeVarona: Gold Medal Winner

ANTHOLOGY

Directors in Action

Clown Prince

of

Hollywood

*The Antic Life and Times
of Jack L. Warner*

BOB THOMAS

McGRAW-HILL PUBLISHING COMPANY
New York   St. Louis   San Francisco
Toronto   Hamburg   Mexico

1 2 3 4 5 6 7 8 9 DOC DOC 9 5 4 3 2 1 0

ISBN 0-07-064259-1

Library of Congress Cataloging-in-Publication Data

Thomas, Bob, 1922–
   Clown prince of Hollywood : the antic life and times of Jack L.
Warner / by Bob Thomas.
      p.   cm.
   Includes bibliographical references
   ISBN 0-07-064259-1
1. Warner, Jack L., 1892–1978.   2. Motion picture producers and
directors—United States—Biography.   I. Title.
PN1998.3.W37T45   1990
791.43'0232'092—dc20
[B]   90-5449
                                                                       CIP

Book design by Eve Kirch

*To Patricia
who insisted I tell this story*

Contents

Contents

Acknowledgments

I entered Warner Bros. studio for the first time on March 4, 1933, the day that Franklin Roosevelt was inaugurated President. My father, George H. Thomas, who was publicity director of Warner Bros.–First National, took my brother Frank and me for a Saturday outing at the Burbank lot, and we visited the set where *Gold Diggers of 1933* was being filmed. I watched with juvenile fascination as Mervyn Leroy directed Dick Powell, Warren William and Guy Kibbee in a scene in a gentlemen's club. Later, all of us posed for a photograph outside the stage.

After I became Hollywood correspondent for the Associated Press in December 1944, I made regular visits to Warner Bros., and the practice still continues. So this biography of Jack L. Warner comes not only from the sources noted below and in the bibliography, but from decades of hearing tales from my father and from Humphrey Bogart, Errol Flynn, James Cagney, Joan Blondell, Mark Hellinger, Jerry Wald, Al Jolson, and many others.

I am grateful to all of the people who have come to the aid of this biography. Foremost—after the object of the dedication—is my editor, Anne Sweeney, who had faith in the project when others did not. Ernest Lehman was especially kind in sharing his journal of the making of *Who's Afraid of Virginia Woolf?* President Ronald Reagan took time out from his own literary endeavor to reminisce about his old boss.

Special thanks to Mark Weinstein and Paula Franklin of the Reagan staff; Leith Adams and Ned Comstock of the Warner Bros. archives at the University of Southern California; Brigitte Kuepper of the UCLA Theater Arts Library; the staff of the Academy of Motion Picture Arts and Sciences library; Deac Rossell of the Directors Guild of America Special Projects; Martha Clonis of the *Youngstown Vindicator*, Ohio; the library of the *London Free Press*, Ontario; Sukie Pett of the Associated Press news library; researchers Janet Thomas and Kristin Schwellenbach.

Any biography of recent figures is dependent on the testimony of those who knew them. In writing about Jack Warner, I enlisted the memories of those who admired or despised him, were amused or appalled by him, and one or two who were neutral. My gratitude to all of them:

Lauren Bacall	Irving Fein	Jack Lemmon
Hugh Benson	Mel Ferrer	Mort Likter
Max Bercutt	Joel Freeman	George Lucas
Milton Berle	Ivan Goff	Sidney Lumet
Ray Bradbury	Samuel Goldwyn, Jr.	Delbert Mann
George Burns	Merv Griffin	Les Martinson
Pat Buttrum	Bill Hendricks	Virginia Mayo
Sammy Cahn	Paul Henreid	Dina Merrill
Robert Cohn	Charlton Heston	Barry Mirkin
Sean Connery	Jean Howard	Dennis Morgan
Warren Cowan	Peter Hunt	Patricia Neal
Owen Crump	Joe Hyams	William T. Orr
Bette Davis	Chuck Jones	Arthur Park
Sammy Davis, Jr.	Hal Kanter	Gordon Parks
Olivia de Havilland	Alan King	Jackie Parks
Kirk Douglas	Howard W. Koch	Gregory Peck
Stan Dragoti	Bill Latham	Ronald Reagan
Blake Edwards	Richard Lederer	Gottfried Reinhardt
Rudi Fehr	Ernest Lehman	Cliff Robertson

Acknowledgments

Jack Rose
Bill Schaefer
Mel Shavelson
George Sherman
Art Silver
Alexis Smith
Robert Solo
Robert Stack

Gary Stevens
George Stevens, Jr.
James Stewart
Daniel Taradash
Jack Valenti
Hubert Voight
Michael Wayne

Michael Wilson
Shelley Winters
Robert Wise
Loretta Young
Richard Zanuck
Efrem Zimbalist, Jr.
Fred Zinnemann

Burbank, July 1967

THE SAN FERNANDO VALLEY burns, in July, with the persistent, all-enveloping heat of a pottery oven. It is a time when the residents spend as many afternoons as possible in the azure pools that dot the valley like a scattering of beach glass. On just such a day in 1967, two symbolic events of Hollywood history occurred—footnotes, perhaps. Both went unheralded and scarcely noticed. The participants were two men separated by two generations and a vast difference in their cultures.

The heat didn't bother George Lucas, who had spent his formative years in the San Joaquin Valley where 100-degree summer days were the norm. On this day Lucas, who was twenty-two years old, hardly noticed the weather. He was too excited about starting a new assignment. As winner of a Sam Warner Scholarship at the University of Southern California film school, he would be able to study all aspects of filmmaking at the Warner Bros. studio for six months. And he would be paid for it: $100 a week.

Lucas wore chinos, sneakers, a plaid shirt and—his one concession to convention—a tie. In keeping with the times, his hair was shoulder-length, and he was growing a brave little goatee. Slim and diffident, he was a deceptively unimposing figure.

"I was self-assured; I felt good about myself," he recalls. "My short films had won a lot of awards, and I knew that I could make movies."

Lucas reported to the production office in a Spanish-style building on the edge of the studio, and he was assigned to a young studio manager for a tour of the lot. It was like a ghost town. Production had come almost to a halt as the studio awaited the arrival of the new Seven Arts owners. Few people were in sight as the two young men wandered the studio streets, peered inside the dark stages, visited the departments presided over by single caretakers. Lucas was especially interested in the animation department, which was occupied only by the executive, Bill Hendricks. He showed the young man how the cameras worked and where the animators created drawings of Bugs Bunny and Porky Pig when the studio was in full gear.

The tour continued to the back lot and encountered the only feature that was filming at the studio, *Finian's Rainbow*. Lucas watched a musical number with Fred Astaire, Petula Clark, Tommy Steele and Keenan Wynn tossing fake coins around a money tree.

"This is the director, Francis Coppola," said Lucas' guide by way of introduction.

"Hi," said Coppola. He was only twenty-seven, but his bushy beard and stout figure made him seem older. He shook his visitor's hand and returned to his duties.

Over lunch in the empty commissary, Lucas admitted that he had no notion of what he wanted to do in his six-month apprenticeship. "Why don't you watch production for a week or two and get your bearings," the young studio manager suggested.

Lucas returned to the *Finian's Rainbow* set after lunch and stood in the background to watch Coppola at work. When he became bored with the endless repetition, Lucas wandered the dusty western and New York streets, remembering the movies he had seen as a kid in Modesto and as a film student at USC. He could imagine the time when these streets, now baking silently in the oppressive sun, were alive with cowboys and gangsters.

Back on the *Finian's Rainbow* set, Lucas spoke with the second assistant director, Howard Kazanjian, a fellow member of the film fraternity at USC. Another set worker approached and remarked, "You know what today is? It's Jack Warner's last day as boss of the studio. Think of that!"

"Who would ever have thought," said Jack Warner with a wide smile, "that a butcher boy from Youngstown, Ohio, would end up with twenty-four million smackers in his pocket?"

Warner was holding forth, as he had a few thousand times before, in the executive dining room of Warner Bros. studio, his audience a group of men over whom he had wielded absolute control. But the number around the lunch table had diminished. Walter MacEwen, his chief assistant, was there, and Bill Orr, Warner's son-in-law and a producer, and Max Bercutt, the publicity head, and a few more. Other chairs were vacant, their occupants having found other jobs as Warner Bros. drifted into its new identity as Warner Bros.–Seven Arts.

Jack Warner had sold his holdings eight months before, and he figured he would collect $24 million after capital gains taxes. If he had any misgivings about loosening his hold on the enterprise he and his brothers had started fifty-five years earlier, he gave no evidence. He presided over the luncheon with the same stale jokes at which his listeners laughed indulgently. He was seventy-four, but he glowed with good health and youthful exuberance.

After lunch, Warner retired to the adjoining trophy room which served as a second office. There he signed a few urgent letters prepared by his secretary, Bill Schaefer. The room was jammed with Oscars, foreign decorations, gold plaques, silver cups, awards of every kind. Back in his office in the executive building, Warner conducted more business, talked on the telephone. For once there were no rushes to see, no contracts to sign.

"I think I'll take a walk," Warner said, and he took along his social secretary, a glib Englishman, Richard Gully. They strolled past the star dressing rooms, the stages, the shops, all of it the princedom that Warner had ruled since the First National merger in 1928. Gully talked steadily, while Warner was uncharacteristically silent.

"Well, Colonel," said Gully, "at least you got a good price for it."

"Yeah," Warner said reflectively. "But today I'm Jack L. Warner. Tomorrow I'll just be another rich Jew."

Jack Warner had seen it all: nickelodeons, silent features, sound (which he and his brothers introduced), musicals, gangster movies, television, 3-D, wide-screen, the new frankness (which he helped bring about), million-dollar star salaries. His stewardship spanned forty-five years, longer by far than any other studio head. During all that time, he was absolute monarch of a motion picture factory, first on Sunset Boulevard and then in the San Fernando Valley flatland, that poured forth some of the most entertaining and innovative, as well as the most banal, of American movies.

His workers regarded him with fear, ridicule and, occasionally, respect. Fear, because he was merciless in his firings. Ridicule for his unending, fruitless attempts at humor. Respect for his showmanly sense and quick judgments. "If I'm right fifty-one percent of the time, I'm ahead of the game," he often said.

Some of those who fought with Warner during his lifetime have now mellowed in their judgment of him. Some have not.

Bette Davis, actress: "In some ways, Jack was a very moral man. He never engaged in any of the dressing-room nonsense. Did you know he never allowed women employees to wear pants? Skirts only. He had another fascinating phobia: He never allowed any chest hair to show on the actors. . . .

"Warner was wonderful to me after B.D. was born. We became father and child, no question about it. He told me I didn't have to come back to work until I really felt like it. He was a thoughtful man. Not many nice things were said about him. All they ever said about Jack was about his bad language at meetings. His language was something."

Gregory Peck, actor: "I kinda liked Jack. He was a gallant old boy. All of those old guys attacked their jobs with relish and gusto. Sure, they made a lot of potboilers, but also they could come up with something truly remarkable."

Billy Wilder, director-writer: "Warner would have given everything he owned to be a stand-up comedian. He tried it all the time, and the results were pathetic."

Gottfried Reinhardt, producer-writer: "What confused the matter was that he always played the clown. He had a trick of juggling the cigar, and he always seemed amiable. He was not amiable at all. He was a very tough son of a bitch. Among the moguls I have known in Hollywood, he was by far the most dangerous. Tricky as hell."

Olivia de Havilland, actress: "Was he a clown or clever man or what? He was all those things. I think he was quite vulnerable. He was, you know, very mistrustful of actors; he just mistrusted them. He was unreasonable; he was tyrannical. I was bitter because he was a father figure and autocratic as the head of the studio. . . .

"I was very well disposed toward him. That's what made it so hard for me: that he didn't seem to understand my goodwill, and that whatever I wanted would actually make me more valuable for him and make him more money."

Max Bercutt, publicist: "He was a son of a bitch to me, but he was a *consistent* son of a bitch. He wasn't nice to people. He hated actors, directors, writers."

Jack Valenti, producers' head: "I thought the clown act was really a mask. He seemed like a man going to a masquerade party, and he wore a different disguise. His was the clown, the jester, the jokester. I thought that Jack Warner, beneath all that, was a shrewd manager, a fellow who was playing poker with you and trying to find a way to put your guard down.

"As a political animal, I admired what I saw even as I was being frustrated by it. In a corner of my mind, I thought, 'This shrewd son of a bitch is playing me like Toscanini, for God's sake. I can hear the strings, he's telling the basses and the percussion what to do, and I'm dancing to his tune.' I thought how marvelous, how wonderful."

Blake Edwards, director-writer: "I found him to be treacherous. He'd say something to your face and then turn around and double-cross you. Harry Cohn was mean and nasty, but if he told you something, you could count on it."

John Huston, director-writer (in his autobiography, *An Open Book*): "There was a funny, childlike candor to the man. He was never guarded in anything he said; words seemed to escape from him unthinkingly. He was accused—and there may be something to it—of playing the fool. He was anything but pretentious and seemed to be constantly laughing at himself, but he was certainly a canny, astute individual when it came to his own interests."

James Stewart, actor: "I thought he was fine, in the same way that Louis B. Mayer and Darryl Zanuck were fine. They loved the business, and they had a tremendous capacity of sort of knowing what would be right for the audience at a particular time."

Robert Solo, producer: "All those dreadful jokes were simply a device to keep people at a distance. He didn't want anyone to get close to him."

Hugh Benson, producer: "The clowning was a defense mechanism. It was a cover-up for his inability to hold an intelligent conversation. I think he doted on his reputation as Jack Warner who told bad jokes."

Ronald Reagan, former actor and former President of the United States: "I don't think the jokes were a [defense mechanism]. I think he just enjoyed it. I understand that somewhere in the past he had been in vaudeville. I remember that when he used to speak at some kind of gathering, he loved to start and then say, 'Oh,' and take the script and throw it over his shoulder. Then he'd go into his stories."

Lauren Bacall, actress: "I thought he was a man who was totally uncomfortable, almost all the time. I think that was the reason for the bad jokes: he felt inadequate, and he *was* inadequate. He was not a man you could talk to. He always wanted to boil everything down to the lowest common denominator.

"When I went on suspension so many times, I always wanted to talk to him, not to anyone else. I would go in his office, and he was so uneasy. He'd take me to the window and look out at all the sound stages, and he'd say, 'Would I have all this if I didn't know what I was doing?' He never cared anything about protecting talent. Talent was the enemy to him."

Virginia Mayo, actress: "I think he was afraid of actresses. I never met him until I had been under contract to the studio for a while. Then I saw him on a studio street and he said, 'I've seen you in the movies!' That was all. He walked away."

Loretta Young, actress: "He was always full of vim and vigor, always the big boss. He loved to show off and preside over lunch in his private dining room. Actors weren't allowed, of course. He was attractive, had a great smile, and his jokes were always terrible."

Dennis Morgan, actor: "I don't think that anybody could honestly say that they loved him. You could say that he was a good picture maker; in other words, he could get pictures made and on the screen—and in a hurry."

Jackie Park, Warner's mistress: "He could be equally charming or cruel. If he could control you, he would destroy you. He was cruel to his executives, making them stay at their desks until eight at night, even though he didn't need them. His formula was: control and humiliate. But in so doing, he humiliated himself.

"The only one he couldn't control was Ann, his wife. He was afraid of her."

Julius Epstein, writer: "I think the best definition of Jack Warner was by [producer] David Weisbart—'affable arrogance.' When he no longer had the studio, the arrogance was gone."

Chapter 1

Krasnashiltz to Youngstown

STORYTELLER THAT HE WAS, Jack Warner in later years romanticized, edited and generally obscured his early life. He did, after all, traffic in illusion, and family stories could always be improved, just like a movie script. Here was a man who could—and did—publish an autobiography without any mention of his first wife or his only son.

He was born in London, Ontario, in 1892, but the date and month were never ascertained. That is understandable, since the Warner family had been on the move in a desperate, unavailing search for prosperity. The arrival of the ninth child of Benjamin and Pearl Warner was not an exceptional event. Later Jack Warner proclaimed his birthday to be August 2. The date proved convenient; he could celebrate his birth in continental style during his annual summer vacation at his Cap d'Antibes villa.

The family originated in czarist Poland, near the border of Germany. In 1857 in the village of Krasnashiltz, Benjamin Warner (the original family name has remained obscure) was born into a hostile world. The night-riding of cossacks, the burning of houses, the raping of women were part of life's burdens for the Jews of the *stetl*. They were not allowed an education, so their learning came in secret from the village rabbi. Unschooled, they could support their families only by menial work or by developing homely skills. Benjamin mended shoes.

He was a tall, powerfully built young man who attracted the eyes of the maidens of Krasnashiltz. He chose Pearl Eichelbaum, a lovely girl with a full figure, one who seemed strong enough to bear his children—there would be twelve. Ben and Pearl were both nineteen years old when they married in 1876. Their first child, Cecilia, died when she was four. Anna was born in 1879, and Hirsch (later Harry) in 1881.

Prompted by his growing family and the ever-present threat of pogroms, Ben gazed toward America. His dream was furthered by letters from a fellow villager named Waleski, who wrote glowingly of riches to be found in the New Land. If a no-good like Waleski could find his fortune in a place called Baltimore, so could he, Ben decided. He left his young family and departed for America in 1883.

The passage was a misery—the immigrants were jammed together for twenty days in a sunless hold that stank of cattle dung. New York wasn't much better; it was noisy and dirty and hostile to a twenty-six-year-old who spoke no English. Baltimore was also clamorous and frightening. Ben searched ten days before finding the shame-faced Waleski. His letters of golden times in the United States had been pure fiction. Waleski was living in poverty reminiscent of Krasnashiltz. He invited Ben to share his heatless basement and found the newcomer piecework in shoe repair shops.

"Shoes Repaired While You Wait"

That was the sign Ben erected on the tiny cobbler's shop he opened at Pratt and Light Streets a few months after his arrival in Baltimore. It was a novel approach to shoe repair, the first instance of Warner showmanship in the New Land. Soon Ben was earning three dollars a day, and within a year he was able to send for Pearl and their two children.

The family grew, babies arriving at regular two-year intervals: Abraham in 1884, followed by Henry, Samuel, Rose and Fannie.

The children were put to work early, helping in the shop or performing chores in the neighborhood.

Ben Warner was a restless entrepreneur. "This is the land of opportunity," he kept telling his doubting wife. A friend wrote from Virginia that crews building a new railroad were a prime market for kitchen goods, hardware and other items. Ben acquired some stock and traveled by horse and wagon to the railroad camps. Business was so good that he hired Pearl's two brothers, newly arrived from Poland. One of them was honest; the other vanished with the week's receipts.

The next escape from shoe repair sent Ben Warner to Canada. Another friend had persuaded Ben of the fortune to be made by trading tin wares to trappers for fur pelts. For months Ben hauled his rattling wagon from one outpost to another, sending the furs he bartered to his partner in Montreal and his paltry earnings to the family in Baltimore. Finally he could stand their absence no longer. He found a large, run-down house in London, Ontario, and sent for Pearl and the children.

During the harsh Canadian winter, Fannie Warner became ill and died. It was a numbing blow to Ben and Pearl, who had lost little Henry the winter before. The only Jews in a strange city, they had never felt more isolated. Then their neighbors began to call, laden with bread and pies and kettles of soup. They arranged for Fannie's burial, and they comforted the grieving parents and their children at the graveside.

Another son was born in London, and he was named Jacob. Later he would call himself Jack L. Warner; the L stood for Leonard, he explained, but it appears to have been invented, along with the rest of the name. A fifth Warner son, David, arrived in Hamilton, Ontario, the following year. After two years of fur collecting, Ben decided to visit his partner in Montreal. The partner had fled, and the boxes in the warehouse contained—shredded paper. Back to shoe repair in Baltimore.

Harry Warner, the eldest son, was a fervent believer in the American Dream, and he was ashamed of his father's failures. At fourteen he was eager to make his own mark in the world. Passionate about politics, he boarded a train for Ohio, ostensibly to hear the Republican candidate for President, William McKinley. En route, he conversed with a man who told him of the growing colony of Poles in Youngstown, Ohio, where the mills were hiring.

Harry found Youngstown to be a restless town eagerly becoming a city, its new buildings already wrapped in a patina of soot and dust from the nearby mills and factories. He rented a cubbyhole on a busy street and opened a shoe repair shop with equipment sent by his father.

Harry realized the publicity value of a fresh-faced boy standing behind a window and mending shoes and boots under the sign "The Baltimore Shoe Repair Shop—Repaired While You Wait." Passersby could not help noticing him, and his business flourished.

"Young man, does that sign mean what it says?" a sedately dressed man with a self-confident air asked Harry one morning.

"Indeed it does, sir," Harry replied. "Have a seat, give me your shoes, and we'll have them ready for you in a jiffy."

Before the gentleman had read three pages of the *Youngstown Vindicator*, Harry had reheeled and shined his shoes. "I'm impressed," said the customer. "Perhaps I can be of assistance some day. Here's my card." He was Henry Garlick, president of the First National Bank and a future ally in the business ventures of the Warner family.

Ben Warner needed little persuasion to join Harry in Youngstown. Soon Pearl and the rest of the Warner children came too. All nine crammed into the space behind the Baltimore Shoe Repair Shop, and for the rest of his life Jack Warner was haunted by the sickening smell of newly tanned leather. Two more children were added to the cramped quarters: Sadie in 1895, and Milton a year after.

Competing cobblers seized the repair-while-you-wait formula, and Ben countered declining business by offering a few groceries at the rear of the shop. He finally saw an escape from the shoe repair business he detested, and with the help of Harry's newfound friend at the First National Bank, he opened a grocery store and meat counter on East Federal Street.

Housing for a family of cleven was a constant problem. For a time they lived above the grocery store, but that was as cramped as the rear of the shoe shop. They lived in small places, first on Walnut Street, then on Belmont Avenue, before finally locating a ramshackle house on West Federal Street, with a privy and water pump in the backyard. Every Saturday night the older boys were assigned to haul buckets of water to the back porch where Pearl Warner ritualistically bathed each of the nine children in a small, lead-lined tub.

Ben Warner discovered why the house had been available: it was scheduled to be demolished. Wreckers descended, removing one room at a time, while Pearl and Ben desperately sought new quarters. The Federal Street house was almost leveled when Pearl rented a house by claiming she had only three children. Several months later when the landlord discovered the size of the family, they were evicted. At last they moved into a permanent home on West Elm Street.

The solidarity of the Warner family, instinctual from the ghetto centuries and further inbred from the years of bare-bone survival in the New Land, was viewed by neighbors with awe and admiration. All earnings of family members were contributed to a common treasury. Everyone worked—at home, in the store, or at jobs or enterprises.

There was a small Jewish community in Youngstown, and the Warners joined the temple but were not notably devout. Ben maintained a kosher section of his meat counter, though he recognized that his main customers were *goyim*. He observed the high holidays and enrolled his sons in Hebrew school.

Jack was a poor student. He enjoyed recounting the story of how the long-bearded rabbi repeatedly berated him for failing to understand Hebrew. Whenever the boy made an error, he received a jab in the leg with a hat pin.

"You are stupid," the rabbi ranted. "If I give you the pin enough, perhaps you won't be so stupid. Your brother Harry speaks Hebrew like English, and he does not need the pin."

Jack continued making mistakes and getting jabbed in the leg. Finally he warned that he would yank the rabbi's beard if the jabbing didn't stop. The rabbi jabbed; Jack yanked. It was the end of Jack's Hebrew studies.

At the age of seven, Jack was placed in charge of grocery deliveries. Every morning at four o'clock, he rose to load the wagon and hitch up the family horse, named Bob. Jack finished deliveries in time to rush to school, and then hurried back in the afternoon to resume his work.

There was time for pleasure, too. All the boys had a dramatic flair, and they joined a theater club that met in the basement of a downtown store. They imitated the popular performer Thomas E. Shea and duplicated the attractions at the Opera House to the acclaim of friends and family. Jack, who had a remarkable soprano voice, sang in school productions of *The Mikado* and *HMS Pinafore*.

With the grocery store thriving and the older boys contributing their earnings—minus fifty cents for expense money—to the family coffers, the Warners at last could celebrate their emergence from poverty. The occasion was the marriage of Anna to a local boy, Dave Robbins. For a week, Pearl Warner and volunteer friends prepared delicacies, both Polish and American. The Ozersky bakery was taken over to produce the wedding cake. On the wedding day, all the taxis in Youngstown were commandeered to drive the family and guests to Diamond Hall, the site of the wedding.

It was the event of the year in Polish-Jewish society. Normally unsmiling, Ben Warner warmly greeted the guests, many of them customers of the grocery. Pearl wept softly as her daughter entered a life of her own. But she delighted in seeing her stalwart sons, handsome in their rented tuxedos. Harry in particular looked dashing as he glided over the floor with a succession of female guests. He was proud, even vain, about his dancing, and he and his sister Rose displayed the skill that won them first prize in every waltz contest in Youngstown.

With typical acumen, Harry stretched his fifty-cent allowance on his dancing dates. Unlike his brothers, who blew the money in a day, Harry saved his allowance until the end of the week. He purposely dated girls who lived within walking distance of his house and downtown. Thus he wasted none of his fifty cents on carfare.

Harry was the go-getter of the family, bristling with ideas to make money. "If you buy in large quantities, you can undersell the other stores," Harry lectured his father. Ben was unconvinced, but he allowed Harry to test his theory by ordering a large supply of pork loins. Not enough customers wanted pork loins, and the meat had to be sold at a loss before it spoiled.

Next, Harry joined with Abe in a bicycle repair shop. Abe had been a star quarterback in high school—he always dropped out at the end of football season—and he had won a few bicycle races. Harry and Abe decided to capitalize on the cycling craze by renting bicycles at fifteen cents an hour. Their business thrived until competing cycle shops opened in Youngstown.

For a time Harry and Abe operated a bowling alley on South Champion Street, and Sam and Jack helped out by setting pins. Like the bicycle shop, the bowling alley suffered from competition, and it closed.

Harry decided that his future lay in selling. One of Ben's meat suppliers admired the young man's persuasive manner and offered Harry a sales job with the company. Harry traveled throughout Ohio and Pennsylvania, and his earnest manner convinced butchers and delicatessen owners to buy more lamb chops and salami than they really needed. Later he sold apple vinegar with equal success, perfecting a style that would later persuade bankers to invest millions in Warner enterprises.

With his athletic build, Abe qualified for work in the steel mill. On his first day at the factory, he saw a worker crushed to death by falling metal. On the second day, a worker's leg was smashed. When Abe told his mother about the incidents, she forbade him to return to the mill. "You may be next," she warned.

Abe realized his future was in selling, not in pouring steel. He took a job in Chicago with Swift, selling the soap that was a by-product of the meat business. After weeks of poor sales, he concocted a scheme: he would raise the price of soap and offer retailers a free box for every five they sold. He quickly became the company's ace salesman, and he claimed to have invented the practice that became widespread in many industries.

Sam was the hustler among the brothers. At twelve he was working the street fairs with a gambling game that involved spinning an arrow for the chance to win a cigar. Since the chances cost a nickel, and Sam paid a penny for the cigars, profit was certain. When Youngstown cops demanded a cut of his take, Sam gave up the enterprise.

He next barked for an egg-dodging attraction at a carnival and managed a snake eater. When ice-cream cones became popular, Sam and a friend bought a cone-making machine and set up a stand outside a penny arcade. Sam lost interest in such humdrum work. He tried boxing but ended up with only a broken nose to show for his efforts. Then he took a job as a fireman on the Erie Railroad. As he hurled coal into the roaring boiler oven, he mulled over opportunities to make a lot of money. Something that didn't require much capital or physical labor. Something the public was eager to buy and would not tire of.

Jack was the son who worried Ben Warner the most. He was a pesky kid, always defying authority, as when he pulled the rabbi's beard. Jack was a poor student, and his education ended after the fourth grade. That didn't concern his father; a full-time hand was always welcome at the grocery store. But Jack seemed to spend his off-work hours with a bad crowd. He became a member of the Westlake Crossing gang, a group of ragtag teenagers who waged wars on rival gangs. After a few rumbles with rocks and fists, Jack resigned. Brave he was not. He turned to pickup games of baseball and football instead.

At home, Jack realized that his youth penalized him in competition with his older brothers for his parents' attention. His only tactic lay in playing the clown. No matter that his pranks and jokes and funny songs drew groans and an occasional box on the ear. He persisted. And for better or worse, he was noticed.

For Harry's nineteenth birthday, his mother collected her savings and presented him with a used upright piano, the kind she had seen in the parlors of her better-off friends. Harry was a smooth dancer, but he was tone-deaf, so Rose became the Warner pianist. When she played for the family in the evening, Jack always joined in by singing a chorus, followed by a dance and a few jokes. His audience was less than enthusiastic, and he later claimed that his mother once offered him twenty-five cents just to be quiet.

Jack's soprano voice had a pure, sweet tone, and when his voice began changing, his song-selling compensated for the loss of tone. With Rose as his accompanist, he became a popular figure at weddings, lodge meetings, sewing bees, benefits and funerals. Except at the funerals, he interspersed his songs with the jokes and wisecracks gleaned from vaudeville stages and pulp magazines. Because Italian singers were then popular, Jack adopted the name of Leon Zuardo for his Youngstown appearances. Leon Zuardo had a brief career, but he reappeared twenty years later as a radio personality.

Jack's formal debut into show business came when two of his father's friends, Christie Dibble and Spitz Renner, hired him to sing with the song slides at their downtown nickelodeon, the Dome. Jack was thrilled with the opportunity and especially the salary, eighteen dollars a week. Rose played while he trilled the song hits of the day; happily he was a quick study and could learn a song on one hearing.

Next came an offer to sing at Youngstown Opera House on Sunday nights for a fee of ten dollars. There he was seen by Gus Sun, the penny-squeezing operator of vaudeville theaters throughout the Midwest. "Gus Sun time" was notorious among vaudevillians for its low pay, decrepit theaters and slave contracts. Sun admired young Warner's style and suggested that he team up with another performer in a song-and-dance act that would include a blackface number.

Jack leaped at the opportunity, enlisting another Youngstown entertainer, Pike Rickard. They choreographed some simple dance steps and a few songs. Jack realized that the lame jokes he told to Youngstown audiences were not good enough on the Gus Sun time. He invested a dollar in Madison's Budget, a pamphlet with bootlegged jokes and monologues performed by vaudeville stars. "If they're good enough for Willie Collier, they're good enough for me," he told his partner.

The two youths toured the Gus Sun theaters in futile search of the magic of show business. The boys' rewards were listless audiences, broken-down hotels and spartan meals. Jack returned home disconsolately after the first tour. He sought advice from the brother who was his closest confidant, Sam.

"Don't go back," Sam argued, reasoning that Jack had learned all he could and that his voice would soon be changing.

"Get out front where they pay the actors," Sam declared. "That's where the money is."

Chapter 2

Beginnings of the Dynasty

SAM WARNER LEFT THE RAILROAD in 1903 for a job that better suited his talents: barker for a penny arcade in Cedar Point, Ohio. There he became fascinated with the kinetoscope, Thomas Edison's invention that flashed moving images on a white screen. Sam wanted to know more about the machine, and he found work as a projectionist at a nickelodeon on Central Square in Youngstown. The owner, George Olenhauser, was patient with Sam's curiosity and showed him how to repair and reassemble the kinetoscope when it broke down.

Nickelodeons were opening in stores and tents all over the Midwest, and Sam had his pick of jobs as a projectionist. He chose Hales Tours at White City Park in Chicago. It was an ingenious attraction in which patrons sat in railroad cars and watched out the windows as scenes of Yosemite, the Grand Canyon and Niagara Falls were flashed on the screen outside. Boys bounced on planks placed under the cars, helping to create the illusion of traveling through the country's wonders.

When Sam learned that Hales Tours would open at the Idora Amusement Park in Youngstown, he applied for the job as projectionist. He admitted the entire family on passes so that they could share his enthusiasm for the new medium of entertainment. Father Ben approved cautiously. Harry surveyed the hundreds of eager patrons and recognized the financial possibilities. Abe had already become entranced with movies during his soap-selling tours. In every new town, he patronized the nickelodeon and spent hours studying the images on the screen and the delighted response of the ticket buyers. As for Jack, he was enamored of anything connected with show business.

Sam loitered at a theatrical boardinghouse near Idora Park because he knew that the landlady's son owned a Model B kinetoscope. After winning her confidence, he learned that the son was broke and was willing to sell the Kinetoscope and all its gear, plus one movie, for a thousand dollars. Sam rushed home to tell his father about the rare opportunity.

Ben Warner, whose own early dreams of fortune had turned to dust, was swept up by his son's fervor. A family meeting was held at the dinner table; only the traveling Abe was absent. All agreed on the investment, and they began totaling their assets. The amount fell short of the thousand dollars, even with the pawning of Ben's gold watch. "There's only one thing left: Old Bob," Ben sighed. Borrowing on the family horse reached the goal, and Sam counted out the small bills that comprised the Warner savings and handed them over to the kinetoscope owner. Happily, the transaction included a print of *The Great Train Robbery*, the most popular attraction in the nation's nickelodeons.

"Let's see what we bought," Sam suggested. In the backyard of the Elm Street house he erected a black tent with a junkyard auto body for a stage. Neighbors were invited to sit on the lawn and watch the western melodrama, while Sam cranked the projector.

The first movie performance presented by the Warner brothers was less than a success. Images on the bedsheet were murky and dim, and the train moved at a snail's pace. Ben feared that he had again invested in a failed enterprise. But Sam conferred with his friend George Olenhauser, and together they repaired the projector's defects.

A carnival was opening in nearby Niles, and Sam proposed

showing *The Great Train Robbery* there. He scouted the main street and found a vacant store that seemed ideal. Harry and Abe took charge of converting the store into a movie house and tacked up fliers all over town. Sam ran the projector. Rose sold tickets and then hurried down the aisle to play piano, while Jack sang with the illustrated song slides.

"We're in business!" Sam exclaimed. "Three hundred bucks in one week!"

After the busy first week in Niles, no more customers came. The Warner traveling show moved on to Hubbard, Steubenville, Girard and Warren, exhausting the ticket-selling possibilities in each town within a week. They plunged into Pennsylvania, playing Sharon, Meadville and New Castle.

At each screening, Sam ran the film through the projector, letting it tumble into a barrel. Then he tediously rewound the footage for the next show. Fortunately, nobody dropped a match in the barrel and exploded the Warners' main asset. The endless screenings, frequent breaks and constant attrition of sprocket holes finally exhausted *The Great Train Robbery*. The Warner brothers returned to Youngstown.

"Where did you make the most money?" Harry asked with customary analysis.

"New Castle," Sam replied. "We coulda stayed three weeks except the film gave out on us."

"Then we should go back there and open a theater of our own," decreed Harry. "We need to get a change of pictures so the customers will come back. Don't worry about money. I've saved some cash, and I'll lend it to you."

Harry, Sam and Abe scouted New Castle and agreed that the expanding factory town could support a permanent movie house. They found a hall that could be converted into a theater, but it lacked seats. That was solved by an agreement with the local undertaker. The brothers rented his chairs at night and returned them for the next day's funerals. They borrowed ninety-nine chairs only; an audience of one hundred would have invited supervision by fire inspectors.

Sam and Dave Robbins, who had married Anna Warner, opened the Cascade Theater in New Castle in 1904. The building's exterior was impressive, with Byzantine arches left over from an earlier life as a penny arcade. The interior was as bleak as a storeroom. "What the hell," Sam figured, "the customers are gonna be sitting in the dark, anyway."

The New Castle factory workers flocked to the Cascade for escape from the squalor of their daily lives. The older brothers decided to join the enterprise full-time. Abe submitted his resignation to Armour, and Harry quit as salesman for the Lucas Pickle Company. Both came to New Castle, and Harry made regular trips to a Pittsburgh film supplier for new attractions to fill the Cascade's screen.

Jack was also needed in New Castle—to "chase" the customers between screenings on busy weekends. Every Friday afternoon, he and Rose boarded the trolley from Youngstown to New Castle. At the theater Rose played the off-key upright, while Jack sang the song hits of the day. He was fifteen years old, and his voice had not yet found its register. He had no trouble convincing the patrons to abandon their seats before the next show.

The Cascade Theater was so successful that the Warners opened another theater in New Castle, the Bijou. Despite the theaters' prosperity, Harry realized that he and his brothers had reached a dead end. As exhibitors of films, they were powerless, ever dependent on suppliers. "That's where the money is—distribution," he reasoned. He proposed selling the theaters and opening a theater "exchange" in Pittsburgh.

The Duquesne Amusement Supply Company, named for the Pittsburgh college and suburb, offered a new concept in the movie business. Theater owners could buy a film and exchange it among themselves, thus avoiding the expense and bother of hunting for product. Abe and Sam agreed to Harry's plan, and the three brothers opened headquarters in the Bakewell building in downtown Pittsburgh.

Harry dispatched Sam to New York to hunt for films. Sam learned that Marcus Loew, the theater magnate, bought films instead of renting, and he stored them in trunks. Sam paid $500 for three trunks and shipped them to Pittsburgh. The Warner brothers film exchange was in business.

Jack was devastated when his brothers moved away. With the family business shifting to far-off Pittsburgh, he would be distanced from Sam, the brother he idolized. Jack envied Sam's quicksilver mind, his devil-may-care approach to life and all its challenges. He longed to be with his dashing brother. He was tired of dipping slaughtered chickens into boiling cauldrons in the grocery basement and plucking the feathers. He hated the lingering stench. Girls shunned him because of it, and his interest in girls was quickening.

"Come and join us," Sam Warner suggested to his young brother. Jack was eager, but he knew his parents would object. In his later years Jack enjoyed telling the story of how he made up his mind—he decided to throw the cleaver at the butcher block. If it stuck, he would go. If it dropped to the floor, he would stay. It stuck.

Now the four brothers were joined in their lifelong partnership. Harry was unquestionably the leader, not merely by primogeniture but by his self-assumed role as the keeper of family morality. He remained a steadfast Jew, while his three brothers edged into the *goyim* world. A business enterprise, even one so freewheeling as the movies, Harry believed, could still be conducted without abusing the tenets of the Torah. With his lean, ascetic face, tight lips and severe nose, Harry looked the part of the God-fearing patriarch.

Abe deferred to his older brother in everything. Although he had been a hearty salesman with his soap customers, Abe was quiet and withdrawn amid the family. He had lost the confidence he'd had as a star athlete. His face had become fleshy, his hair thin, his body no longer hard and disciplined. He seemed willing to play a latent role with his more aggressive brothers.

Sam was totally unlike his two older brothers. He was quick and emotional, always ready to hatch an idea and pursue it, sometimes to impractical limits. With a strong jaw, thick hair and dancing eyes, he could charm the girls as well as potential clients. Everyone liked Sam. Jack adored him.

Jack adopted Sam's snappy dress, his clever line, his delight in the pleasures of life. But Jack was no carbon copy. He had his own style of wisecracking and joke-making that had exasperated his father. More than any of the brothers, Jack was entranced with the performing side of the entertainment business. Although he had detested the hardships of the Gus Sun tour, he had never felt more alive than when he faced audiences, no matter how indifferent they were.

Both Harry and Abe had married Jewish girls and had settled in the Pittsburgh suburbs. Jack boarded with Harry until his steady patter wore out his welcome; then he moved to Abe's house. His duties for the film exchange were nebulous. Harry decreed that Jack was too young to run the projector; several projectionists had died in fires caused by the explosive nitrate film. Jack was in charge of inspecting and shipping prints to the customers.

Theater owners were constantly complaining that they weren't receiving enough product. Harry bawled out Jack, who explained that he didn't have enough films to ship. To Harry that was no excuse. Jack found a way to ease the shortage. He figured the titles for each film ran about thirty feet, so he scissored fifteen feet from each title and filed the excerpts alphabetically. When a theater requested a popular title that was not in stock, he spliced the film's title onto any other film and shipped it out. Theater owners rarely noticed that they had received the right title but the wrong film.

With the Pittsburgh office of Duquesne Amusement Supply thriving, Harry decided it was time to open a branch. He dispatched Sam and Jack to Norfolk, Virginia.

Virginia proved to be fertile ground for the two sporting brothers. The Norfolk office in the Monticello Arcade showed an immediate profit, and Sam instructed Jack in the pleasures that money could provide. No longer under the surveillance of their father and their stern older brother, they savored good times with the southern belles. Sam's brand-new Buick White Streak provided the magnet, and Jack tagged along with his own date in the rumble seat. Though he drank no alcohol, Sam was always the life of the party. To impress a girl he walked across the room on his hands and performed a standing backflip.

Both Sam and Jack were born salesmen, and they ingratiated themselves to the film buyers. One of their innovations was a publication called *The Duquesne Film Noise*—"We are the only film exchange with its own magazine—watch others follow." It carried photographs of Sam, "editor and manager, Norfolk office," and Jack, "assistant editor and manager, film and supply department." Both posed in high collars and dark suits with serious expressions, seemingly trying to look older than they were.

The April 1909 issue advertised Pathe's *Passion Play*, 3,200 feet in length and "highly hand-colored"; Pathe's *Earthquake*; and the services of Duquesne's vaudeville booker, Mr. Harry Mitchell. Misspellings in the *Noise* betrayed the editor's and assistant editor's lack of schooling, but their zeal was apparent:

EXPERIENCE

is a good teacher, but her tuition fee is heavy. You get the benefit of our experience in the moving picture line—particularly service, which saves you expense, time and worry of experimenting with unknown exchanges.

The same issue carried a portent of future disaster. An item attempted to assuage theater owners' concerns about a new dictate by the Patents Company. Brave talk, because the Warners already feared that their enterprise was doomed by the far-reaching arm of the Patents Company.

It had been formed in 1908 after Thomas Edison concluded that many producers and exhibitors were making millions from his inventions without paying any royalty. He found willing partners— Vitagraph, Biograph, Kalem, Lubin, Essanay, Gaumont, Melies, Selig, Pathe—in the formation of a monopoly. The "Edison Trust" decreed that no film could be produced or shown in the United States unless it was licensed by the corporation. All cameras and projectors were subject to a schedule of fees.

This was ruinous to independent producers and theater operators. To tighten its grip, the Patents Company in 1910 formed the General Film Company to distribute films of its member companies only to licensed theaters. The Warners' exchanges in Pittsburgh and Norfolk were being throttled, film supplies diminishing to a parcel of overplayed attractions.

One day a stranger entered the Warner office in Pittsburgh and announced: "I'm buying out your business today."

"Our business is not for sale," Harry declared.

"Oh yes, it is," the man said. "I'm from the General Film Company, and we are not going to supply you with any more films."

"We'll sell," Harry replied.

General Film dictated the terms: $10,000 in cash, $12,000 in preferred stock, and payments over a four-year period for a total of $52,000. "How about a job managing this office for you?" Harry inquired. "Come to New York and we'll take care of you," the emissary promised.

But when Harry and Abe called on the General Film president, J. J. Kennedy, he told them the Pittsburgh job had been filled. "Very well, Mr. Kennedy," said Abe Warner, "then we will put you out of business."

"Personally, I wish you luck," Kennedy commented, "but in business, I hope you break your neck." Kennedy opened a box of cigars but didn't offer any to his visitors.

Despite the loss of the family business, Sam and Jack planned a triumphant march home. They packed their belongings into the Buick White Streak and embarked on the perilous journey, slogging for days through rainstorms and over mud-thick roads, sleeping in haystacks at night. They arrived at the Elm Street house in early morning and roused the entire family.

"Come look outside," Sam insisted, and the parents and children trooped down the front steps in their nightclothes to marvel at Sam's Buick. Nothing like it had been seen in Youngstown. With Sam as chauffeur and Jack as footman, they regally drove their mother and father around the block.

*   *   *

The brothers scattered, though they remained in contact with each other. Jack drifted from city to city, finding work in film exchanges. Sam pursued his own interests in New York City, and Abe returned to selling. Harry decided that his father Ben had worked long enough in the family grocery. With the money from the General Film sale, he bought a large store on Federal Street and installed a modest version of a modern supermarket. Ben could supervise a staff of clerks, relieved of the dawn-to-dusk toil of the old store. Harry also bought the Rex Theater in Youngstown and supplied it with films left over from the exchange. When the films ran out, he sold the theater at a profit.

Sam had ingratiated himself with the crowd of salesmen who hung around the film exchanges in New York. A friend told him of the chance to acquire the New Jersey and Connecticut rights for *Dante's Inferno* for a modest sum. The five-reeler had been filmed and hand-colored in Italy, and its depictions of the suffering of sinners in the netherworld had proved a sensation in the United States, especially in areas where hellfire and damnation were preached from pulpits. The spectacle scenes, not yet attempted in American films, dazzled audiences accustomed to small casts in comedies and melodramas. Best of all, the foreign origin of *Dante's Inferno* placed it outside the stifling clutch of the Patents Company.

Sam returned to Youngstown and enthused to Jack, "Kid, I got a great deal for us." Jack needed no persuasion. He was tired of menial work in film exchanges, and would have followed Sam anywhere.

They opened in Hartford. With customary showmanship, Sam devised ways to make *Dante's Inferno* a theatrical experience. He stationed Jack behind the screen with sheet metal to create the effect of thunder, and a wind machine that sounded like a hurricane. Sam hired a professorial man with a booming voice to intone the Dante poem from the wings. The performance was a sensation, and the two Warners marched from town to town with their allegory on the wages of sin. Their only problem was the professor. Afflicted by his own alcoholic hell, he staggered to each performance and could barely get through his recital of the Dante masterpiece. Sam finally was forced to fire him.

The tour ended in Atlantic City. Sam figured he and Jack had earned $1,500 and saved countless souls. Their accomplishment merited a celebration, he told Jack, and he booked a room at the Normandie Hotel in mid-Manhattan. After a full-course dinner, Sam and Jack retired for the night. Unfortunately, they heard the unmistakable sounds of a crap game in the next room. Most of their $1,500 fell victim to the dice, leaving barely enough for the night train to Youngstown.

Harry summoned his three brothers to a meeting. He was tired of being under the fist of the Patents Company and subject to the whims of independent producers. It was time for the Warner brothers to make films of their own. After all, there was no secret to making movies. He proposed that Sam and Jack produce a couple of two-reelers—cheaply, of course.

"But where can we go?" Sam asked. "The Patents Company detectives are everywhere."

"I've heard about an abandoned foundry in St. Louis," Harry said. "You could set up a studio there."

Sam and Jack boarded the train for St. Louis, fashioning movie plots on the way. Their first film was *Peril of the Plains*, a reworking of the old settlers-vs.-Indians plot for which the brothers enlisted members of the Missouri National Guard to battle the fake Indians. Sam and Jack handled production matters, and Sam directed the film in three days. They followed with *Raiders on the Mexican Border*. Both films were hits with the Warner family but no one else. At least the Warner brothers had made a tiny step toward producing their own movies.

A little man from Germany, called "Uncle" Carl Laemmle because of his fondness for hiring relatives, had declared war on the

Patents Company in 1909. Refusing to cave in to the trust, he formed the Independent Motion Picture Company (IMP), which gathered other filmmakers into its fold and established exchanges in major cities. In 1912, Laemmle beat back legal efforts to stop him, and the government soon began moves to end the monopoly.

Still smarting over the forced sellout to the trust's General Film Company, Harry Warner lent his support to IMP. Seeing a more favorable climate for independents, Harry decided to exploit the growing market for films in California. He sent Sam to Los Angeles and Jack to San Francisco with instructions to open exchanges.

San Francisco in 1912 was an aphrodisiac for a pleasure-seeking twenty-year-old like Jack Warner. Still rebuilding from the earthquake and fire, the city throbbed with vitality. The Barbary Coast offered its gaming tables and painted ladies twenty-four hours a day. Restaurants displayed delicacies Jack had never heard of in Youngstown. Market Street glittered with vaudeville houses and legitimate theaters and movie temples. On his own for the first time in his life, Jack Warner was eager to experience all of it.

Jack opened the Warner exchange at 217 Taylor Street, within walking distance of theaters, night spots, pool halls and gambling clubs. The joking young man, who sometimes dressed like a burlesque comic, became a popular figure among San Franciscans in the entertainment world. Among his many good friends was sprightly little Sid Grauman, son of a vaudeville theater owner and, like Jack, a perpetrator of elaborate practical jokes.

Business at the San Francisco exchange fluctuated with the supply of films that Harry was able to send from New York. During one prosperous period, Jack bought a small movie house on Fillmore Street, the All-Star, using his own money, together with a loan from Sam. Jack delighted in standing outside the All-Star, cigar in mouth, watching the patrons pay money to see movies in his own theater.

Despite the ready access of the San Francisco ladies, Jack decided at age twenty-three that it was time for him to marry. The girl he chose was Irma Solomons, the lively teenage daughter of one of San Francisco's pioneer Jewish families. Her parents were unimpressed by the smart-talking young man whose business was selling motion pictures. But Jack and Irma were desperately in love, and their wedding took place on October 14, 1914.

When Jack took his bride home to Youngstown, neither she nor his parents were impressed with each other. Ben and especially Pearl considered the girl snooty and much too young for their son Jack. After her refined upbringing in San Francisco, Irma found the parents' Polish accents almost unintelligible, and she was repelled by Pearl's peasant meals.

On March 27, 1916, Irma Warner gave birth to a son, who was named after his father. This was in defiance of Jewish custom, which required a boy to be named after a deceased relative. Jack M. Warner has been called Junior all his life, even though his father bore a different middle initial.

Once again Harry decided that the Warners should engage in production. He took matters into his own hands, buying rights to a poem by a popular writer, Ella Wheeler Wilcox. *Passions Inherited* was the kind of subject Harry favored in films: sentimental, heartwarming, with solid family values and a strong moral. He hired a British director of melodramas, Gilbert P. Hamilton, and gave him $15,000 to make the film in Santa Paula, a small ranching town near Santa Barbara.

The only word Harry received from Santa Paula was Hamilton's insistence that he needed another $5,000 to finish the film. Weeks passed without communication from Hamilton and the *Passions Inherited* company.

"Find out what the hell's going on down there," Harry instructed Jack.

Jack drove his used Cadillac 300 miles down the coast to Santa Paula. There he could see that not only was Hamilton malingering; he had also used Harry's money to buy new cars for himself and the actress he was bedding.

Leaving the film location, Jack motored to Hollywood where the exposed film had been sent for processing. He screened it and decided Hamilton had shot enough for a complete film—except for the ending. Jack reviewed all the film and found an embrace between the leading man and woman in the third reel. He duplicated the scene, attached it to the end, and sent *Passions Inherited* into release.

It failed. America in 1917 had no patience with the kind of lachrymose morality tale that Harry found so comforting. The war had quickened the nation's pulse, requiring a new kind of film entertainment. The Warner brothers, like many other producers and distributors, were slow to adjust to the new market.

Abe enlisted in the army, where he rose to the rank of sergeant. Harry at thirty-seven was too old for the service. Jack wrote in his autobiography that he and Sam tried to join the military but were assigned to make an informational film for the Army Signal Corps.

Open Your Eyes was their major production. The subject: venereal disease. The Warners agreed to produce the film with their own money, provided they could own the rights to show it in theaters after the war. Against their better judgment, Sam and Jack hired Gilbert P. Hamilton, the lothario of the Santa Paula pecan orchards, to direct. Space was rented at the Biograph studios in the Bronx, where Jack was omnipresent to assure no delay in production.

During the filming of an outdoor scene, snow began to fall, and Hamilton stopped filming.

"The hell with the snow," Jack commanded, instructing the director to aim his camera upward so that the whitened ground wouldn't show. Hamilton resigned on the spot, and Jack and Sam took over the direction. Jack even made the only screen appearance of his career. He portrayed a young soldier buying a ten-dollar bottle of a bogus cure for syphilis from a quack doctor.

With *Open Your Eyes* delivered to the government, the Warner brothers returned to their enterprise of buying films from producers and selling them to theaters. Business was good, because of the wartime need for entertainment. But the three civilian brothers, Harry, Sam and Jack, all deeply patriotic, felt the need to do more for their country than make instructional films and promote Liberty Bonds. They also burned with the desire to elevate themselves from the merchandizing of small-time movies and to earn a place with giants of the industry like Zukor, Laemmle, Lasky and Fox.

Happily, in 1918, the brothers were able to achieve both goals.

Chapter 3

Foothold in Hollywood

TWO YOUNG BLADES IN HOLLYWOOD, Sam and Jack Warner joyfully plunged into the creative excitement of the burgeoning film community. Jack had left San Francisco to join his favorite brother where the film trade churned feverishly to satisfy the need for wartime amusement. Jack made his headquarters at the Alexandria Hotel at Fifth and Spring Streets, first stop for producers, directors and actors arriving by train from the East. The Alexandria's lobby contained the "million-dollar rug," so called because of the movie deals that were made there. The negotiators seldom noticed the dapper twenty-five-year-old film salesman who strained to overhear information that might prove of value to him.

Jack spent most of his daytime hours at the Warners' exchange on Olive Street, seeking films to distribute and customers to buy them. At night he attended screenings of the new films and accompanied Sam to parties given by Sam's host of friends. Sometimes Jack brought along Irma; more often she remained alone in their apartment with their son. Jack found that having a young wife at his side slowed down the pace of a movie executive on the rise.

Sam often traveled to New York for conferences with Harry and Albert. Wherever he went, Sam read voraciously, as if to compensate for his meager education. He consumed everything available—newspapers, magazines, trade journals, books—to satisfy his curiosity about the world around him and, particularly, the movie business. While glancing over the *Philadelphia Public Ledger*, he saw the serialization of a book called *My Four Years in Germany*. He became fascinated with James W. Gerard's dramatic account of his service as American ambassador to Germany. Gerard witnessed the buildup of the German war machine and negotiated fruitlessly with Kaiser Wilhelm II, first to avoid war, and then to stop the sinking of Allied ships by U-boats. Each succeeding chapter confirmed Sam's belief that the book contained the basis for a gripping and timely motion picture.

"This is it!" he exclaimed to Harry. "This movie could make us a fortune!"

Harry viewed his proposal thoughtfully and came to the same conclusion. Harry now assumed the responsibility of consummating a deal. He paid a call on Ambassador Gerard.

Harry introduced himself to the urbane, well-educated Gerard and began his sales pitch on why the Warner brothers should produce *My Four Years in Germany*. Harry spoke eloquently about his parents' struggles in Poland, his father's efforts to support his large family in America, the brothers' prosperity in the film business, only to be crushed by the trust.

"Soon we will be a force to be reckoned with in the movie business," Harry declared. "Being able to film your book would confirm that. We can give you the intense, specialized effort that you won't get from the bigger companies."

Gerard admitted that major producers, including Lewis J. Selznick, had sought rights to his book. But he liked Harry's style and the Warner zeal. He agreed to assign the rights to the Warners for $50,000, plus twenty-five percent of the profits. The purchase price was less than what he had been offered by other producers.

Now Harry faced the challenge of raising the money to pay Gerard and the production costs. The major companies, ever vigilant against upstart competition, managed to shut off the normal avenues of financing. Harry scrambled to find smaller investors, including the family's old friend, Henry Garlick of Youngstown's First National Bank. Still he lacked enough to pay for the making of *My Four Years in Germany*. Finally he made a deal with Mark M. Dintenfass, a colorful, scarred veteran of the movie wars, to back the film.

Sam and Jack hurried east to manage production. As always, they had to cut costs everywhere. They saved on set building when Arthur Brisbane, the renowned Hearst editor, donated the use of his New Jersey farm, which was designed like a German village. William Nigh, who had filmed Keystone Kops two-reelers, directed the interiors at the Biograph studio in the Bronx. Sam and Jack hired unknown Broadway actors, reasoning that the attraction of *My Four Years in Germany* would be the title, not stars. To lend reality and save money as well, they bought newsreel footage of the war, interspersing it with the story.

My Four Years in Germany was something new for American audiences. Never had documentary footage been incorporated into a feature film. The result was gripping, especially in scenes of German atrocities. Field Marshall Hindenburg's instructions for treatment of Belgian civilians appear in the titles: "Healthy ones to the farms; use your discretion with young and old."

A young woman on a farm tells Gerard, "We are slaves." A German soldier kicks a Belgian girl and leaves her crippled for life. Another soldier separates a girl from her family—with rape obviously in mind. British soldiers are caged behind barbwire and guarded by dogs. Gerard himself appears in the film to lend credence to the depictions.

Gerard sat in a theater box at the New York premiere on March 21, 1918, and accepted the thunderous applause at the conclusion. *My Four Years in Germany* inflamed audiences wherever it played, contributing immeasurably to the war fever. First National distributed the film, which attracted more than a million dollars before the Armistice but little afterward. Everyone profited: Gerard, First National and the Warner brothers, who collected $130,000 to finance their future plans.

For the Warner brothers, the triumph meant more than money.

They had made a significant, patriotic contribution to their country, which they revered. For the rest of their lives and careers, they would make similar contributions, more so than any other film company. Americanism to the Warners, and especially to the foreign-born Harry and Jack, became a religion, something to be duly honored and devoutly proclaimed.

Equally important to the brothers was the status that *My Four Years in Germany* conferred. They had been something of a joke in the movie trade, a quartet of Youngstown hustlers who scraped through the film barrel for remnants that would bring them a few bucks. No more. With a single hit movie, the Warner brothers had emerged as a significant new force.

My Four Years in Germany proved such an elemental success that the Warners felt emboldened to try another film in the same vein. They produced *Kaiser's Finish*, which made no pretense of being a true-life story. The plot centered on a bastard son of Kaiser Wilhelm II, raised in the United States, a double for the crown prince. The U.S. government enlists him as a spy to enter Germany and assassinate both the Kaiser and the crown prince.

Even amid wartime fervor, *Kaiser's Finish* would have overtaxed credulity. Completed after the Armistice, it was a movie without a market. It disappeared into the Warner vault, erasing much of the profit from *My Four Years in Germany*.

The brothers did not lament for long. Harry continued to preach the unlimited future of the motion picture business, predicting a postwar prosperity that would bring new millions flocking to the box office. He strove to ingratiate himself to the moneymen who were willing to take chances on movie ventures—at a handsome rate of interest, of course. The major banking houses were closed to him; they were operated by conservative gentiles who held the immigrant, movie-making Jews in low regard.

Sam and Jack returned west with instructions to establish a studio to produce Warners features. They found a rundown property at 18th and Main Streets, a few blocks south of downtown

Los Angeles. The place had been converted into a primitive studio with a few outdoor stages. Sam and Jack noted that the studio had one major attraction: a menagerie of trained circus animals.

"A serial! Girl threatened by jungle beasts! A natural!"

Their minds worked almost in unison. Serials were popular and easy to make. All you needed was a continuous story and a Perils-of-Pauline cliff-hanger to induce the customers to return the next week to see how the heroine escapes. Jack and Sam devised a story line for *The Tiger's Claw* and hired an attractive blond actress, Helen Holmes, who had appeared in serials for Kalem.

All Sam and Jack needed was money. Sam was always on the lookout for potential backers, and he found one in a man named Motley Flint. Not much older than Sam, he was an executive with the Security First National Bank. Unlike most bankers, he was a visionary, and he saw a future in the motion picture business in general and in the Warner brothers in particular. He agreed to finance *The Tiger's Claw*.

The serial proved a money-maker, and it was followed by *The Lost City*, also starring Helen Holmes. The Warners had another release in 1919, *Open Your Eyes*. It was the venereal disease tract they had produced at their own cost for the Signal Corps, retaining the postwar release rights. The public displayed no interest in the subject, and the film, along with Jack Warner's sole screen appearance, quickly disappeared.

Sam and Jack tried a fifteen-chapter serial in 1920, *A Dangerous Adventure*. This time two actresses faced repeated peril from ferocious animals, but the formula didn't work. *A Dangerous Adventure* failed, but two years later Jack trimmed its thirty reels down to seven, and it earned a nice profit for the Warners.

A pair of young brothers, Kenneth and Howard Hawks, called on Sam and Jack to propose a comedy to star an Italian discovery of Fatty Arbuckle's. His name was Mario Bianchi, but Arbuckle had changed it to Monty Banks. The Warners hired Banks away from Mack Sennett and cast him in the Hawkses' story, *His Night Out*. After two days of filming, the director mysteriously disappeared, and Jack finished directing the comedy himself. He was in his glory, hamming away behind the camera and injecting gags stolen liberally from Sennett.

Four more Monty Banks comedies were produced. Harry arranged for their release through a young company operated by Jack Cohn, Joe Brandt and Harry Cohn. The firm's name, CBC, was later changed to Columbia because the trade referred to it as Corned Beef and Cabbage.

The Warner operation moved from downtown to a small lot across the street from the Thomas Ince studio in Culver City. The new quarters were no improvement. The open spaces were littered with junk, and the two small stages appeared on the edge of collapse. Sam and Jack tidied up the place as much as they could, but they were unhappy about working in such tawdry surroundings.

"We gotta get out of this rat hole," Sam declared. He and Jack scoured Los Angeles for a new location, and they found a ten-acre lot in the heart of Hollywood at Sunset Boulevard and Bronson Avenue. The owners were old-line Los Angeles financiers who, unlike others of their class, had a tolerance for the parvenu movie people who had descended on their placid city.

Sam and Jack agreed to a purchase price of $2,500 per acre, nothing down, with payments of $1,500 per month. On the first of each month, one of the brothers drove downtown to hand over $1,500 in cash. Sometimes they had nothing but promises, but the owners were surprisingly amenable to postponing payments.

With money borrowed from Motley Flint, the brothers erected a studio from the ground up—one large stage, an office building, a set-building shop. Sam and Jack themselves helped things along by pounding nails and digging trenches. After rains, the ground became a morass, and the budget made no allowance for cement. A studio worker wangled a truckload of gravel at a bargain price, and it was dumped on the Warner property. Sam and Jack removed their jackets and helped shovel gravel along pathways. During a break in filming, Monty Banks and other actors and set workers pitched in to help.

The brand-new studio required new productions to fill its cavernous stage. Jack made a scouting tour of Mack Sennett's Edendale studio and spotted Al St. John, a lean, country-hick comic who was a nephew of Fatty Arbuckle. Jack hired St. John for $500 a week and cast him in *Speed*, which exploited his skill as a trick bicycle rider.

With both of his comics, Jack Warner encountered a vagary of the acting breed that would haunt him to the end of his career. Monty Banks' outbursts of Italian temperament could only be assuaged when he was assured that he was as great a comedian as Charlie Chaplin. During the third Al St. John comedy, the star failed to report for work. Jack traced him to his Fremont Place house. St. John would not return to the studio until he received a bigger salary, a better dressing room and more publicity.

In his autobiography, Jack diagnosed the "virtually incurable disease" that afflicts actors. The symptoms: "the swelled head no hat in town will fit, the itchy autograph finger, the uncontrollable impulse to demand better pay, the angry plea to be let out of a contract, the eyestrain from reading and rereading newspaper puffs."

He concluded: "The sickness becomes progressively more acute, and has been known to bring on professional suicide."

The Warner brothers' production accelerated with the addition of Harry Rapf as production manager in 1921. He had a colorful background, having emerged from minstrel shows and vaudeville to become head of production for Lewis Selznick. He was a lean, cadaverous man with a hawkish profile that made him the butt of many jokes. Once while he and Irving Thalberg were walking on the MGM lot, Thalberg asked, "Do you smell smoke?" When Rapf replied that he didn't, Thalberg said, "Then there is no smoke."

Rapf pursued the trend to racy films about America's loosening morality in the postwar times. Rapf produced *Why Girls Leave Home*, which starred Anna Q. Nilsson, and *Ashamed of Parents*. A boy actor named Wesley Barry attracted notice in *Why Girls Leave Home*, and he became a Warner brothers star in *Rags to Riches* and *School Days*.

While his younger brothers frolicked in Hollywood, Harry Warner methodically pursued the company's financial matters in New York. He had been distributing Warners features through First National, CBC and Paramount Pictures, but he was convinced that all of the companies cheated on payments.

"We can no longer be at their mercy," Harry told his brothers. "We must distribute our own films, and buy theaters, too."

In 1923, Warner Bros. Pictures was established with Harry as president, Sam and Jack as vice presidents in charge of production, and Albert (as Abe now called himself) as treasurer. Harry and Albert would remain in New York to deal with financiers and distributors; Sam and Jack would produce the movies in California.

Financing for the new corporation came from Motley Flint in California as well as from the Bank of Italy run by the Giannini brothers, with whom Jack had become acquainted during his San Francisco days. Flint also introduced Harry to his Wall Street friends, the most important being Waddill Catchings of the Jewish firm of Goldman, Sachs. Catchings helped round up backers for the Warner Bros. expansion. Harry began opening exchanges in major cities to distribute the Warner Bros. films. He also started buying theaters, the first being in Youngstown, Ohio. Thus his parents and sisters would be assured of seeing all the Warner Bros. movies at no charge.

The quality of the films needed to be elevated, drastically. Harry paid high prices for literary works: F. Scott Fitzgerald's *The Beautiful and the Damned*, Sinclair Lewis's *Main Street*, Charles G. Norris's *Brass*, George M. Cohan's *Little Johnny Jones*. Harry entered a $250,000 contract with Broadway impresario David Belasco for three hit plays, including *The Gold Diggers*. Sam and Jack were delighted to have such important works to produce. Albert, the treasurer of Warner Bros. and chief worrier, was not.

During a visit to Hollywood, Harry discovered that the company's bank account was overdrawn by nearly a million dollars. He relayed the information to New York, and Albert, who had none of his brothers' gambling propensities, wrote Harry:

"I'm telling you frankly that I will have no confidence in anything you say or do, and I will take the train to Los Angeles and let you come back to New York with a guardian. I get disgusted when I find that we are O.D. $990,000, and receive a wire from you to buy *Rain* or some other bunk titles, or tackle a million-dollar theater property or a lot of other things that run through your wild mind. . . ."

Harry backed down from bidding for the stage hit *Rain*, but Albert's fury prompted only a brief halt in Harry's buying fever. Warner Bros. acquired forty theaters in Pennsylvania, the beginnings of a nationwide chain.

Jack Warner breezed into Youngstown in December of 1923, a returned hero. He visited his parents and sisters, called on a few friends and gave an expansive interview to the *Vindicator*. He told the reporter that he had once been a newsboy for the *Vindicator* and remembered sleeping at the newspaper office on the night of a presidential election so that he could hawk the extra edition as soon as the paper rolled off the presses.

Main Street was opening at the Liberty Theater, and Jack bragged that the major set of the midwestern town had cost Warner Bros. $32,000. "Why not use a real-life street?" the reporter asked.

"It's too dangerous," Jack explained. "Toward the end of the movie there is a snowstorm. We stage this mechanically, by means of airplane motors with the propellers reversed. When ten of those get going, they create a tremendous wind. I happened to get in front of one, and you bet I stepped aside mighty quick. When the storm began—we used confetti, of course, for snow—there were a hundred people in the scene. At the end there were a dozen people left on the stage, and our Main Street had been blown nearly to pieces."

Jack took his mother and his sister Rose to California so that they could witness the glory of the Warner Bros. studio, which now featured a stately white colonnaded building alongside Sunset Boulevard. Pearl Warner admired her grandson Jack, now a fat-cheeked seven-year-old, but could barely disguise her contempt for his mother. Nor could Irma restrain her own distaste for the elder

Warners, with their heavy accents, their old-world homilies and their unappetizing food. Privately, Pearl had a designation for Jack's wife: she was the *shiksa*, the gentile woman.

Both Rin-Tin-Tin and Darryl F. Zanuck arrived at Warner Bros. in 1923, with equal impact.

It was Harry Rapf with his nose for promising properties who brought Rin-Tin-Tin to Jack Warner. Rapf had met a man named Lee Duncan who owned a remarkable German shepherd. Duncan told the story, never verified, about finding the dog in a trench during the war in France. After his discharge from the army, Duncan returned to America with Rin-Tin-Tin (the nickname for the good-luck yarn dolls pilots hung over their cockpits) and taught him an amazing catalogue of tricks.

"I'm telling you, Jack, it's uncanny," enthused Rapf. "The dog can do anything. And Duncan has a story he wants to sell us."

The story, *Where the North Begins*, concerned a pup who is adopted by wolves and later rescues a fur trapper and becomes his friend. Jack had his doubts about the project until he met Rin-Tin-Tin, who seemed to display more intelligence than some of the Warner comics. Jack ordered a script to be written from Duncan's outline.

Where the North Begins proved a sensation at a preview, and Jack summoned Hal Wallis, who had recently been elevated to publicity chief after three months at the studio. Like Jack, the Chicago-born Wallis had left school at fourteen to help support his family. He had traveled across the country selling electric heating and was working as a theater manager in Los Angeles when Warner Bros. hired him. Jack appreciated Wallis's direct manner and his quick mind that brimmed with ideas.

"I think we've got the makings of our first real star with this mutt," Jack said. "I want you to give him one helluva buildup, as much or more than we do for our two-legged actors."

Wallis held a press conference to announce the signing of Rin-

Tin-Tin for a three-picture contract at $1,000 a week. Included in the provisions, Wallis insisted, was a five-piece orchestra for mood music while the star was working, a diamond-studded collar and chateaubriand steaks for lunch. Rin-Tin-Tin appeared at the conference and shook hands with all the reporters. They were issued an extensive biography of the new Warner Bros. star, filled with fanciful details of his dramatic life.

After the premiere of *Where the North Begins* at the Loew's State theater in downtown Los Angeles, Rin-Tin-Tin came onstage to a roar of applause. Wallis took him on a sixteen-week tour across the country, and the dog star astounded the press and public at every stop. Duncan had taught him to pick up a coin with his nose and place it in a small cup, to count to ten with his paws, and even to bark to ragtime music. As often happens with publicists, Wallis was disillusioned by close contact with his star. He found Rin-Tin-Tin to be foul-tempered and snappish when out of the spotlight.

Where the North Begins became the biggest hit for the Warner brothers since *My Four Years in Germany*. Even Albert, the keeper of the Warner conscience, was smiling.

The country went gaga over Rin-Tin-Tin. Hal Wallis minted thousands of Rin-Tin-Tin badges to be handed out to boys at Saturday matinees. The star's face appeared on millions of boxes of Ken-L-Ration Dog Biscuits. Fan mail poured into the studio at the rate of twelve thousand pieces a week.

Jack wanted a quick follow-up to Rin-Tin-Tin's hit. He offered the directing job to Mal St. Clair, a fast-working graduate of Mack Sennett's Keystone comedies. St. Clair suggested that a young friend, Darryl Zanuck, write the script; they had recently collaborated on a serial, *The Leather Pushers*.

Zanuck had accomplished much in his twenty-one years. Lying about his age, he'd left Wahoo, Nebraska, to join the army at fifteen. In France he fought as a bantamweight prizefighter and submitted letters to the *Stars and Stripes*. Determined to become a writer, he worked his way across the country, writing stories which magazines rejected. In Hollywood, he had four short stories printed as a book by a vanity press, sold all four to studios, then worked as a gag writer for Mack Sennett, Harold Lloyd and Charlie Chaplin.

Four days after Jack Warner suggested the Rin-Tin-Tin picture, Mal St. Clair (whom Warner referred to as "our seasick director, Mal de Mer") and Darryl Zanuck appeared in Warner's office with a completed script. Jack was at first taken aback by Zanuck's looks; he seemed more like a scrawny, buck-toothed farm boy than a screenwriter.

"Tell me the story," said Jack, who like most production heads was semiliterate and could judge a project better by storytelling than by reading.

His two visitors began. Since St. Clair was inarticulate, Zanuck assumed the responsibility of relating how Rin-Tin-Tin witnesses a murder and sees his master falsely accused of the crime. Now it is up to Rinty to bring the killer to justice. Zanuck acted out every scene in dramatic style, descending to all fours to bark out Rinty's dialogue.

Jack was overwhelmed, not so much by the plot of *Find Your Man*, as by the histrionic invention of young Zanuck. Jack sent the company to a location at Klamath Falls, Oregon, and Hal Wallis organized a junket of newsmen to observe Rin-Tin-Tin in action. Rinty obliged. For one scene, he was to intervene at a court trial just as the hero was being wrongly sentenced for murder. Unable to enter the door to the courtroom, the dog climbed to the roof, slid down the chimney, burst into the courtroom and delivered a message absolving the hero of the crime.

Find Your Man proved another triumph for Rin-Tin-Tin, whom Jack Warner termed "the mortgage lifter." The dog remained at Warner Bros. for nineteen profit-making films, offsetting losses created by more prestigious films. Ever afterward Jack referred to Rin-Tin-Tin as his favorite star: undemanding, punctual, always delivering a good performance and never asking for a raise.

Actually he meant Rin-Tin-Tins. When he realized how valuable the German shepherd was to the Warner Bros. fortunes, Jack asked Lee Duncan to provide duplicates. One dog had expressive eyes and appeared in close-ups. Others had their own specialties:

running, jumping, fighting, playing dead and so forth. Eventually there were eighteen Rinties available for film work.

Darryl Zanuck wrote several of the Rin-Tin-Tin features and almost anything else that needed writing. He was indefatigable, pounding out scripts on his typewriter into the night and on weekends. All Jack Warner had to do was throw out a story idea or a title, and Zanuck would come back in a few days with a finished script.

During one dazzling year Zanuck wrote more than half of the studio's thirty features. When Jack reported on the year's product at a sales convention, a theater owner complained, "Why do you charge so much for your pictures? You've only got one writer."

Jack didn't want to lose his prolific scenarist, but he worried about the multiple credits. Zanuck supplied the solution: "I'll use phony names." He would be Darryl F. Zanuck for the more important films, Gregory Rogers for comedies, Mark Canfield for melodramas, and Melville Crossman for contemporary subjects. Zanuck was amused that Crossman drew the best notices and was even offered a contract by MGM.

Zanuck took over the duties of production manager, which had been vacant since Harry Rapf left for MGM. Zanuck was to remain at Warner Bros. for ten years, rising to a $5,000-a-week salary and the highest post achievable without being a Warner brother. He and Jack became lifelong friends, though with a few lapses. Zanuck never became friends with Harry Warner.

Reflecting on his former employers in later years, Zanuck observed: "Harry, being president, was prone to jump on Jack for any film that did not come out well. . . . Sam was the bridge between them. Harry hated Jack. Jack played a role like Louis B. Mayer to a certain extent. It was a gentleman's role. He could captivate you. Harry was just the opposite. Anyone who got over two thousand dollars a week he hated instantly even if he never met him. In Harry's mind, everybody was a thief, including Jack for condoning extravagances.

"What a boring guy Harry was. Jack was unreliable, but never boring."

*　　　*　　　*

Where was Sam Warner during these crucible years of the Hollywood studio? He divided his time between Hollywood and New York, a calming force between the combative Jack and the ever-complaining Harry and Albert. Sam shared responsibility for production with Jack, but he preferred to let his effusive brother enjoy the spotlight and assume the day-to-day dealings with actors, writers and directors. Sam was a visionary. Though equally unschooled, he had more elevated taste than Jack. Sam was always seeking ways for Warner Bros. to achieve the status of Zukor's Paramount Pictures and the newly formed Metro-Goldwyn-Mayer, with its dynamic leadership by Louis B. Mayer and Irving Thalberg. That could never be accomplished when a German shepherd was the studio's biggest attraction.

"We gotta get more class into our pictures," Sam preached to Jack.

The Warner Bros. directors were mostly graduates of two-reel comedies and serials whose major attraction to Jack was their swiftness in filming. It was Sam's idea to hire Ernst Lubitsch, the wily Berliner who had emerged from Max Reinhardt's theater to direct German films of dazzling wit and sophistication. Mary Pickford had brought him to Hollywood to direct her in *Rosita*, one of her best films.

Lubitsch came to Warner Bros. in 1924 to make *The Marriage Circle*, a comedy of manners set in prewar Vienna. The film drew the best reviews accorded a Warner Bros. film; *The New York Times* named it one of the year's ten-best movies. Lubitsch followed with four more stylish films: *Three Women*, *Lady Windemere's Fan*, *Kiss Me Again* and *So This Is Paris*.

Jack was not accustomed to employing a director with leisurely ways. His spies reported that Lubitsch often stopped shooting in the middle of the afternoon to serve the company coffee and cakes. Jack hurried down to the stage and fulminated over such loss of valuable production time. The pint-size director merely smiled, "Stay and have some coffee, Jack."

Jack decided that prestige bore too high a price. "The Lubitsch touch" moved to other studios. Although his films produced no profit for Warner Bros., the studio had gained in two important ways: Lubitsch had contributed much-needed refinement to the product; he left behind his valued assistant, Heinz (later Henry) Blanke, maker of prestigious films in future years.

It was Sam's notion to bring John Barrymore to Warner Bros. The youngest of the famed acting family had astonished the New York theater world with his Hamlet and would soon repeat his triumph in London. Sam convinced Harry to offer Barrymore a contract to appear in *Beau Brummell*.

Sam and Jack decided to visit their new star backstage at the Sam Harris theater. As Jack related in his autobiography, the two brothers knocked on Barrymore's dressing room door. He peered out with steely eyes and asked, "You saw the play?"

"Yes," Sam replied. "You were marvelous."

"In that case, you two bastards," the actor muttered, "you've seen enough of me for the day." He gave them the bum's rush out the stage door.

"Don't be alarmed; he's a great kidder," Sam assured in the theater alley. Jack wasn't certain.

Beau Brummell was acclaimed by audiences and critics, another Warner Bros. film on *The New York Times*' ten-best list of 1924. Over Albert's strenuous objections, John Barrymore was signed to a long-term contract according him $76,250 per film, with an additional $7,625 a week if filming exceeded seven weeks; plus script approval, solo top billing unless he approved a costar, travel expenses for his entourage, hotel accommodations and meals in Los Angeles, a limousine, and publicity that would adhere to his "standing, reputation and prestige." Barrymore himself handwrote such stipulations into the contract.

Sam Warner had become a familiar and well-liked figure among the movie crowd in Hollywood and New York. An insatiable gambler, he could shoot craps for hours with other studio executives;

neither he nor Jack had learned any lesson from the loss of their *Dante's Inferno* profits that night in Manhattan. Sam squired many of the screen's beauties to premieres and parties, but none held any permanent attraction. He was now in his mid-thirties, and still the only unmarried brother, a fact that pained Pearl and Ben Warner. They were even more distressed, however, when he chose his bride.

She had been born Lena Baskette in San Mateo, California, and had danced as a child ballerina at the 1915 San Francisco World's Fair. A year later she was starring in *Lena Baskette Featurettes* for Universal Pictures. Her vivacity and dark girlish beauty made her a popular young actress in films. In 1923 she left Hollywood for the New York stage, and soon she was a featured dancer in the *Ziegfeld Follies* with the more stagy name of Lina Basquette. Florenz Ziegfeld admired her dancing so much that in 1925 he cast her in two of his shows at the same time; every night a waiting taxi drove her from the *Follies* to *Louie the 14th* and back again.

Sam Warner saw Lina performing in *Louie the 14th* and was entranced by her lithe beauty. He met her at a party given by a newspaper publisher, and he became a nightly visitor at the stage door of the New Amsterdam Theater. After a few midnight dinners, he proposed marriage. The eighteen-year-old Lina was reluctant; Sam seemed like an old man at thirty-seven. Lina's ambitious mother favored the match, believing that since Sam was one of the famous Warner brothers he must be rich (she was wrong).

Lina cried and cried, but her mother insisted that marriage to Sam meant security for the future. Lina and Sam were married in 1925 at the home of Dr. Nathan Krass, rabbi of the Reform Temple Emanu-El in New York.

Flo Ziegfeld was furious that Lina had married a "third-rate picture man." Like most Broadway impresarios, he had nothing but contempt for the movies.

Pearl and Ben Warner were desolated by the marriage. The fact that the wedding had been solemnized by a rabbi did not erase the shame that a Warner had married a non-Jew. Harry and Albert sided with their parents, and the two brothers and their wives would have nothing to do with Sam's *shiksa* child bride. Jack was more tolerant. Religion meant little to him; besides, he believed Sam could do no wrong.

Lina was pregnant in August of 1926 when she accompanied Sam to Youngstown, where she was the outsider at the golden anniversary of Pearl and Ben Warner. Even though the elder Warners had moved to California in 1925, they chose to celebrate their anniversary among the friends they had made during their thirty years in Youngstown. All the brothers were there: Harry, Abe, Sam, Jack and David, as well as their sisters. A dance was held in the ballroom of the Hotel Ohio, the music supplied by the orchestra of the Warners' Dome Theater. It was the last time the entire family would be together.

On October 10, 1926, scarcely ten months after the wedding, Lina Basquette Warner gave birth to a daughter, named Lita after Lita Grey Chaplin, Charlie's nineteen-year-old wife. Little Lita would later become the focal point of a bitter episode in the Warner family history.

Beau Brummell had been filmed without incident, but Jack Warner worried about John Barrymore's future behavior under his new, liberal contract. Jack's concerns were soon realized. Barrymore arrived with his entourage, which consisted of his butler Blaney and his rhesus monkey Clementine. All three lived at the Ambassador Hotel in a four-room suite which Barrymore redecorated with items from the Warner Bros. prop department. He entertained lavishly, providing food and drink for brother Lionel and other visitors, charging everything to his hotel bill. Barrymore's most pressing need was happily solved when he gained entrance to a heavily locked closet. It was stacked high with champagne and liquor bottles, a boon in prohibition America.

Warner Bros. had sought to capitalize on Barrymore's reputation as a lover by casting him in *Don Juan*. The actor agreed to the role, *after* he played in a movie of his own choice: *Moby Dick*. He was tired of portraying "scented, bepuffed, bewigged and ringletted" characters and wanted to be seen as a real he-man for a change.

Jack paid a visit to the Ambassador Hotel to discuss the sea-faring movie. He found Barrymore in the early stages of a monster hangover, bleary-eyed, unshaven and unkempt. Clementine leaped onto Jack's head and relieved herself. When Jack rushed to the bathroom to wash, he found the bathtub filled with champagne bottles. Barrymore proudly exhibited his lucky find: the well-stocked closet.

During the making of *The Sea Beast*, as the Melville saga was called, Barrymore seemed intent on emptying the closet. Jack Warner hired an old-time prizefighter to maintain a twenty-four-hour watch on the star and make sure he reported to the set on time.

One day on the Warner Bros. lot, Barrymore encountered "the most preposterously lovely creature in all the world." She was Dolores Costello, the blond daughter of tragedian Maurice Costello. She had appeared in films with her father and had been dancing in the road company of George White's *Scandals* with her sister Helene when both were spotted by a Warner Bros. casting agent.

Barrymore burst into Jack Warner's office and proclaimed that Dolores Costello would be his leading lady in *The Sea Beast*.

"But there is no role for a woman," Jack protested.

"Write one," said Barrymore.

Dolores Costello became Barrymore's costar and later his wife, the wedding postponed until his divorce from Michael Strange.

The Sea Beast cost $800,000, more than any Warner Bros. film, but it produced a healthy profit. John Barrymore remained a Warner Bros. star for five years through seven features, with accompanying headaches for Jack Warner.

Under the aegis of Waddill Catchings of Goldman, Sachs, Harry continued his program of borrowing so that Warner Bros. could expand. He paid $800,000 for the faltering Vitagraph Company, which dated back to 1896. The glory days of stars like Rudolph Valentino and Norma Talmadge had faded, and Vitagraph had been reduced to little more than a couple of studios and a distribution system. But Harry believed that such assets strengthened his company's position, and the move helped to foster the impression within the industry that Warner Bros. was on the rise.

Sam Warner was in an acquisitive mood as well, but in a surprising direction: radio.

Other film companies had shunned radio, fearing it would become competitive with movies. Sam thought otherwise, reasoning that radio was simply another form of entertainment that could stand alongside the legitimate theater and motion pictures. Besides, radio would be a good medium to advertise Warner Bros. movies.

Harry gave his blessing, and Sam and Jack established Los Angeles' third commercial radio station, KWBC, which stood for Warner Bros. Classics, the title given to the studio's more prestigious films. Later it became KFWB, and Jack always insisted the call letters stood for "Keep Fighting, Warner Brothers." A studio and transmitter were set up on the Sunset Boulevard lot by a remarkable sound engineer named Nathan Levinson. He had been a signal corps major during the war, and now was in charge of Western Electric's Pacific division.

KFWB became Jack Warner's playground. All his barely repressed ham emerged once more, and he took to the airwaves as the long-lost Youngstown tenor, Leon Zuardo. His rendition of "When the Red Red Robin Comes Bob Bob Bobbin' Along" always finished to huge applause, largely because the studio was filled with Warner Bros. employees. All the studio's performers were introduced to say a few words, and Rin-Tin-Tin contributed barks. Old vaudeville chums like Mervyn LeRoy and Bryan Foy dropped in and exchanged ancient jokes with the master of ceremonies.

Leonard Levinson often called at the studio to check on the KFWB facilities. One day he arrived excitedly at a meeting of Sam, Jack, and the studio engineer, Frank Murphy. Levinson blurted out the news: he had seen a wonderful thing, a talking motion picture.

"No! Where?" Sam asked.

"In our Bell lab in New York. Damnedest thing you ever saw. You've got to go East and take a look for yourself."

Chapter 4

Triumph Amid Sorrow

WHAT SAM SAW IN NEW YORK was a man in formal clothes on a movie screen in a small studio. The man smiled at the camera and removed his gloves. Sam was startled to hear the snap of the buttons. Then the entertainer set aside his cane, his hat and coat, and the sounds were just as natural as if he had been in the room. He sat down at a piano and began to play. Sam could scarcely believe it. The music filled the room with perfect fidelity, the notes matching the finger movements.

"Fantastic!" Sam exclaimed. "This isn't a phony, is it?" Always wary of con artists, he peeked behind the screen to make certain there was no hidden piano.

Sam, the only one of the Warners who understood mechanical things, insisted, "Tell me how it works."

The grinning Nathan Levinson and the engineers of Western Electric explained. Two synchronized motors ran side by side. One propelled the film through the camera, the other operated a wax recording of the sound, which was played on a loudspeaker behind the screen.

Sam lusted for the talking machine just as he would not rest until he had acquired the kinetoscope in Youngstown. His inventive mind raced with the possibilities. Someday Broadway musicals could be photographed and shown to the hinterlands. Movies could have recorded musical scores, relieving theaters of the expense of employing orchestras. Opera singers and vaudeville stars could be brought to the masses.

Harry Warner listened to Sam's outburst of enthusiasm with a granite face. Harry had hocked the company to the limit in order to acquire Vitagraph. Making and releasing sound movies would be ruinously expensive. And where would they be shown? Silent movies were prospering as never before; theater chains would be loath to spend millions to install sound equipment.

"It's out of the question," Harry decreed. "You know as well as I do, Sam, that these talking pictures have been tried before and have never worked."

Harry was right. Movies with sound had been attempted since the last century, when Thomas Edison tinkered with devices to help his growing deafness. He had tried unsuccessfully to couple film with cylinders, instead of the two disks used by the Bell engineers. Lee de Forest invented the audion amplifier in 1906, and by 1923 he was showing films with speeches by Calvin Coolidge and monologues by Eddie Cantor. But only a few theaters had installed his equipment, and Hollywood had ignored de Forest's device.

Sam would not be defeated by his brother's intransigence. "I want you to meet the people over at Western Electric," he told Harry.

"I am *not* going to look at your talking machine," Harry declared.

"No, no, I just want you to meet these guys. They might come in handy some day."

Harry reluctantly agreed. On the way to the Bell lab, he paid a call on his financier Waddill Catchings at Goldman, Sachs. When Harry mentioned where he was going, Catchings remarked, "I'd better go along with you to make sure you don't buy Western Electric."

When they arrived at the Bell lab, Harry was surprised and irritated that Sam had arranged a demonstration of the new invention. The engineers gave a brief explanation of how the system worked, and then the room darkened. The first attraction on the screen was a stuttering comedian. "Wonderful! Wonderful!" Catchings exclaimed. Harry agreed, although he remained silent. He didn't want to disclose any enthusiasm to the Western Electric people.

The climax was a performance by a full symphony orchestra. The woodwinds, brass and strings resonated through the room with the fidelity of a European concert hall. Harry was overwhelmed.

Back at the Warner Bros. offices, Harry admitted to Sam, "Yes, something might be done with it." He spoke of the possibility of bringing fine music and the best of entertainment to Americans everywhere.

"But don't forget you can have actors talk, too," Sam suggested.

"Who the hell wants to hear actors talk?" Harry replied. "The music. That's the big plus with this."

Waddill Catchings, who was more enthused than Harry, agreed to seek financing for the venture into sound. The next step was to reach an agreement with Western Electric. That was not easy, because the higher-ups of the corporation were anti-Semitic.

Lina Basquette recalled accompanying Sam to a dinner with Western Electric executives at an old-line Manhattan club which banned Jews from the premises. Sam asked her to wear a gold cross so that they would be acceptable. That night an agreement was reached between Western Electric, which was a subsidiary of AT & T, and Warner Bros.

Harry signed the contract on June 25, 1925. Western Electric would provide the technical skill and equipment for a series of sound films; Warner Bros. would supply the entertainment. Cautious in his statements during the negotiations, Harry was now free to express his optimism about the future of motion pictures augmented by music.

Western Electric suddenly had misgivings about surrendering such a valuable discovery to a company that was considered second-rate in its industry. The chief of the talking picture division tried to renege on the agreement and seek a bigger company. Waddill

Catchings went directly to the president of Bell to forestall such a move.

The Warner brothers decided on a strategy. Jack would supervise the creation of a musical score synchronized to the action of *Don Juan*, the John Barrymore vehicle which had begun filming in Hollywood. Sam would take over the newly acquired Vitagraph studio in Brooklyn and make a series of musical shorts to accompany *Don Juan*. Harry and Albert in the New York office would make preparations for the film's release.

At last Sam had a clearly defined and vital role to play in the company. He plunged into the work, devoting long hours to conceiving new ideas and solving constant problems. There were no rules, no precedents for making a series of sound films. The only method possible was trial and error.

The errors were many. The old Vitagraph studio had been built for silent films, and passing trucks sounded as if they were coming through the board-and-batten walls. Subway trains resembled earthquakes as they rumbled underneath the stages. Sam had planned to record Metropolitan Opera singers at Vitagraph, but obviously that was impossible. He moved operations to the old Manhattan Opera House on 34th Street and set up a studio in what had been John McCormack's cubicle for warming up before a performance.

Sam himself directed all the filming and recording. Synchronizing the camera and recorder proved incredibly tedious. Each of the musical numbers had to be filmed without interruption—ten or twelve minutes apiece. The only way to achieve different angles was to film with two or three cameras simultaneously.

Harry was determined that this boldest venture of Warner Bros. would be crowned with success. He instructed Jack to add $200,000 to the budget of *Don Juan*. To record the *Don Juan* score, Harry wanted the best: the New York Philharmonic Orchestra.

William Axt and David Mendoza fashioned the score from romantic themes and classical works, composing music to match what was happening in each reel of film. Henry Hadley conducted the Philharmonic at the Manhattan Opera House, timing the music to the split-second changes of mood on the screen. Just as recording started, blasting began for the construction of the 8th Avenue subway. Hadley tried to record between blasts, but take after take was ruined, and each time all the equipment had to be readjusted. Sam was frantic, yet he would not compromise; the recording had to be perfect.

When Sam poured out his frustration to Jack in California, Jack provided the solution to the subway blasts: record at night.

Sam worked day and night to complete the short films and record the symphonic score to *Don Juan*. Harry acquired a $4-million loan through Waddill Catchings and established the Vitaphone Company to franchise the sound system to theaters and producers, completing the contract with Western Electric for exclusive rights to the system. Harry also bought the Picadilly Theater in Manhattan and renamed it the Warner Theater.

August 6, 1926. The small, high-collared figure of Will Hays appeared on the huge screen of the Warner Theater. In his dry Indiana monotone, he welcomed the bejeweled audience and assured them they were about to witness a historic event. His listeners sat in hushed astonishment despite the banalities of the movie czar's speech. When he finished, applause filled the theater, and Hays made a discreet bow.

The New York Philharmonic launched into the *Tannhauser* overture, not from the orchestra pit or the stage but from the screen. Sam Warner, who held tightly to Lina's hand, was convinced he could hear all 107 instruments. Sam and his wife sat apart from Harry and Albert and their wives, and Ben and Pearl Warner, who had come to witness their sons' triumph. Jack remained in California to prepare for the Hollywood premiere.

A parade of virtuosi followed. Marion Talley singing "Caro Nome" from *Rigoletto*. Mischa Elman on violin with Dvorak's *Humoresque*. Popular musician Roy Smeck on banjo, ukulele, Hawaiian guitar and harmonica. Violinist Efrem Zimbalist in Beethoven variations. Giovanni Martinelli with the clown's lament from *I Pagliacci*. Finally Anna Case singing "La Fiesta" with the Cansino dancers, the Metropolitan Opera chorus and the full orchestra.

The dazzled first-nighters, who included Warner rivals William Fox, Adolph Zukor, Lewis Selznick and Nicholas Schenck, could scarcely recover their breaths before the curtain reopened for the start of *Don Juan*. The talkless movie was almost a letdown. But the viewers were soon enthralled by the lush spectacle, the magnetic Barrymore, and the fluid direction by Alan Crosland. The final duel between Barrymore and Montague was thrillingly choreographed, and the audience cheered Don Juan's victory.

Most of those in the Warner Theater had been stirred by the music that lent an almost constant accompaniment to the action, realizing only afterward that no orchestra was present. It had all been done through the magic of Vitaphone.

"Perhaps the most brilliant motion picture premiere that was ever held," declared H. David Straus in the *Morning Telegraph*.

"Vitaphone Bow Is Hailed As Marvel," headlined *Variety*.

"A marvelous device," wrote Mordaunt Hall in *The New York Times*. "The future of this new contrivance is boundless. . . ."

Everyone in the movie business was talking about Vitaphone, and Ben and Pearl Warner were never prouder of their four sons. "We never dreamed that we would live to see such a performance," they wrote to Jack in California.

"When four marvelous boys like you stick together through thick and thin, there is no question but that you will attain all the success you hope for."

While his brothers thrilled over the press notices, Sam Warner started preparing another program of Vitaphone talking shorts. This time he aimed at popular tastes. The Philharmonic played a patriotic medley, "The Spirit of 1918." George Jessel delivered his famed monologue of a telephone conversation with his mother, followed by an Irving Berlin song. Elsie Janis, who had entertained the troops during the war, sang with an army chorus. A concert baritone delivered "A Long, Long Trail" and other familiar songs. Willie and Eugene Howard performed one of their dialect skits, and Al Jolson sang in blackface.

Harry Warner puzzled over the reaction to the Vitaphone premiere. Despite all the rave notices, no other producers were lining up for the Vitaphone franchises. Harry was heartened by the performance of the Warner Bros. stock, which climbed from fourteen to fifty-four within a month. But releasing *Don Juan* and the musical shorts had proved to be an expensive process. Warner Bros. had few showcase theaters in major cities, and none of the theater chains would undertake the expense of installing sound systems. In some cities, Warner Bros. had to rent theaters "four-wall" to exhibit the *Don Juan* program in sound.

In Hollywood Jack prepared the next film for Vitaphone, *The Better 'Ole*, a war comedy with Charlie Chaplin's less talented brother Sydney. The sound track included a patriotic score and the sounds of cannons, rifles, tanks and other effects. *The Better 'Ole* and Sam's short subjects opened at the Colony Theater in New York on October 5, 1926. Again the reviews were congratulatory, with Jolson's three songs attracting the greatest praise.

The third Vitaphone offering was *When a Man Loves*, a romance based on *Manon Lescaut*, with John Barrymore and Dolores Costello. Sam returned to opera for the musical shorts. The novelty of sound was waning, and the reception to *When a Man Loves* was tepid.

The Vitaphone revolution was faltering. After promising to equip theaters for $5,000, Western Electric raised the figure to $25,000. Theater owners balked at such a fee. Meanwhile William Fox announced that his company was developing its own sound process, Movietone. The Warner Bros. stock began sinking. Harry reached the end of his bank loans and was forced to sell four million dollars worth of his own stock to keep the company solvent.

The Warner brothers' paranoia about their competitors seemed justified. Leaders of the Big Five—Paramount, MGM, Universal, First National and Producers Distributing—met secretly in December 1926. Flaunting the antitrust laws, they agreed none would enter sound pictures until all did. And when and if that happened, all would adopt the same system. The intent was obvious: the Big Five would never license a sound system from Warner Bros.

Western Electric was now wondering if it had made a mistake

in committing to an outsider like Warner Bros. Harry Warner would not allow Western Electric out of their deal. But in April of 1927, Harry was faced with heavy losses and no bank loans. He had to sell more of his stock, and he was forced to negotiate a new contract giving Warner Bros. less exclusivity to the Western Electric system.

The Warners found themselves in a wrenching predicament. They had harnessed their fortunes, even the survival of their enterprise, to a device that had attracted public acclaim in a few big cities. But they had failed to reach a mass audience because theaters would not bear the expense of installing sound equipment. Now the brothers were in a desperate race against William Fox and his Movietone. And the Big Five companies welcomed an opportunity to crush the upstart Warner brothers.

The savior came in the form of an egomaniacal mammysinger.

Samson Raphaelson had been partly inspired by the life of Al Jolson when he wrote his short story and play *The Jazz Singer*. The fathers of both Jolson and Raphaelson's hero, Jackie Rabinovich, were immigrant rabbis whose sons defected to popular entertainment. The play, starring George Jessel, opened in New York on September 14, 1925, to a lukewarm response from the critics. Like *Abie's Irish Rose*, its schmaltz caught on with the playgoing public, and *The Jazz Singer* ran thirty-eight weeks, closing only because Jessel had a contract with Warner Bros.

"I love that play," Harry Warner admitted wholeheartedly. He was moved by the parallel to the Warner saga and by the play's message of tolerance. Harry bought the film rights for $50,000 and signed Jessel to star at the same amount. First, Jessel would appear in three ethnic comedies for Warners, *Private Izzy Murphy*, *Sailor Izzy Murphy* and *Ginsberg the Great*.

By the time *The Jazz Singer* neared production in early 1927, Warner Bros. was enmeshed in Vitaphone. According to Jack Warner's autobiography, Jessel wanted $10,000 more to sing and dance in the movie. Jack agreed, but Jessel insisted on getting Harry's approval of the additional payment. Jack balked at being forced to ask his older brother for a decision he could make on his own. The deal was off.

George Jessel lived fifty-four more years, and his life ever after was clouded by his loss of *The Jazz Singer*. The role he had created had gone to his fiercest rival, Al Jolson, and Jessel never did become a star in a mass medium. In 1927, he claimed that he had declined *The Jazz Singer* because the movie script had diluted its Jewishness, portraying Jack Robin (né Rabinowitz) returning to show business after singing "Kol Nidre" for his dying father.

For decades Jessel was a member of the famed Comedians Round Table at the Hillcrest Country Club in Los Angeles. Also sitting at the table was Al Jolson, the man who had stolen Jessel's prize. Acknowledged by Jack Benny as the fastest wit at the table, Jessel always had a clever riposte when needled about losing *The Jazz Singer*. But his companions understood the inner hurt.

George Burns has another explanation of why Jessel lost *The Jazz Singer*: "Georgie wanted his salary in cash, and Jack Warner wouldn't give it to him. Probably because the company didn't have it."

Eddie Cantor was Jack Warner's first candidate for replacing Jessel. Cantor declined out of loyalty to his good friend Jessel. Al Jolson was the only other choice. He wanted $75,000, one-third on signing, the rest at the rate of $5,250 a week. Jack agreed.

Sam Warner was omnipresent during the filming of *The Jazz Singer*. He seemed to sense that this was the one great chance, perhaps the last chance, for him to justify persuading his brothers to tie their destinies to "Sam's toy phonograph," as they called it. Lina worried that Sam, with his long days at the studio, was exhausting himself. For more than a year he had been pouring his energies into perfecting sound techniques, meanwhile producing and directing all the musical shorts. During that time he suffered from devastating headaches, and he had undergone surgery to relieve the pain. His brothers were accustomed to Sam's feverish enthusiasms and saw no lessening of his vigor at thirty-nine. Lina did.

One day when Jolson was recording a song, he prefaced it with his trademark comment: "You ain't heard nothin' yet, folks! Just listen to this!"

When Sam heard the playback, he was electrified by Jolson's words. In an instant Sam realized why he had crusaded for sound pictures. Jolson's dynamism in that one brief phrase changed the whole dimension of the scene.

Sam instructed the director, Alan Crosland, to inject a monologue in the scene of Jolson's return to his parents after a long absence. He was to sing "Blue Skies" for his mother, and then repeat the song in a jazzy version. The scriptwriter, Alfred A. Cohn, wrote the speech, and Jolson provided his own ad libs:

"Mama, darlin', if I'm a success in this show, well, we're gonna move from here . . . Oh, yes, we are . . . We're gonna move up in the Bronx. A lot of nice green grass up there. A whole lot of people you know. . . ."

Jack shared Sam's enthusiasm for *The Jazz Singer* dialogue. The final scenes in the film were completed on August 7, 1927. Harry was pressing for a quick release date, and Jack and Sam agreed to a premiere at the Warner Theater in New York on October 6.

Sam's work wasn't done. There remained the delicate process of synchronizing *The Jazz Singer* film to the sound records. The original wax records were shipped to the Victor Talking Machine plant in Oakland where they were covered with graphite and electroplated with copper. When the records were returned to Hollywood a week later, they were combined with the edited film.

Finally in mid-September, *The Jazz Singer* was completed. Couriers transported the film and records to New York with the delicate care accorded a Ming vase.

Jack could see the fatigue in Sam's face. Sam had lost weight, and his eyes were rimmed with shadows. But then, Sam had worked furiously on projects before, and had always regained his strength.

Not this time. Jack departed for the New York premiere not realizing how sick Sam was. Jack was conferring with Harry and

Albert about sales plans for *The Jazz Singer* when they received word that Sam had entered California Lutheran hospital with a sinus infection. The infection was spreading, and Sam would have to undergo an operation. Jack left for California immediately. Harry and Albert followed soon afterward, accompanied by a pair of medical specialists.

None of the brothers reached Los Angeles in time. Sam died of pneumonia on October 5, the day before *The Jazz Singer* premiere.

Jack was desolate. Death in the family had struck before, but Sam was special. Throughout his life, Jack had been warmed by Sam's sunshiny optimism, his thirst for excitement, his inventive mind, his gambling nature. Sam had always served as a cushion between the sternness of Harry and the jocularity of Jack. Now Jack would have to face his oldest brother alone.

The response to *The Jazz Singer* was greater than even Sam could have dreamed. On the day after the New York premiere it was proclaimed a monumental occasion. The sheer power of Jolson's screen presence assured that silent pictures were dead, though some studio bosses were slow to recognize this. Overnight the Warner brothers were kings of the movie business. But now there were three.

Chapter 5

The Great Expansion

THE REVOLUTION DIDN'T HAPPEN OVERNIGHT. By early 1928, *The Jazz Singer* was being seen—and heard—by packed audiences in a hundred theaters across the nation. Filmed for $500,000, it would eventually produce a $3-million profit.

But there was no headlong rush by other theaters to install sound equipment. The Big Five agreed not to show talkies, as they were now being called, in any of their theaters. And they controlled most of the theaters. The entrenched rulers of the industry hoped their strategy would propel the overextended Warners to ruin.

It could have happened except for Harry's astute maneuvering. He was embattled on both sides, from the powerful Big Five and from his nervous partner, Western Electric. A new executive of Western Electric was trying to break the contract with Warner Bros. so that the company could deal with better-established producers. Harry fought his every move and in the end won a $4-million breach-of-contract judgment against AT & T.

Warner Bros. announced it would produce twelve talkies in 1928 in addition to twenty-six silents. The first three of the talkies were silents which included a few scenes with dialogue. They attracted good business as novelties.

Still grieving for Sam, Harry and Jack decided to leave their business worries and travel to Europe, ostensibly to arrange for openings of *The Jazz Singer*. Before leaving, Jack appointed a new production manager. Darryl Zanuck had proved a dynamo at the studio, his salary rising to $1,000 a week in recognition of his avalanche of scripts and story ideas. Now Jack chose him as his chief lieutenant.

After announcing the news to Zanuck, who still had a farm-boy look at twenty-six, Jack counseled: "Even if you don't need glasses, get some window panes and grow a mustache. It'll give you a little age."

The next important player in the Warner Bros. saga was a wisecracking rogue named Bryan Foy.

He was the eldest of the Seven Little Foys who had delighted audiences and terrorized backstages during vaudeville tours with their father Eddie Foy. Because Eddie paid his kids only in nickels, Brynie earned money elsewhere, principally from back-alley crap games and writing gags and songs for other acts. His most noted contribution was "Mr. Gallagher and Mr. Shean," which he gave to his friend Ed Gallagher and partner Al Shean.

Brynie outgrew the family act and drifted to Hollywood, where he acted and wrote gags at Fox, and then produced his own shorts. He became well-known for his ability to turn out a short subject in a day's shooting. Such prowess attracted the admiration of Jack Warner, who hired him to produce shorts for the studio. A big, solid man who could mutter gags out of the side of his mouth by the minute, he was Jack's kind of guy.

When Jack was in Europe, Brynie assigned a couple of writers to overhaul the script for a two-reel melodrama, *The Lights of New York*. "We're gonna blow it up to five reels," Brynie announced. "And it's gonna be all-talkie."

Brynie himself directed the picture on borrowed sets, instructing the actors to remain close to the potted plants or chandeliers where the microphones were placed. Foy completed the film in two weeks at a total cost of $75,000.

"I sort of overshot *The Lights of New York*," Foy confessed to

Jack Warner on the boss's return to the studio. Jack agreed to look at the fifty-seven-minute movie and was not displeased.

The Lights of New York was a bundle of banalities crudely performed by actors who sounded like voices on an Edison cylinder record. Released in August of 1928 as "the first all-talkie" (even though it still contained titles), it earned $2 million.

Brynie Foy's little quickie wrote the last death notice of the silent movie.

In 1928 Harry Warner cannily exploited the film industry's disarray by launching a two-year spending spree that confused and confounded his competitors. Not even the stock market crash deterred him.

The acquisitions were fueled by loans through Waddill Catchings, and also by sales of the brothers' stock, the proceeds being lent to the company. Since the stock had risen from 39 to 139 in the summer of 1928, the proceeds were considerable.

The first and most important purchase was the Stanley Company of America, which controlled 250 theaters. Harry continued buying theaters at the rate of one a day until Warner Bros. boasted a chain of 500. Now at last Harry no longer had to plead with the big theater chains to play the Warner Bros. product.

The Stanley Company owned a one-third interest in First National, the production company founded in 1917 by theater owners fighting Adolph Zukor's attempt at monopoly. After ten years, Zukor was able to weaken First National by wresting away one of its biggest theater chains. Harry Warner recognized that First National was floundering, a ripe target for takeover. He bought out other stockholders for $4 million, and then paid $10 million for William Fox's third of First National.

Harry's competitors were astounded by Warner Bros.' grab of First National. "It would have made more sense," one of them said, "if First National had bought Warner Brothers."

The addition of First National enhanced Warner Bros.' prestige. Despite its enormous success with talkies, Warner Bros. was still considered a penny-pinching studio specializing in schlock. First National had class, as exemplified by its stars: Richard Barthelmess, Colleen Moore, Loretta Young, Billie Dove, Constance Bennett, the Talmadge sisters, Kay Francis, Milton Sills, Harry Langdon. First National also had a first-class studio nestled on the valley side of the Hollywood Hills.

Harry continued his reach, acquiring Witmark, Remick, Harms and other music publishers. He placed his son Lewis in charge of Warner Bros. Music. Although Lewis was only twenty, Harry was already grooming him to inherit leadership of the Warner empire.

The Brunswick-Balke-Collender Company with its radio, phonograph and record divisions was added to Harry's loot, along with radio stations, foreign sound patents, Broadway musicals and a lithograph company. By 1929, Warner Bros.' gross assets had mounted to $230 million and the company showed a profit of $14.5 million.

The film industry's official recognition of Warner Bros. came on May 19, 1929, at the first awards presentation of the newly organized Academy of Motion Picture Arts and Sciences. *The Jazz Singer* was not nominated for best picture because the governors believed it was unfair for a talkie to compete against silents. Instead, Warner Bros. was given a special award for revolutionizing the industry with sound. The banquet at the Hollywood Roosevelt Hotel began with a demonstration of Western Electric's portable sound-projection machine.

Jack Warner was out of town, so Darryl Zanuck accepted for him, declaring, "This award is dedicated to the late Sam Warner, the man responsible for the successful usage of the medium."

After all the flowery speeches, Al Jolson rose to sing for the 300 dinner guests.

"I notice they gave *The Jazz Singer* a statuette, but they didn't give me one," Jolson said. "I could use one; they look heavy, and I could use another paperweight. For the life of me, I can't see what Jack Warner would do with one of them. It can't say yes."

*   *   *

Jack Warner moved swiftly to establish his sovereignty over First National. He was appalled by the overmanned staffs and lavish production budgets, compared to the cut-to-the-bone operations of Warner Bros.

In the first week after the merger, he fired a hundred First National employees. He decreed that First National's cost per picture, then seventy percent higher than Warner Bros.', must be brought to parity. First National had been spending $300,000 and up on its class-A films and $135,000 to $175,000 for program pictures. Jack pointed out that Warner Bros. films averaged $100,000, and the company realized good earnings from those costing $50,000.

Jack fired the production manager of First National and placed his publicity man, Hal Wallis, in charge of the Burbank studio. After seven years of promoting the Warner Bros. product, Wallis realized his dream of entering production. Jack himself would have preferred to move into the modern, efficient Burbank studio, but he was forbidden by the government. As part of the agreement allowing the merger, the justice department decreed that production by Warner Bros. and First National had to remain separate for two years.

Wallis faced an immediate problem: First National had no sound equipment. That was solved by transmitting sound by telephone lines to the Sunset Boulevard studio, where it was recorded. Since the sound equipment could only be employed for one movie at a time, Warner Bros. filming extended from nine in the morning until six at night and then First National began shooting at seven and concluded in the early morning. The system continued until First National could be wired for sound.

Jack Warner reveled in his newfound eminence as ruler of two major motion picture studios. In 1929 he presided over the production of eighty-six movies, more than half of them from First National.

At age thirty-seven he was wielding more power than he had ever dreamed of. His words were listened to not only by Warner Bros.–First National employees, who had no choice, but by journalists, investment bankers, and his counterparts at other studios. Not that his new position added dignity to his demeanor. Now he merely had a bigger audience for his jokes.

They came in endless profusion, good jokes, mostly bad jokes, painful puns, plays on words that would have baffled James Joyce. Jack could hardly utter a serious sentence unless he was firing someone; even then, the employment could end with a gag. He enjoyed the company of old vaudeville hands like Brynie Foy and Mervyn LeRoy, who could exchange snappy dialogue with him for hours.

Jack idolized Jolson. "The World's Greatest Entertainer" was just that to Warner, on the screen and off. Both were heavy gamblers, and they enjoyed trips to the Agua Caliente casino and race track just across the border. To the end of his life, Jolson was the only actor who could enter Warner's office unannounced. Jack was invigorated by Al's highly charged talk, his breezy manner, his cynical views of movie executives and of women.

Jolson received $150,000 for a second Warner Bros. film, *The Singing Fool*, and Jack didn't squawk. The new movie combined maudlin sentiment with the Jolson dynamism and sold $5.5 million worth of tickets to a public primed by the hit of *The Jazz Singer*. Millions cried when Jolson sang "Sonny Boy" to his dying son, played by Davey Lee. Three million song sheets were sold, and the box-office total of *The Singing Fool* remained an industry record for years to come. In lieu of salary, Jolson agreed to accept Warner Bros. stock. It proved a valuable investment, and he became the company's biggest stockholder, after the founding brothers.

Jack Warner fashioned himself after Jolson and other star performers. He admired their easy air, their aplomb and their capacity to turn even the most serious situation inside out with a gag. You can take the boy out of vaudeville, but Jack would never forget his brief span on the Gus Sun circuit. He was always out there in front of the advertising backdrop, purveying his endless bag of borrowed jokes, striving for the belly laugh that never came.

Newcomers to the studio sometimes mistook his jocular manner for softness. A grave error. When Jack thought that his prerogatives as studio ruler had been breached or even lightly questioned, he would fire the miscreant in an instant. Often he needed no excuse whatsoever.

Jack's appearance reflected his personality. He often appeared in the straw hat, white pants and blazer of a song-and-dance man. In photographs he always posed the same: wide, tooth-filled grin, body askant, one hand in pocket, the position at the left-hand side of the photo. "The captions always read left to right," he reasoned.

Because of his status as head of a studio newly emerged as an industry power, Jack was accepted into Hollywood's upper crust. He was considered a jester, but an affable one, and his lack of social polish went unnoticed by Louis Mayer, late of Minsk, and Sam Goldwyn, the onetime Polish glove maker. Jack and Irma Warner mingled on equal footing with such royalty as Mary Pickford and Douglas Fairbanks, Norma Shearer and Irving Thalberg, Marion Davies and William Randolph Hearst, and Charlie Chaplin.

Irma Warner played a latent role in Jack's life. She was generally seen in public on Jack's arm at social gatherings. At other times she remained at home with young Jackie. If she was aware of Jack's philanderings, she made no complaint.

As chief of two major studios, Jack had ample opportunity for dalliance. Most of the affairs were brief encounters. The exception was Marilyn Miller.

She had been Florenz Ziegfeld's most brilliant star, a lovely blond dancer who starred in *Sunny*, *Sally* and the *Follies*, and nearly shattered the producer's marriage to Billie Burke. Marilyn had married and divorced Mary Pickford's wastrel brother Jack, and her name had been connected with other well-known men. She was one of a host of Broadway performers engaged by Warner Bros. when the movie musical became possible because of sound.

Jack was captivated by Marilyn's petite beauty, her vivacious manner and absence of inhibition. He readily acquiesced to demands and behavior he would never have tolerated from another star. When she arrived on the train in Pasadena, she insisted on a Rolls Royce to take her to the studio.

Sally, the Ziegfeld musical in which she sang "Look for the

Silver Lining," was scheduled for her first Warner Bros. film. She looked at her costumes and sniffed, "Flo would never allow anything like that." She ordered an entirely new set of gowns and a chinchilla coat. A star's dressing room had been remodeled for Marilyn, but she found it wanting. She supervised a total makeover, including paneled walls, French antiques and a Roman bath.

Studio workers were amazed that Jack Warner would authorize such extravagances. Soon they realized that Marilyn was sleeping with the boss. *Sally* was a First National picture, so it was filmed at night in Burbank. Jack found an excuse to visit the studio during the filming, and his presence often resulted in Marilyn's absence from the set.

Production managers and assistant directors were faced with a dilemma: how could they maintain their rigid schedules while the star was dallying with the boss? None wanted to confront Warner and face certain termination. So they chose underlings for the perilous job.

George Sherman had worked for First National in New York from the age of thirteen, earned his way to California on a boat and was hired by the studio at sixteen, rising from the mail room to become a second assistant director. Ben Silvey, a big, burly first assistant director, called the tiny Sherman and told him, "Miller's gotta report to wardrobe for a fitting. She's already been told, but she still ain't there. Take this memo down to the rehearsal stage and tell her she's gotta report."

Memo in hand, Sherman entered the stage and found the star dancing to the music of a rehearsal pianist. Sherman walked toward her when he heard a gruff voice demand, "What do you want?"

Sherman swung around and saw the angry face of Jack Warner.

"Oh," said Sherman cautiously. "I got a memo here says Miss Miller has got to report to wardrobe."

"Gimme that." Warner snatched the memo away. "I'll see that she gets to wardrobe. And don't interrupt us again."

As Sherman was driving out of the studio that evening, the gate man called, "Hey, Sherman. Mr. Warner says don't come back tomorrow."

Sherman, who needed the eighteen-dollar weekly salary, came back. He consulted the production manager who told him, "Look, I got orders to fire you. I don't wanna do that because you didn't do anything wrong. So just stay outa Warner's way. If you see him coming, duck."

Luckily Sherman was assigned to Corinne Griffith's company, and she barred all executives from her sets. But one day, when it was raining and Sherman was driving in a limousine on his way to pick up Miss Griffith, he suddenly saw Jack Warner and Hal Wallis, with raincoats and umbrellas, walking toward the car.

Wallis waved down the limousine and opened the door to find the second assistant inside. "What the hell are you doing?" Wallis demanded. Sherman explained his mission. Warner stared at the little man as if thinking he looked familiar. Then the door closed and the limousine drove on.

Harry's spies in California soon reported to him about Jack's affair with Marilyn Miller. Harry responded with Old Testament fury. He castigated his brother for violating his marital vows. Further, if the affair became public knowledge, as was certain in a place like Hollywood, it would be ruinous to the family honor and the very foundation of the company.

Jack responded in his usual lighthearted manner. Boys will be boys, he said. The time when his eldest brother could lecture him about his behavior was long gone.

Like most musicals of the period, *Sally* was successful, and it was followed by *Sunny*. A third Marilyn Miller film, *Her Majesty, Love*, flopped. Miller's onstage radiance failed to transfer to the screen. Her film career, and the affair with Jack Warner, terminated. Her turbulent life ended five years later when she died of blood poisoning at the age of thirty-seven.

Two shattering tragedies befell the Warner brothers in 1930 and 1931.

Early in 1930, the Warners' faithful banker, Motley Flint, was sued by David O. Selznick, who was outraged when Security First

National Bank refused his request to withdraw $250,000. After testifying in court, Flint stepped down from the witness stand and paused to speak to Selznick's mother. A man leaped up and laid a gun on Mrs. Selznick's shoulder. He fired directly into Flint's face, killing him instantly. The judge ran to the killer and demanded the gun. The man fled but was quickly apprehended. His name was Frank Keaton, and he blamed Flint for the collapse of an oil company that had left him penniless.

All three Warner brothers grieved for Flint, who had been the antithesis of the hard-hearted banker. He had helped finance them in their earliest Hollywood days and had guided them over the perilous years, introducing Harry to New York financial sources that had helped build Warner Bros. into an empire.

Flint's murder was a personal loss for Jack. Not only had the banker stood behind the Warners in the worst of times, he had also been a wise counsel to Jack, softening Jack's rage at Harry's bossiness.

Among the few things that brought joy to Harry's life was watching his son Lewis grow up into a stalwart, intelligent young man. Harry had brought his son into the company early and was pleased to see the boy assume responsibility. Despite his youth, Lewis had blended the music publishing companies into a profit-making subsidiary of Warner Bros. Harry had more challenges in mind for Lewis who would some day lead the company after the founders had retired.

On a vacation to Havana in 1931, the twenty-three-year-old Lewis had fallen ill with infected gums. The infection poisoned his blood, and his father was informed of his serious condition. Harry and Albert chartered a plane to Cuba and brought Lewis to Miami and then to New York by train.

For six weeks Lewis's condition declined at Doctor's Hospital, with Harry ever-present. On April 5, Lewis died of septicemia and double pneumonia.

Harry was inconsolable. He railed against God for robbing him of his greatest treasure. All his dreams of Lewis leading a second generation of Warners into a new era were shattered forever. Harry and his wife Rea still had two daughters, Doris Ruth and Betty May, but daughters were not the same as sons.

Actually the Warners had three daughters. The third was Lita Basquette Warner, their adopted daughter and niece. The adoption was a curious aftermath of the death of Sam Warner.

Harry made no effort to conceal his distaste for the Ziegfeld dancer Sam had married, despite Sam's obvious love for Lina and his delight in their daughter Lita. Immediately after Sam's death, Harry moved swiftly to wrest the girl from Lina, then twenty and in Harry's eyes too wild to be a fit mother. Sam and Lina had agreed that if they had a son, he would be circumcised and raised a Jew; a daughter would be baptized and become a Catholic, Lita's faith. Harry could not countenance Sam's daughter as a Christian.

The wrangling began soon after the funeral. Harry was backed by Albert in arguing that Lita deserved a more stable upbringing than Lina could provide. Sam had left a $100,000 trust fund for the baby, but it provided an income of only $85 a week. Harry and Albert offered a $300,000 trust fund if Lina would give up custody of Lita.

Lina was confused and grief-stricken. Because of legal maneuverings, she had been denied her share of Sam's estate, now worth millions. She would need to work, and indeed, she wanted to continue performing. That meant Broadway and Hollywood and on the road in vaudeville—not the best circumstances to raise a young daughter. The Warners' proposal would assure Lita's future. With heavy heart, Lina agreed.

The regrets began almost immediately. In 1930 she sued Harry Warner, claiming he would not allow her yearly three-month custody of Lita despite his agreement to do so. She told reporters that Hollywood friends had snubbed her because she "had sold her baby."

"I am still her mother," Lina declared. "It is cruel for people to say I gave her away for adoption or 'sold' her."

Harry and his legal forces were too strong for her. "We have legal control of the child until she reaches twenty-one," said Rea Warner, "and she will remain with us until then."

It was thirty-two years before Lina Basquette saw her daughter again. She returned to her movie career and had a brief vogue in films like Cecil B. DeMille's *The Godless Girl*. Then, she claimed, she was blacklisted in the industry by the Warners. She remained in the news over the years with five more marriages, two suicide attempts and nervous breakdowns. She made her final film in 1943, and after working as mistress of ceremonies in a Las Vegas night-club, she retired from show business. In 1949 she started breeding Great Danes in Bucks County, Pennsylvania. Still active at eighty-two, she was the subject of a *New Yorker* profile in 1989. One matter gave her satisfaction: she had survived all the Warner brothers.

Chapter 6

Mobsters, Molls, Hoofers and Others

THE 1929 CRASH SCARCELY made a dent in Warner Bros.' fortunes. True, the company profit dropped to $7 million in 1930, a fifty percent reduction from 1929. But Warner Bros. appeared in better condition than most of the other film companies, some of which were lurching toward bankruptcy. Harry had amassed 51 subsidiaries, 93 film exchanges, and 525 theaters in 188 American cities, the majority in the populous East. Warner Bros. could withstand the vagaries of the film market with more ease than the companies that were less diversified.

In 1930 Warner Bros. became free of the justice department's requirement of two separate studios. Jack now moved all major production into the gleaming white Burbank studio, relegating the Sunset Boulevard lot to B pictures and shorts. Darryl Zanuck came along as head of production, and Hal Wallis became a producer under Zanuck's supervision.

Warner Bros. faced one major problem: lack of star power. The studio had a number of recognizable names, including those inherited from First National, but most of them were holdovers from silent films. None guaranteed box-office success, as did the big stars of MGM and Paramount. Albert Warner, who headed the sales division, complained to his brothers that his salesmen repeatedly heard the same thing from movie buyers: "We need stars. You guys don't have 'em." As a result, Warner Bros. films rented at lower prices than those of other major studios.

"Let's do something about it," said Harry, and he and Jack devised a daring plan.

One morning Hollywood was startled to learn that three important Paramount stars, William Powell, Kay Francis and Ruth Chatterton, had switched to Warner Bros. at double their salaries.

Adolph Zukor, Louis Mayer, William Fox and other industry leaders were outraged. All of them had adhered to a gentleman's agreement never to raid each other's contract lists. To do so would elevate star salaries and invite a ruinous bidding war. Now the Warner brothers, whom most of the leaders never trusted anyway, had broken that agreement.

Jack Warner bore their fury with total disdain. He and Harry had gambled and won. Film buyers now displayed greater respect—and offered higher percentages—for the Warner Bros. product.

One of Warner Bros.' new stars was an aging Britisher named George Arliss. For twenty years he had been a favorite of American theater audiences with his melodramas and plays about historical characters such as Disraeli, Alexander Hamilton and Richelieu. In the early 1920s he had transferred a few of the plays to the silent screen.

In 1929 Arliss was touring the country in *The Merchant of Venice*, and Jack Warner brought a party to see the play at the Biltmore Theater in Los Angeles. Afterward Warner, Zanuck and their party joined Arliss in his room at the next-door Biltmore Hotel.

Arliss had starred in *Disraeli* for United Artists in 1921, and Warner suggested remaking it as a talkie.

"Great idea!" Zanuck exclaimed, leaping up and striding back and forth as he expounded on a new opening for the movie. Arliss nodded his approval. Zanuck continued through the whole story until Arliss began thinking, as he wrote later, "You talk too much, young man. I should have more faith in you if you didn't have quite so much to say."

Jack Warner smiled over his assistant's exuberance. "He does all the work at the studio now," Jack confided. "I just add up the figures."

Disraeli proved a box-office success to everyone's surprise, including Harry Warner's. He had expected to lose money on the film, but had gone along with Jack's decision, hoping that *Disraeli* would attract the more serious-minded audience that scorned movies.

George Arliss, at age sixty-one, became a film star. *Disraeli* won him the Academy Award as best actor, and he made nine more films for Warner Bros. in the following four years. Arliss was amused by Jack's clowning and awed by Zanuck's invention, but he reserved his biggest praise for Harry.

In his memoirs Arliss wrote: "Harry Warner is the one who spends a great deal of time in New York, and as far as I am able to judge, never goes to sleep. His eyes are permanently open; his most sensitive finger he places on the pulse of the picture-going public and keeps it there. . . . But he also has a finger in a great many pies; if he sees a pie that he thinks his brothers might like, he puts a finger in it and doesn't take it out unless he finds it too hot—in which case he doesn't whistle but withdraws it noiselessly.

"His whistling is reserved for the time when his brother Jack, in Hollywood, telephones that some large sum is required to finance a few million-dollar pictures that are to be made; and then Harry strolls into the fertile fields of Wall Street and whistles the money off the trees."

Exactly who deserved credit for *Little Caesar* depends on whose memoir you read. Jack Warner claimed in *My First Hundred Years in Hollywood* that he was given the W. R. Burnett book by a songwriter he encountered in a train station after a duck hunting trip in Mexico. Warner said he read the gangster yarn on the train and wired his New York office from San Diego, ordering the purchase of the film rights.

Hal Wallis, in his autobiography, declared that he had been overwhelmed by reading *Little Caesar* and had recommended it to Warner, who bought it on Wallis's say-so. In *his* life story, Mervyn LeRoy recalled enthusing about the book after Warner had given him galley proofs to read. Warner, according to LeRoy, reported that others at the studio opposed buying *Little Caesar* because its harsh realism ran counter to the studio's light, entertaining pictures of the talkie period. After an hour of argument, said LeRoy, he won his case and ended up directing the film.

Darryl Zanuck made no claim of discovery, but with unaccustomed modesty he declared that *Little Caesar* was ninety percent LeRoy and ten percent Zanuck.

The casting of Edward G. Robinson as the Capone-like Caesar Bandello is also clouded by old men's memories. Warner remembered that an agent had suggested Robinson, who was playing a gangster on Broadway in *The Racket*.

Robinson recalled in his memoirs that Wallis had offered him a minor role in *Little Caesar*. After reading the script, he walked into Wallis's office in a mobster's uniform—homburg, heavy overcoat, white scarf, a cigar in his mouth.

"If you're going to have me in *Little Caesar* as Otero, you will completely imbalance the picture," Robinson announced. "The only part I will consider playing is Little Caesar."

Little Caesar was a landmark for Warner Bros. films, instilling a sharper edge that fit the depression times. An endless wave of gangster movies followed, many of them with the studio's unorthodox new star, Edward G. Robinson.

During rare admissions of fallibility, Jack Warner always remarked, "Don't forget I'm the guy who turned down Clark Gable."

Jack Warner wanted Douglas Fairbanks, Jr., for the role of Joe Masara in *Little Caesar*. Mervyn LeRoy objected, saying Fairbanks was too refined to play a Chicago racketeer. LeRoy had another actor in mind. He had seen Clark Gable as Killer Mears in *The Last Mile* at a Los Angeles theater and was struck by the animalistic power of his performance. LeRoy directed screen tests of Gable as Mears in *The Last Mile* and Joe Masara in *Little Caesar*. LeRoy later recalled the studio's reaction.

"What the hell have you done, Mervyn?" exclaimed Zanuck. "I'll tell you what you've done: you've just thrown away five hundred bucks on a test. Didn't you see the size of that guy's ears?"

In later years Jack Warner claimed responsibility for rejecting the actor who would be king. "Gable's ears stood out like a couple of wind socks," said Jack, "and I told Mervyn I didn't want him."

Clark Gable wasn't the only star who got away. A few years later, Mervyn LeRoy was preparing *They Won't Forget*, a daring film about two men falsely accused of the rape and murder of a young girl in a southern town. He auditioned fifty girls before making his choice: a dark-haired, poorly dressed, scared fifteen-year-old named Judy Turner. Leroy changed her name to Lana.

She made an unforgettable entrance on the screen, striding down a small-town street with her breasts bobbing rhythmically underneath a sweater. LeRoy didn't want to repeat the mistake with Gable. He signed Lana Turner to a personal contract. Jack Warner expressed no interest in adding her to the Warner Bros. contract list, and she spent her starring years at MGM.

In 1930 the Warner brothers were charged with extravagance and mismanagement by a stock trader who collected shareholder proxies in an attempt to unseat the company founders at the annual meeting in Wilmington, Delaware. Harry and Albert urged Jack to attend the meeting, which was scheduled for the Warner Theater because of the expected crowd. At Harry's suggestion, Jack delivered a speech tracing the family's beginning in Poland, the nickelodeon days in Ohio, the struggle against the movie powers to gain a place in the industry. It was Jack's finest hour, and the revolt was quelled.

Before returning to Hollywood, Jack saw a New York play,

Penny Arcade, and reaped a harvest from the cast: James Cagney, Joan Blondell and Frank McHugh. The greatest prize was Cagney.

Cagney came west with a three-week contract at $500 a week. Along with Blondell, he appeared in a movie version of *Penny Arcade*, retitled *Sinner's Holiday* and filmed in fifteen days. During the shooting, Jack Warner received the first inkling of the nature of his new actor.

The script called for Cagney, as the cowardly killer Harry Delano, to weep on his mother's breast and utter, "I'm your baby, ain't I?" He refused. When the director threatened to report him to Zanuck, Cagney replied, "I don't give a shit what you tell him, but I'm not going to say that line." And he didn't.

Cagney was immediately cast in *Doorway to Hell* as henchman to mobster Lew Ayres. During the filming, Warner Bros. offered Cagney a year's contract at $500 a week. Even though the actor could see that the terms favored the studio in every regard, he needed the security in depression times. He signed the contract, but then found himself languishing in supporting roles, including a two-minute scene with George Arliss in *The Millionaire*. Jack Warner offered to lend Cagney to Howard Hughes for the role of Walter Burns in *The Front Page*. "No thanks," Hughes replied brusquely. "He's nothing but a little runt."

Zanuck had already cast Eddie Woods as the mobster Tom Powers in *Beer and Blood*, and he announced that James Cagney would play the secondary role of quiet-spoken Matt Doyle. The director, William Wellman, had seen Cagney in *Doorway to Hell* and knew he was miscast in the new film. Wellman convinced Zanuck to switch the roles of Norris and Cagney.

The film industry's self-censoring Hays Office termed *Beer and Blood* an offensive title, and the film was renamed *The Public Enemy*. The Hays Office was keeping a close eye on sex and violence in films, and Jimmy Cagney was amused by the restrictions. His necking scene with Jean Harlow was kept so pure that Cagney offered his own grace note at the end. When he rose from the couch, he put his hands in his pockets and shifted his pants for greater comfort.

Whoever inspired Cagney's smashing a grapefruit in Mae Clarke's face is anyone's guess. Both Zanuck and Wellman claimed the idea. But Cagney said it derived from an actual happening. A Chicago gangster, Hymie Weiss, had wearied of his moll's constant chatter over breakfast and plastered her with an omelet. The grapefruit was considered less messy on the screen.

Public Enemy was a huge success, bestowing the star status that Jack Warner had been reluctant to accord Cagney. The actor was rushed from one three-week movie to another with never a raise in his $500-a-week salary. He took his grievances to Jack Warner, arguing that actors with far less drawing power were being paid $1,000 a week. Besides money, Cagney was irritated by being forced into personal appearances to tout other people's movies as well as his own.

Warner was deaf to Cagney's arguments, snapping, "You got a contract; I expect you to honor it." Cagney took the next train for New York.

"Cagney will never work in any studio again unless he returns immediately," Warner fumed to Bill Cagney, who had become his brother's manager. As the receipts came in from *Public Enemy*, *Smart Money* and *Blonde Crazy*, Warner relented. Cagney was given a new contract that paid him $1,000 a week and provided more favorable working conditions. This was the first of a long series of skirmishes, battles and all-out wars between Jimmy Cagney and Jack Warner. Cagney had no compunction about using a sneaky weapon on his opponent. Whenever Warner castigated him, Cagney responded in Yiddish obscenities, which he had learned in his Hell's Kitchen youth. When Warner was rendered apoplectic by the stream of Yiddish vulgarisms aimed at his character, Jimmy breezed out the door with a smug grin on his Irish face.

Bette Davis was packing to leave town, a conspicuous failure. She had made six films for Universal and on loanout to other studios, most of them flops. Junior Laemmle, the boy regent in charge of his father's studio, had remarked within Davis's hearing, "She has as much sex appeal as Slim Summerville." In September of 1931 her contract was terminated.

In their autobiographies, Jack Warner and Bette Davis give differing opinions about who brought Davis to Warner Bros. Warner claimed that she had been recommended by an underling, Rufus LeMaire, and Warner agreed to try her out for a role in *The Man Who Played God*.

Davis had a more romantic version. She related that while she packed for her retreat to New York, she received a telephone call from George Arliss. "And how are you, old boy?" she replied in a phony British accent, believing him to be an imposter.

It *was* George Arliss, and she had been recommended for the role of the young fiancée of the deaf concert pianist in *The Man Who Played God*. They met, and Arliss approved her for the role. Under Arliss's astute guidance, she performed with grace and subtlety, and a studio contract resulted.

After a series of unrewarding secondary roles, Davis was cast opposite Richard Barthelmess in *Cabin in the Cotton*. As the down-south spitfire, she had her first meaty role in a major production. The only drawback was being directed by Michael Curtiz, the Hungarian workhorse whose mauling of the English language became legendary. Curtiz gazed at Davis through the camera and muttered, "Goddamned nothing no-good sexless son of a bitch."

Despite a hostile director, Davis made the fickle Madge into an indelible figure, epitomized by the deathless line, "Ah'd love to kiss you, but ah just washed mah hair."

Bette Davis's dreams of greatness were soon dashed by films like *Three on a Match* and *Parachute Jumper*. The years of humiliating frustration mounted into a fury. Jack Warner would soon discover a tigress in his midst.

Paul Muni was no newcomer to films. The Academy had accorded him a nomination as best actor for his first film, *The Valiant*. *Scarface* established him as a film actor of extraordinary power.

Zanuck picked Muni for Warner Bros.' most searing social drama, *I Am a Fugitive from a Chain Gang.*

Robert E. Burns wrote the book about the savage cruelties of a Georgia chain gang, to which he had been wrongly condemned. Still a fugitive, Burns made a secret trip to California to advise on the script. Mervyn LeRoy directed the film with even harsher realism than *The Public Enemy.*

I Am a Fugitive previewed well, except for the ending which left Burns' fate ambiguous. Zanuck wrote a new scene in which the fugitive's girlfriend asks how he lives. "I steal," he replies. When LeRoy rehearsed the scene, the klieg light fuse blew, plunging the set into darkness before the final line. "Do it just that way when we roll," the director instructed.

It was an electric finish for a stirring film, as effective as Jimmy Cagney's corpse falling through the doorway in *The Public Enemy*. *I Am a Fugitive* became a critical and popular success, awakening the nation's conscience to the brutality of the penal system. Warner Bros. was praised for its public service, and as the honors poured in, Jack Warner offered no resistance to film projects with social consciousness, nor did Harry.

Muni remained at Warner Bros. for seven years, making the studio's most prestigious films. He specialized in biographies but never achieved his dream of playing Beethoven. "Nobody wants to see a movie about a blind composer," Jack Warner declared.

Loretta Young was one of the holdovers from First National, an exquisitely beautiful teenager who was ideal casting as the hero's girlfriend or younger sister. From 1929 to 1931 she appeared in twenty-one films, yet she was only earning $100 a week—not enough to buy a car so that she could avoid three streetcar transfers from her home in Carthay Circle to the studio in Burbank.

The actress waited in Jack Warner's outer office for two days before she was admitted. She explained her plight to the boss and asked if the studio could lend her the money to buy an automobile. "You can take it out of my salary," she said.

"I'll have to think about it, Gretchen," he replied, using her real name.

Loretta heard nothing from him. She and the rest of the Warner Bros.–First National contract players were ordered to appear at a spectacle that the studio was staging for a Shriners convention at the Los Angeles Coliseum. She was assigned to a convertible car that bore her name in large letters, and she began the circle of the track, waving to the thousands in the Coliseum.

Jack Warner suddenly appeared on the runningboard of the convertible, dressed in white pants, striped coat and straw hat.

"Okay, kid, you get the money for the car," he shouted. "But you gotta pay it back." He jumped onto the track and dashed away to continue his role as ringmaster for the pageant.

By 1932 the movie musical was dead, having been destroyed by industry excess and public apathy. In the wake of the sound revolution, the studios believed they could sell anything that was "all-talking, all-singing, all-dancing."

Warner Bros. poured out revues such as *The Show of Shows*, old musicals like *The Desert Song, The Gold Diggers of Broadway*, new musicals, *On with the Show, Say It with a Song*. The studio imported a host of musical personalities: Fanny Brice, Sophie Tucker, Jack Buchanan, Vivienne Segal, Irene Bordoni, Alexander Gray, Texas Guinan. Most of them were soon on the train back to New York.

Choreographers, stage directors, conductors, arrangers, lyricists and composers also came to California. Among them were Richard Rodgers, Lorenz Hart and Herbert Fields, who were assigned to write an original musical, *Hot Heiress*.

Upon his arrival, Rodgers got a taste of the playfulness of Jack Warner. The composer was summoned to the executive lunchroom where he found Warner, picture of the movie mogul, sprawled over the table with a large cigar in hand.

"Vell, now you're here, you got to get to work," said Warner in his best vaudeville Dutch accent. "And I don't vant any of your highbrow song-making. Muzik mit guts, ve got to have—songs mit real sentiment like 'Stein Song' and 'Vit Tears in My Eyes, I'm Dancing.' " It took a few minutes for Rodgers to realize that he was being put on.

After three years of one musical after another, the public cried "Enough!" Theaters began advertising on their marquees "Not a Musical." Harry Warner forbade the studio from making any films that were even suggestive of singing and dancing.

Then came *42nd Street*.

Zanuck claimed the idea. He came across a backstage story that was more tart than saccharine, and he had two scripts written, one with musical numbers, one without. He showed the script that contained no musical sequences to Jack Warner. Lloyd Bacon directed the musical version, according to Zanuck, on the Sunset Boulevard lot, away from the gaze of Jack Warner.

"Then the time came when we had to screen the picture," recalled Zanuck. "Jack went out of his mind. He never knew until it was screened that it was a musical. Only one thing, he loved it! He said, 'But what am I going to tell Harry? Have you got another version?'

"But he sent the musical version to Harry in New York and Harry wired back, 'This is the greatest picture you've sent me in five years.' "

42nd Street was an amalgam of unique talents, the most extraordinary being the choreographer's. Busby Berkeley was a former actor who had staged dances for Broadway shows, and then had come to Hollywood to choreograph numbers for Eddie Cantor musicals at Goldwyn. When the film musical fell into disrepute, he was reduced to directing stage presentations at Fanchon and Marco movie theaters. Then Zanuck summoned him for *42nd Street*.

During rehearsals, Zanuck wanted to view what Berkeley was preparing. Berkeley outlined the "Young and Healthy" number and had Dick Powell and the ensemble perform it in sections. He couldn't show how it would look, said Berkeley, because he planned it all in cuts. Zanuck was impressed and he gave Berkeley carte blanche—"anything he wants, he can have."

42nd Street started the musical cycle all over again. Warner Bros.

led the way with a stock company that included Jimmy Cagney, Dick Powell, Ruby Keeler, Joan Blondell, Ginger Rogers, Al Jolson and a host of second bananas. Busby Berkeley rose from choreographer to director, dazzling the film world with his musical numbers. They could cost $10,000 for a minute of screen time, as Harry Warner often noted.

Musical geniuses could be as much trouble as actors, Jack Warner discovered. Berkeley raced from one film to another, marrying and divorcing in between. His taste for alcohol matched John Barrymore's, and one night in 1935 he landed in serious trouble. Driving from a party at the home of Bill Koenig, production manager at Warner, he swerved his sports car across Pacific Coast Highway and smashed into an oncoming car. Three people died.

"Fix it," Jack Warner muttered to an underling. The great defense lawyer, Jerry Geisler, was hired to defend Berkeley. He argued that a blown tire had caused Berkeley to lose control. Guests at the Koenig party testified that Berkeley had not been drinking. After two hung juries, Berkeley was acquitted. And the officer who had investigated the accident became a member of the Warner Bros. security force at a handsome salary.

Chapter 7

Exit Zanuck, Enter Wallis

THE DEPRESSION CAUGHT UP with Warner Bros. in 1932. Neither Harry's financial mumbo jumbo nor the magic of Jack and Zanuck could prevent the company's slide into the red. The $8-million loss in 1931 mounted to $14 million in 1932. Jack listened to the alarm signals from New York.

The studio payroll, already lean, was cut further by layoffs and firings. Film schedules would be limited to eighteen days. Incensed by the troublemaking of newcomers like Cagney and Davis, Jack Warner issued a proclamation: henceforth no artist under contract would be allowed to say anything about any aspect of a film's production. To emphasize his ukase, he issued another round of salary cuts.

The stiff economies added to Darryl Zanuck's restiveness. Other studios began courting him, despite the industry's no-raiding policy. One night Zanuck attended a preview with Jack and his good friend, Columbia's bombastic Harry Cohn. When they were alone together, Cohn asked Zanuck, "How long has your deal with Warners got to run?"

Zanuck was shocked that Jack's good friend would attempt to

steal his prized lieutenant. Cohn advised him: "Don't ever forget that they're the Warner *brothers*. You can never go too far there. It's different at Columbia."

Zanuck reminded Cohn that Columbia was also a brother act, with Jack Cohn heading the New York office. "We operate differently," Harry assured him.

With Paramount and RKO in bankruptcy and Fox and other studios near it, industry moguls were in a panic. Five thousand of the nation's 16,000 movie houses had closed, and many were offering cut-rate admissions and free dishes. The Roosevelt bank holiday of March 1933 brought theater business to a standstill.

The movie moguls gathered together and decided on a fifty percent pay cut for all studio personnel. Zanuck was disturbed by the ruling, which did not apply to the bosses themselves. But he accepted his cut (from $5,000 a week to $2,500), and he urged his fellow workers to do likewise. Most of them had no choice.

By agreement, the Academy of Motion Picture Arts and Sciences and the Price, Waterhouse accounting firm would decide when normal salaries would be resumed. When the decision was made after eight weeks, Harry Warner balked. He refused to restore the cuts.

Darryl Zanuck felt betrayed. He had encouraged the studio employees to acquiesce to the cuts, promising a quick end to them. Zanuck and Harry engaged in a shouting match, and afterward Harry told his brother, "Jack, I don't think this is the kind of man you want around here."

"He isn't going to be around here," Jack replied.

On April 15, 1933, Darryl Francis Zanuck ("three charming fellows," Jack called him) announced his resignation as head of production at Warner Bros.–First National. He had accepted an offer from Joe Schenck to join Twentieth Century, which would merge with Fox two years later.

The next day, Jack summoned Hal Wallis to his office. Both Harry and Jack rose to shake Wallis's hand. "Well, Hal, you're it," Jack grinned.

*   *   *

"Working for Warner Bros.," said Wilson Mizner, "is like trying to fuck a porcupine. It's one prick against a hundred."

During his two years at Warner Bros.–First National, Mizner left a pure-gold legacy of one-liners that the studio's writers repeated for decades. His respect for authority was nil. Mizner described his boss, Jack Warner, as "the only man who has rubber pockets so he can steal soup."

Mizner's notoriety preceded him. He had been born near San Francisco in 1876, had spent his early years in Mexico where his father was U.S. ambassador, and then had studied at Santa Clara College. Whatever the Jesuit fathers taught him was soon forgotten in the Klondike, where he entertained gold miners with marked cards and diseased floozies at a Nome resort he called the Mc-Question.

When his Alaska luck ran out, he shifted operations to the silver fields of Nevada. In 1903 Mizner landed in New York where he read of the death of a traction magnate who had left $7.5 million to his widow. A month later New Yorkers were startled to read that the widow, Mrs. Charles T. Yerkes, fifty, had married Wilson Mizner, twenty-nine. For a fortnight he lived in the splendor of her Fifth Avenue mansion until he was kicked out. "The next time I marry," he vowed, "it'll be an armless midget. She won't be able to fight back." He had learned a priceless lesson: "Always treat a whore like a lady and a lady like a whore."

Prized for his witticisms, Mizner became a well-known man about Manhattan, hobnobbing with Diamond Jim Brady, Lillian Russell, Bat Masterson (then a New York newspaperman) and O. Henry. Irving Berlin dedicated a song to him with the title "The Black Sheep Has Come Back to the Fold." Mizner resented the implication that he would ever allow himself to be caught "in the fold." He coauthored three plays about the underworld and complained of one reviewer, "If that man can criticize plays, then I can make a watch that'll give milk."

Mizner managed a middleweight champion boxer, Stanley Ketchel, and from 1907 until the war he made thirty crossings of the Atlantic. It was not because he liked ocean travel; he traveled as a "greyhound," exercising his unparalleled chemin de fer skills among the rich passengers. He amended P. T. Barnum's line by expounding, "There's a sucker born every minute—and two to take him."

Back in Manhattan he operated an art gallery that specialized in fake old masters, meanwhile adding to his reputation for cynical wit. H. L. Mencken prized Mizner's line, "I respect faith, but doubt is what gets you an education." Of Mencken he said, "I liked the guy, but he talked me out of it."

He was a huge man, six feet four, and powerfully built with a deceptively bland face and hands that were broken and gnarled. "From punching out whores in the Klondike," he explained. His appetites were large and his habits bad; hence his health was often wretched. He distrusted all doctors. Faced with an appendectomy, he was visited at his hotel by a friend who assured him that the surgeon had never had a fatality. Mizner took a roll of bills from under his pillow and instructed, "Take these down to the lobby and see what odds you can get that I don't break his string."

Mizner liked to tell of one illness that appeared so serious that concerned friends summoned a priest. Mizner was too weak to protest. He closed his eyes and began reciting what he considered to be his sins. "When I opened my eyes," he said, "there was a cop standing by my bed. The priest had gone into the street to get him."

From 1918 to 1927, Mizner and his brother Addison, a noted architect, operated a land development scheme in Florida. They amassed $30 million in sales until their backers abandoned them and the Florida land bubble burst. The Mizners were sued for fraud, and their company was forced into bankruptcy.

Wilson figured Hollywood would be fertile ground for a quick buck. Now that the movies could talk, maybe they would pay for some of the prized dialogue he had been giving out for free. His hunch was correct. Darryl Zanuck hired him to add dialogue to Warner Bros.' scripts about crime and big-city life.

There was one problem about Mizner's employment as a studio writer: he didn't write.

"How come this guy is getting five hundred bucks a week for writing, and I've never seen anything he's written?" Jack Warner demanded.

"Mizner's a gag man," Zanuck explained. "He doesn't write anything. He just sits in the story meetings and contributes gags."

"Well, goddammit, if I'm paying him five hundred smackers to write, I'd sure as hell better see something," Warner declared.

Zanuck conveyed Warner's decision to Mizner. The next day Warner looked out of the bay window of his office toward the Writers Building. Mizner sat on the steps in the sunshine, surrounded by a few hundred pencils. He was methodically sharpening them with a knife. He soon resumed his normal duties.

Warner found Mizner handy on one social occasion. It was a party for Eddie Mannix, the MGM executive who looked like a bouncer, which he once was. Louis B. Mayer and Irving Thalberg invited their own staffs to the Ambassador Hotel, as well as those from other studios, including Warner Bros.

Mannix got drunk soon after the guests arrived and mounted the bandstand to beat out a joyful tattoo on the drums. The crowd was amused for a few minutes. Then the guests wanted to dance, and the bandleader was unable to pry Mannix away from the drums.

"C'mon, Eddie," Jack Warner coaxed, "be a good fellow and go back to your table."

Eddie muttered a threat, and Jack retreated. An amateur boxer, Joe McCloskey, was nearby, and Jack persuaded him to intervene. McCloskey grabbed Mannix and was escorting him across the dance floor when Mannix smacked him in the mouth with a hard right. MGM and Warner Bros. men, long engaged in bitter competition in the marketplace, poured onto the floor and began swinging at each other. Fists, plates and furniture were flying, and the delighted Eddie Mannix slugged any Warner man in sight.

Wilson Mizner, who had been watching the fray with an indulgent eye, rose to his height and approached the wildly swinging

Mannix. With one well-aimed punch, he felled Mannix and ended the battle.

Jack Warner became more tolerant of his undisciplined writer. Both invested in a new restaurant founded by Herbert Somborn and named by Mizner The Brown Derby. He explained that if the service and food were good enough "people would probably come and eat it out of a hat."

Every night Mizner occupied the number-one booth, which the Hollywood greats visited to share his wit. When Al Jolson asked him the state of the restaurant's business, Mizner replied, "Draw your own conclusions. Last night my waiters were arrested for vagrancy." When Douglas Fairbanks complained of a tilting table, Mizner said, "Now, actor, you wouldn't expect anything in Hollywood to be on the level, would you?"

Despite his poor work habits, Wilson Mizner proved to be an asset for Warner Bros. films. He contributed much of the bright dialogue in *One Way Passage* and served as the model for the con man played by William Powell. *Frisco Jenny*, about phony mind readers, was a natural for the Mizner touch. He collaborated with warden Lewis E. Lawes on the adaptation of Lawes' book, *20,000 Years in Sing Sing*. When they met, Mizner commented, "Warden, I never expected to talk to you without an iron grill between us."

In late 1932 word came from Florida that Wilson Mizner's brother Addison was not expected to live. Wilson wired, "Stop dying. Am trying to write a comedy." Addison, the only man whom Wilson truly loved, defied his brother's instructions. The deep loss Wilson felt was something he revealed to no one.

Since he refused to change his lifetime habits of booze and late hours, Wilson's health began to decline. But he continued reporting to the studio in what he called the San Infernal Valley.

Not quite fifty-seven, Wilson Mizner suffered a heart attack in the writers' building in mid-March 1933. He declined to be hospitalized, preferring the comfort of the Ambassador Hotel. As his condition worsened, a nurse asked if he wanted to see a priest. "I want a priest, a rabbi and a Protestant minister," he replied. "I want to hedge my bets."

He got a priest. When the priest asked if he could provide any spiritual consolation, Wilson said, "Much obliged, padre, much obliged. But why bother? I'll be seeing your boss in a few minutes."

The priest chided him for levity when he might be dead in a few minutes. "What? No two-weeks' notice?" Wilson protested. He died at 11:04 p.m. on April 3.

His feelings were expressed in a 1916 interview: "Death is the final guffaw of life; the funeral is only a Pullman ride straight through to the last stop. Death is a habit. You can't break yourself of it—it's rather a good one."

Jack Warner was a political ignoramus, but he was certain that he was a Republican. So it was surprising in 1932 when he supported the presidential candidacy of Franklin Delano Roosevelt.

As Jack later told it, he was summoned to New York on the urgent command of Harry. Jack, Albert and Harry met secretly in their offices with a powerful group including James A. Farley, Roosevelt's political manager; Joseph P. Kennedy, head of RKO Pictures and a Democratic power; Alfred E. Smith, former New York governor and presidential candidate; John J. Raskob, former General Motors executive, now chairman of the Democratic National Committee.

The purpose of the meeting: to assure the election of Franklin Roosevelt as President.

"The country is in chaos," Harry explained to his brother. "There is revolution in the air, and we need a change."

The Republican Warner brothers enlisted in the Democratic cause. Jack's assignment was to help Roosevelt become better known on the West Coast and to seek important supporters, including William Randolph Hearst.

After Roosevelt's nomination, Jack sought financial and political support from his friends. He failed, of course, with Louis B. Mayer, who was an intimate of President Hoover. When Roosevelt came to California, Jack staged a glittering pageant at the Los Angeles Coliseum. He offered Marion Davies a share of the profits for her favorite antivivisection charity, and she guaranteed the backing of the Hearst newspapers.

Jack booked Will Rogers to make the principal speech, and he telephoned Hollywood's biggest stars to assure their attendance. Jack joined the candidate's train in Santa Barbara, and the famous Roosevelt charm overwhelmed him. The Coliseum pageant was a roaring success, and Roosevelt won California by a landslide.

For his efforts, Jack won easy access to the White House—he even slept in Abe Lincoln's bed. Roosevelt won even more. Years later when he needed public support in the coming war against the Nazis, he found a willing propagandist in Jack Warner.

The marriage of Jack and Irma Warner had withered into a charade of formality and custom. After Harry's outrage over the Marilyn Miller affair, Jack became more discreet about his liaisons. Unlike Louis Mayer, Harry Cohn, Darryl Zanuck and other libidinous studio bosses, he no longer demanded sex from actresses under contract. It was bad studio policy, he concluded, and impossible to keep secret.

Irma was resigned to the traditional role of the Jewish wife. She maintained the home, cared for young Jack, did work for her favorite charities—and waited for her husband to return. Those times were rare in the early 1930s. Jack Warner had tremendous responsibilities as studio head and community leader, and his limited leisure did not include Irma.

Jack found a convenient way to hide his romantic adventures. Sam and Pearl Warner regularly invited the family to share the Sabbath on Friday evenings. Irma didn't attend because she'd never felt welcome by Jack's mother and father. Jack went reluctantly— he had never shared his parents' devoutness. He discovered that he could sneak out after dinner and call on one of his mistresses. "Cover for me," he instructed Milton Sperling, a junior studio executive who had married Harry's daughter, Betty.

At last Jack's roving eye landed on someone who beguiled him. She was Ann Page, a ravishingly beautiful brunet who had appeared in a few movies. With her raven hair and slender figure, she had the bearing of an Egyptian princess. She had come from New Orleans, where she'd had a Catholic upbringing and had been, according to publicity, a "society belle." To Jack's inconvenience, she had a husband.

Jack had known Don Alvarado since the early 1920s. He had come to the studio as Don Page (né Paige), a darkly handsome man from Albuquerque who was half Latin. He seemed ideal as a Rudolph Valentino clone, but not with the name of Don Page. He took his mother's maiden name, Alvarado. He had starred briefly as a Latin lover, but the vogue faded with Valentino's death, and he became a supporting player. Don and Ann were married in 1924, and their daughter Joy was born the following year.

Jack was determined to possess Ann despite their two marriages. Harry learned of the infatuation and preached against it. Jack would not be dissuaded. Unwilling to wait the year between divorce and final decree in California, he persuaded Ann in 1932 to divorce Don in Chihuahua, Mexico, where the decree would be immediate and the grounds secret. On September 15, 1933, he separated from Irma. Everyone at the studio was aware that Warner and Ann were living under the same roof.

William Randolph Hearst was boiling mad.

His relations with MGM had been deteriorating ever since Irving Thalberg had given *The Barretts of Wimpole Street* to his wife, Norma Shearer. Hearst had had his heart set on having his mistress, Marion Davies, play the Elizabeth Barrett Browning role.

Hearst felt he deserved some consideration from MGM. His Cosmopolitan Productions, with Miss Davies as its principal asset, had been with MGM ever since the merger in 1924. Most of the Davies films were losers, but Louis B. Mayer continued financing them and paying the star $10,000 a week. The reason was clear: Hearst was an immense power, both socially and politically.

After returning from a tour of Europe's grand palaces, Hearst and Miss Davies were convinced that she should portray Marie

Antoinette. MGM had bought screen rights to the popular Stefan Zweig novel about the fated French queen in 1933. Thalberg had started preparations for Norma Shearer to star. Hearst confronted Mayer, demanding the property for Marion.

Mayer was in a delicate position. If he caved in to Hearst, he would add to the growing rift between himself and Thalberg. Also, the studio would face a certain loss on a huge production starring Marion Davies. If Mayer sided with Thalberg, the studio would probably lose Cosmopolitan Productions and Hearst's great influence. As usually happened, financial considerations made up his mind.

"Tell you what I'll do," Mayer told Hearst. "Even though it would hurt you and Marion, I'll let you have *Marie Antoinette*, if you'll pay the full cost of production. What's more, we'll distribute it free, until you've got back your money. Then you'll pay us double the usual distribution costs."

As Mayer had expected, the proposal was rejected. Hearst placed a call to his friend Jack Warner, who said he would be proud to welcome Marion and Cosmopolitan Productions.

Moving the Marion Davies bungalow from Culver City to Burbank was a production in itself. The twenty-room building had long been a landmark on the MGM lot, and Marion would not leave without it. The building was sliced into sections and hauled across Los Angeles and through the Cahuenga Pass, stopping traffic and requiring utility wires to be raised along the route. It was a symbolic transfer of Hearst's power from one movie mogul to another.

Jack Warner reveled in the new association. He became a frequent participant in the fabled weekends at San Simeon. He enjoyed an affable relationship with the fun-loving Marion and closely studied the workings of an American tycoon. Jack did everything possible to make Hearst and Marion happy at Warner Bros.

For the climax of *Cain and Mabel*, a spectacular scene was planned for the wedding of Marion and Clark Gable. The camera would pan up a gigantic pipe organ with dozens of tap-dancing chorines playing musical instruments, the shot ending on high with fifty choir boys dressed in angel robes.

Hearst was enthusiastic about the scene and called in Jack Warner and Busby Berkeley.

"It's all so beautiful, but I can't do it," said Berkeley. "We don't have a stage high enough to fit it all in."

"Nonsense," replied Hearst. He asked Warner how much it would cost to raise a stage high enough for the *Cain and Mabel* finale.

"About a hundred thousand dollars," said Warner.

"Done!" Hearst exclaimed.

Studio workers watched with amazement as Stage 7 was sawed at its base and then raised with huge jacks. Berkeley's number was staged as he envisioned it, and to this day Stage 7 towers above the others on the Burbank lot.

Warner Bros.' partnership with Cosmopolitan proved unsatisfactory. All of Perc Westmore's makeup magic could not conceal the fact that Marion Davies had passed forty and the years of secret boozing now showed (Hearst did not tolerate drinking). The stammer which meant nothing in silent films hampered her in talkies, and her scenes required short takes.

Marion realized that her lover's long-ago promise to take her out of the Ziegfeld chorus and make her a star was now being pushed beyond her capacities. She started drinking heavily. On *Page Miss Glory* she developed a crush on costar Dick Powell, and he was forced to hide from her. Production costs rose because Marion was too drunk to report to the set in the morning.

Surprisingly, Warner Bros. lost no money on the four Cosmopolitan films. But after *Ever Since Eve* in 1937, Marion pleaded with Hearst to end her movie career. He reluctantly agreed.

Hearst had been thwarted in his plan for Marion Davies to star in *The Miracle*, the Karl Vollmoeller play that had become a classic through the inspired direction of Max Reinhardt. Warner Bros. owned the film rights, but Jack Warner had avoided handing them over to Hearst, realizing the folly of casting Marion Davies as a sainted nun. (Warner Bros. finally filmed *The Miracle* in 1959, badly.)

Reinhardt was greatly admired by Hearst, who had seen the director's mammoth productions in Europe and America. Hearst was among those sponsoring Reinhardt's *A Midsummer Night's Dream* in San Francisco and Los Angeles, and he helped convince Jack Warner to transfer it to film.

Hal Wallis had persuaded Jack to attend a performance of *Dream* at the Hollywood Bowl. Wallis had two things in mind: he wanted to transfer the play to the screen, and he thought Warner Bros. should sign the actress playing Hermia. Although Jack had little comprehension of the dialogue, he was impressed by the visual imagery of the Reinhardt production: silvery forests, gossamer costumes, tableaux lighted by torches.

Of Hermia he could see little but a tiny figure on the Bowl's immense stage. She was Olivia de Havilland, a delicately beautiful Saratoga, California, schoolgirl who had joined the play after the original Hermia and her understudy had left the cast for movie roles. Wallis brought her to the studio, and Jack remembered his first impression: "She had a voice that was like music to the ears. Like a cello, low and vibrant, and the Hollywood wolves would be milling around, hoping she could be had." In just six years that voice would be raised in protest over studio servitude, and the gentle Olivia would upset the film industry's contractual applecart.

Max Reinhardt was ecstatic about converting *A Midsummer Night's Dream* into a motion picture. He had directed four films in Germany from 1908 to 1914, and had always wanted to do more. His directors and actors—F. W. Murnau, Ernst Lubitsch, William Dieterle, Conrad Veidt, Emil Jannings, Marlene Dietrich—had succeeded in movies, but there had been no room for their mentor. Now he would have three sympathetic collaborators: Henry Blanke as production supervisor, Dieterle as codirector, Erich Wolfgang Korngold to adapt the Mendelssohn score.

Reinhardt's son Gottfried had been working as assistant director and writer in Hollywood, and he helped in the *Dream* casting, which came mostly from the Warner Bros. contract list. Fourteen-year-old Mickey Rooney was borrowed from MGM to repeat the role of Puck that he had played at the Hollywood Bowl.

Max arrived two weeks before production began and had little preparation in the ways of filming. Once the cameraman asked, "Would you like to look at the scene through the lens, Mr. Reinhardt?" The crew members could scarcely contain their laughter when Reinhardt put his eye to the camera handle. He relied on Dieterle to supervise the logistics of filming, while he concentrated on the actors and the visual aspects.

Although Shakespeare was Greek to him, Jack Warner put the studio's entire support behind *A Midsummer Night's Dream*. Harry agreed that the film would add prestige to Warner Bros., which was often scorned as a maker of fast-talking melodramas and leggy musicals. A lavish premiere was held at the Warners' Beverly Hills Theater, followed by a party given by Hearst at his Santa Monica mansion, Ocean House. The tennis courts were tented; two orchestras played for dancing; caviar and champagne were served.

Overshadowing the gaiety of the premiere and party was the feeling that *A Midsummer Night's Dream* would fail despite its beauty and cleverness. It did. American ears were untuned to Shakespeare's lyricism. Most critics were scornful, decrying the use of the Warner Bros. stock company, especially James Cagney, Joe E. Brown, and Hugh Herbert. The critics ignored Shakespeare's own use of clowns for comedy scenes.

The failure of *A Midsummer Night's Dream* devastated Max Reinhardt. He had been paid $150,000 for the film and was scheduled to make two more, Dostoevski's *The Gambler* and a French Revolution story. Scripts were being prepared, but Warner canceled Reinhardt's contract.

The remaining eight years of Max Reinhardt's life were laced with tragedy. The Nazis confiscated his string of theaters and his magnificent castle near Salzburg. Unable to find work in the United States worthy of his soaring talent, he was reduced to teaching classes in acting and directing in Hollywood while his wife played bit parts in B movies.

Both of Reinhardt's sons had become Hollywood producers, Gottfried at MGM and Wolfgang at Warner Bros. Wolfgang's work habits ran afoul of Jack Warner, who enforced a 9 a.m. starting time for writers and producers. Warner issued several warning notices to Wolfgang, who believed he was safe from firing because of good reports about his production *The Male Animal*. He was wrong. On the morning after the preview, Wolfgang was fired.

Warner circulated reports that Wolfgang was unreliable, and no other studio would hire him. This worried his father Max, whose health had deteriorated. In 1943 he was hospitalized after a stroke in New York.

A Reinhardt friend suggested to Elsa Maxwell, the party giver and a social acquaintance of Jack Warner, that Max's spirits would be revived if the studio rehired Wolfgang. In a telegram addressed "Dear Professor," Warner sent his wishes for a quick recovery. He added: "Know you will be happy to learn that Wolfgang is returning to our studio and we are very happy to have him back here. He is a lovely gentleman and an able craftsman and the Lord knows there are not enough of them around so we can always use a man of his ability."

Soon after Max's death a few weeks later, Jack Warner fired Wolfgang once more.

Firings became a major hazard for anyone who worked at Warner Bros. Mass firings. Department firings. Firings for economic reasons. Firings for no reason. A wave of fear swept studio workers every time Jack Warner boarded a train to New York. It was his custom to fire employees after he had left the state, thus avoiding any possibility of confrontation.

Once an order to discharge a hundred employees was rescinded. The studio gag went: "Harry Warner made a mistake. He thought it was Christmas."

Another favorite studio story concerned the "happy gate man." During one of Jack's nighttime prowls of the lot to determine that lights were turned off, he encountered a gate man who was warbling Verdi arias in a soaring voice. Jack engaged him in conversation and learned that the gate man studied voice during the daytime. "What would you rather be, a singer or our gate man?" Jack asked. "A singer," the man replied. "You're fired," said Jack.

Even Rin-Tin-Tin, the mortgage burner, was fired. In late 1929, the star's trainer, Lee Duncan, received a letter through his lawyers from a Warner Bros. executive in New York. After the next Rin-Tin-Tin movie, the dog would have to seek other employment. The letter explained that the making of animal pictures "is not in keeping with the policy that has been adopted by us for talking pictures, very obviously, of course, because dogs don't talk."

Douglas Fairbanks, Jr., had been a serviceable leading man ever since the merger with First National. Although he didn't fit the tough-guy mold of Warner Bros.' gangster era, he could be cast in romantic leads and in light comedies. When young Doug was threatened with an alienation of affections suit, Jack Warner was delighted.

"That guy Fairbanks has so goddamn many faggot friends that I was beginning to wonder about him, too," Jack said. "This kinda thing is a relief and it'll prove he's no fairy. Let 'em print the story. I don't care." Rather than embarrass his wife Joan Crawford and his parents, Doug decided not to press charges against his blackmailing accusers.

By the end of his five-year contract in 1933, Fairbanks' salary had grown to more than Jack Warner was willing to pay. He proposed a new contract at a lesser amount, arguing that other stars had accepted such a proposal. He claimed that young Doug's pictures had done so poorly that theater owners in the East had been taking his name off their marquees. Realizing that Warner was seeking any means to sign him for less money, Doug decided to let the contract lapse.

Kay Francis, one of the three stars snatched in the raid on Paramount, established herself as a Warner Bros. favorite until her salary mounted to $4,000 a week during the last year of her contract.

Jack Warner now put Bette Davis in the roles intended for Francis, and the studio announced that she would play out the end of her contract in B pictures.

The star tried to shrug off such treatment by claiming she'd been thinking of retiring, anyway. Later she admitted that Warner's actions had broken her heart. Her career never recovered.

If Jack Warner's abuse of Kay Francis was designed to make other stars compliant to his will, he failed. They recognized that the studio's treatment of Francis would befall themselves as their careers ran down. They resolved to get what they could while they could.

Jack Warner's separation from Irma and his liaison with Don Alvarado's wife had been topics of Hollywood gossip since the Warners parted in 1933. Finally in January 1935, Irma sued for divorce, charging desertion. She testified that her husband had left home and refused to live with her. A property settlement was agreed on, with Irma to retain custody of Jack Jr., who was eighteen. Warner would provide him with spending money, college expenses and a car. Mrs. Warner was granted an interim decree, under which neither party could remarry for a year.

Don Alvarado had been well rewarded for giving up Ann. He enjoyed a lifelong job at Warner Bros., first as an actor and then as an assistant director. For nine years until his death in 1967, he was manager of the Warners' huge ranch in Arizona.

Exactly a year after Warner's divorce, he and Ann were married by a rabbi in the village of Armonk, New York. Also making the motor trip from New York City were a few friends, including Jack Dempsey and his wife Estelle Taylor, moneymen A. C. Blumenthal and Jules Brulatour, and Irving Netcher and his wife, one of the Dolly sisters.

Significantly, Jack's brothers and their families were not present. "Thank God our mother didn't live to see this," exclaimed Harry. Pearl Warner had died in April 1935 after marking her fifty-eighth wedding anniversary. On a return to Youngstown two years later, Ben died of a stroke while playing cards with old cronies.

The family sided with Irma and refused to countenance Ann as a member of the family. That put Jack Jr. on their side, and the rift between father and son grew. Warner was smitten with Ann and was proud of her regal presence at their parties. He didn't even protest when she decided to put her own stamp on their Angelo Drive mansion, buying European marbles and antiques to convert it into a French palace. Jack accepted Ann's daughter Joy as his own, and in 1937 the Warners announced the adoption of a two-year-old girl they named Barbara.

Jack Warner was elated. He now possessed a consort befitting his position as a prince of Hollywood.

Chapter 8

The Trouble with Actors

PAT O'BRIEN IN *CEILING ZERO*

Jᴀᴄᴋ Wᴀʀɴᴇʀ ᴡᴀs ʜᴏʀʀɪғɪᴇᴅ when he drove past the Warners' Beverly Theater and saw the marquee. He was well aware that James Cagney's contract required top billing in all his films, and here was a blatant violation right in his own backyard. As soon as Warner arrived home, he telephoned the theater manager.

"Damn it!" Warner barked. "I told you about Cagney. Now get out there and change the billing before he sees it and blows a fuse."

Too late. A newspaperman had already seen the marquee and had informed Cagney, who ordered a photograph taken. Cagney had completed five films in 1935, one more than his contract called for. He had been cast in yet another prison picture, *Over the Wall*. The title was apt; that's where he went.

The Cagney rebellion was inevitable. Even though his earlier walkout had raised his salary to $4,000 a week, he rankled under the rigid paternalism of Jack Warner. The actor felt that he was being rushed from picture to picture so that Warner Bros. could profit from his status as one of the top-ten box-office stars. He knew that most of the films were potboilers.

Cagney realized his value to Warner Bros. when a theater owner told him, "I have to take five dogs to get one Cagney film." Translation: under the policy of block-booking, theaters were forced to buy five routine movies in order to acquire one with a star of Cagney's caliber.

Working conditions at Warner Bros. inevitably clashed with Cagney's underdog spirit. Actors often performed in two pictures at once, literally bicycling between sound stages. The shooting week extended from Monday through Saturday and often ran into early Sunday morning as directors raced to complete sequences and meet schedules. Warner Bros. directors were chosen for their speed, not their artistic talent. It was usual for Jack Warner to hand them scripts on Friday with instructions: "Start shooting Monday."

Actors frequently worked until midnight and were told to report back early the next morning. Even Christmas and other holidays meant no respite. The time had to be made up by working the following Sunday.

Soon after the Screen Actors Guild was founded in 1933, James Cagney became a member. This was a daring move, because Jack Warner, Irving Thalberg, Harry Cohn and other studio bosses were united in fierce opposition to unionizing of the studios. Company unions, retaliation and threatened blacklisting were among the weapons used by the producers. Cagney, Boris Karloff, Robert Montgomery and a few others would not be intimidated.

Cagney filed suit against Warner Bros. for breach of contract. Jack Warner recognized that Cagney had an open-and-shut case with the billing gaffe, but he decided to extend the dispute through the courts. He anticipated that Jimmy, like any actor, would grow apprehensive about his absence from the screen and seek a settlement. But Jimmy Cagney wasn't like any actor. He and his wife returned to the East, and he made no conciliatory overtures toward Jack Warner.

While lawyers on both sides prepared their cases, Bill Cagney received offers from Sam Goldwyn, David Selznick and other producers. Warner squelched such proposals as soon as he heard of them, threatening injunctions if anyone tried to hire his wayward star. Then Jimmy and Bill Cagney found a company that wasn't afraid of Jack Warner.

Edward Alperson, who had been general sales manager of Warner Bros., had formed Grand National Films, an independent with grandiose plans. He offered Cagney $100,000 a picture plus ten percent of profits for two movies. The Cagneys accepted.

Great Guy featured Jimmy as a former prizefighter who combatted the cheaters as an agent for the Bureau of Weights and Measures. In *Something to Sing About* he was a bandleader who became a movie star. Jimmy enjoyed both films because he could play something besides a criminal.

The two Grand National films were well received by critics, who welcomed Cagney back to the screen after a year's absence. But after the big outlay for the star, Grand National had little left for production values, and the films looked skimpy in comparison to the Warner Bros. product.

Jack Warner made certain that *Great Guy* and *Something to Sing About* did not succeed. Warner Bros. salesmen instructed theater owners that if they booked Grand National films, they would not receive any Warner Bros. product.

Cagney was scheduled to make a third film for Grand National, *Dynamite*, but the company ran out of money. He decided it was time to return to Warner Bros.—on *his* terms. They were $150,000 per picture, profit participation, two pictures a year with right of refusal.

Jack Warner's other major headache, Bette Davis, continued to assert her Yankee will. She railed against threadbare scripts and hack directors. When Warner cast her as a lumberjack in *God's Country and the Woman*, she rebelled. He tried to persuade her, arguing that it would be a Technicolor movie made on location in Washington with George Brent as costar.

"I won't do it!" she exclaimed. "*Satan Met a Lady* was bad enough, but this is absolute tripe!"

She stormed off to her Laguna Beach home. Warner placed her on suspension for three months and enjoined her from working for any other producer. But a different kind of producer appeared at her door. He was Ludovic Toeplitz, a fast-talking English-Italian who had coproduced *The Private Life of Henry VIII* with Charles Laughton and *Elizabeth the Great* with Elizabeth Bergner.

Toeplitz offered Davis two movies, a romance to be made in Italy and a film with Maurice Chevalier in France. The producer was aware that Jack Warner would probably file a lawsuit to stop her, but he was willing to take the chance. So was Davis. She and husband Ham Nelson packed to leave for London, eager to escape the Warner lawyers.

Jack and Ann Warner left at the same time for a European holiday. He met with Toeplitz in Venice and each tried to con the other. The meeting ended in a shouting match. Toeplitz was determined to proceed with his American star; Warner vowed to prevent him. Davis had returned from wardrobe fittings in Paris when she was served with an injunction by Warner Bros. lawyers in England. Now she would be faced with huge legal fees as well as a loss of salary. Davis would not halt her crusade.

The Warners were hobnobbing with William Randolph Hearst at his Welsh castle when he was served with the subpoena to appear in the case. "I like Bette, why don't you settle with her?" Ann asked. Jack refused. He was as stubborn as Davis.

The London dailies headlined the case of the recalcitrant star versus the big movie studio. The setting was the tradition-laden English court of law, with bewigged Britishers who looked and sounded like C. Aubrey Smith and Nigel Bruce. Warner Bros. had retained the crafty Sir Patrick Hastings, whom Agatha Christie used as a model for *Witness for the Prosecution*. Davis employed the towering, stentorian Sir William Jowitt.

"I think, m'lord," Sir Patrick began, "this is the action of a very naughty young lady." Across the courtroom, the Bette Davis eyes flashed a look that had withered many an actor.

Hastings argued that if one willful actress would be able to abrogate her contract, the entire film industry would end in disarray. To Davis it was clear: she was fighting not only Jack Warner and his brothers, but all the major studios. Hastings pooh-poohed the allegation that Miss Davis's contract amounted to slavery. He would be willing to face slavery, Sir Patrick averred, if someone would pay him $2,400 weekly, the salary she would be receiving at the end of her contract in 1942.

"Call Mr. Jack L. Warner to the stand."

Warner answered the summons hesitantly, awed by his surroundings. But he soon gained his bearings and began defending the studio's position, explaining that Warner Bros. had spent a great deal of money to make Miss Davis a star. She bridled at his implication that the studio raised her from nothing to her present eminence.

Under cross-examination, Warner testified, "I'll admit that an actress could be heartbroken if she had to play parts that were not fitted for her." He defended the studio's right to present Davis's likeness in ads, like the current one for Quaker Oats, to be able to force her to attend the Republican National Convention even though she was a Democrat, and to be able to restrain her from divorcing her husband for three years.

Sir William presented a near-nude poster of Miss Davis and asked if Warner would want any woman he was fond of to be presented thusly.

"If she was a professional artist, it would be part of her duty," Warner replied.

After three days of testimony and arguments, the judge took the case under consideration. Davis, who had faced the trial alone after her husband returned to America, retired to a seaside resort to await the verdict. She lost. Warner Bros. was granted an injunction for three years or for the contract's duration, whichever was shorter.

The suit had already cost Davis $30,000 she didn't have, but she was determined to appeal. Then George Arliss came to call. His Hollywood career over, he had retired to England.

"Go back, my dear Bette," said the frail old actor in his clear, measured tones. "You haven't lost as much as you think. Go back gracefully and accept the decision. See what happens. I think good things."

Jack Warner greeted her with welcome arms. "Let's forget all about it, Bette," he said. "We've got work to do."

It started with *Marked Woman* and continued with *That Certain Woman*, *Jezebel* (her second Academy Award), *Dark Victory* and a dizzying number of unforgettable performances.

"Jack was very gracious after the suit," she recalled fifty years later. "If you lose a case, you have to pay both fees. He didn't make me pay the studio's fee. He was very, very good to me when I came home. I got better directors, better scripts. I think he respected me a great deal."

Two newcomers to the Warner Bros. contract list arrived in Burbank during the mid-thirties, each of them destined to provide Jack Warner with a bountiful supply of headaches for years to come.

Jack fully expected Edward G. Robinson to play Duke Mantee in *The Petrified Forest*. The role of the gang leader who holds a desert cafe hostage was obvious casting for Robinson. But Humphrey Bogart, a onetime Broadway juvenile and failed film actor, was determined to repeat his New York triumph as Mantee. He communicated with his friend Leslie Howard in London.

"I will not play in *The Petrified Forest* unless Humphrey Bogart appears as Duke Mantee," Howard notified Jack Warner. Warner needed Howard to repeat his Broadway triumph. Jack grudgingly agreed to sign Bogart to a contract.

Bogart was widely praised when *The Petrified Forest* was released in 1936, but neither Warner nor Hal Wallis perceived him as a leading man. He hadn't the face for it, and despite his gruff manner, his slight lisp was distracting. "He sounds like a fairy," Warner complained. Bogart languished for the next five years; in twenty-eight films he seldom did more than play a henchman or enemy of Cagney or Robinson.

During those years Bogart reserved his off-screen fights for his third wife, Mayo Methot. A sometime actress who specialized in blowsy blondes, she had a violent temper that erupted when she and Bogart drank, which was continuously. At the height of one argument, they hit each other over the head with whisky bottles. Bogart stormed out of the house and headed for a Sunset Strip night spot. The doorman pointed out that Bogart was bleeding from his back. He hadn't noticed that Mayo had stabbed him on his way out.

Bogart found someone else to fight with: Jack Warner.

Warner-baiting became a sport for Bogie; he was constantly devising new mischief to infuriate the boss. Once he was quoted in an article as calling Warner a creep.

"How dare you call me that?" Warner railed. "I looked it up in the dictionary. A creep is a loathsome, crawling thing."

"But I spell it with a "k": k-r-e-e-p, not c-r-e-e-p," Bogart explained. "It's a different word entirely."

For all of Bogart's alcoholic playfulness over the years, he remained professional on the Warner Bros. stages. Only once did he transgress. One morning an assistant reported to Jack Warner that Bogart had refused to appear on the movie set. After a long night's journey into booze, he was crazily riding his bicycle, yelling "No hands!" to everyone he saw. Later Bogart faced the reproving Warner and said, "I apologize. It'll never happen again." It never did.

In 1931 the acquisitive Harry Warner rented Teddington Studio in London. He bought it outright in 1934. The studio was used by Warner Bros. to produce program pictures, mostly for the British market. Irving Asher, who was in charge of the studio, engaged a young actor for a minor role in a routine film, *Murder at Monte Carlo*. Asher was impressed by the tall, debonair Errol Flynn, who had come from Tasmania with fanciful tales of his adventures in the South Seas. He had played a few small parts on the London stage, and in a screen test he displayed amazing presence.

"I recommend that you sign Errol Flynn," Asher cabled Jack Warner, sending along the test. When he received no reply, Asher sent an urgent message. Finally Jack responded, "She stinks." Obviously he hadn't viewed the test. Hal Wallis did, and he sent for Flynn.

Flynn arrived in Hollywood in early 1935 and for weeks did little but play tennis at the Los Angeles Tennis Club. Jack Warner was always distressed when contract actors were not working on pictures, and he suggested casting Flynn in *The Case of the Curious Bride*. When the director, Michael Curtiz, balked at using the inexperienced actor, Warner instructed Wallis: "When we bring a man all the way from England, he is at least entitled to a chance, and somehow or other we haven't given him one. I want to make sure he is in the picture."

Curtiz provided Flynn with a role—as a corpse. Warren William, playing the lawyer-sleuth Perry Mason, looked at Flynn's motionless body and said, "That's him, all right."

Warner Bros. had cast Robert Donat as the pirate leader in *Captain Blood*. Now Donat refused to leave England for California, claiming that the weather might aggravate his asthma. The truth was that he didn't want to leave his mistress, and she refused to make the trip.

The studio desperately sought another star. Leslie Howard declined the role. Brian Aherne, Ian Hunter and George Brent were tested, but Warner dismissed them as not dashing enough for Rafael Sabatini's Captain Blood. Then he remembered the cocky Tasmanian.

"It was Jack Warner who had the guts to take a complete unknown and put me in the lead of a big production," Flynn later declared, dismissing all others who claimed to have discovered him.

In his memoirs Flynn recalled an incident in the filming of *Captain Blood*. Swinging from one boat to another, sword in hand, he suddenly collapsed on the deck. He feared a recurrence of the malaria or blackwater fever that afflicted him in the Pacific. For an antidote he swallowed a jigger of brandy. Then the whole bottle.

When Warner saw the rushes, he summoned Flynn. The actor languished in the waiting room until he was finally admitted to the inner office.

"Listen, Flynn, there's one thing I won't have around this god-damn lot—drinking!" Jack ranted. "I don't drink. My brothers don't drink. Another thing, Flynn, you can't screw around with the broads."

The tirade continued until Warner rose and said genially, "How is everything else going?" The startled Flynn said "Fine," and he departed with promises to behave.

Flynn had learned a valuable lesson: all Jack Warner's rantings about studio behavior were pure bluster. A star who was valuable to Warner Bros. could do what he wanted, exact any terms. "I should have asked for a raise," mused Flynn, who was being paid $300 a week. He resolved never to make such a mistake again.

By the mid-1930s, Warner Bros. had escaped the financial doldrums. A modest $674,158 profit in 1935 ended four years of red ink. The figure mounted to $3.2 million in 1936, and the company would remain profitable for twenty years. The studio had survived the depression as well as a fire in late 1934 that had destroyed dozens of back-lot sets and caused the heart attack death of the fire chief.

As the company prospered, so did Jack Warner. His salary rose from $88,333 in 1935 to $137,333 two years later. His actual wealth climbed as the rebounding of the Warner Bros. stock price added millions to the value of his holdings.

Despite their wealth, both Jack and Harry Warner continued their penny-pinching ways. Harry was noted for his habit of picking up nails whenever he found them on studio streets or stages; he would see that they were returned to the carpentry department. Jack's penchant for turning off lights became part of the Warner Bros. legend. Ray Stark recalls his first job in Hollywood, writing photo captions in the publicity department for 15 dollars a week. One night he forgot the office rule to switch off the lights as he left. The next morning a handwritten note from Jack Warner appeared on Stark's desk: "When not in use, turn off the juice."

Similar messages were left for offenders during Warner's nightly prowl of the offices. One night he found a ceiling light aglow and was unable to locate the switch. As he later admitted to his mistress, Jackie Park, he climbed a ladder to unscrew the bulb, lost his balance, fell and broke a leg.

Jack Warner was in his heyday. He loved being pope of the ever-bustling Burbank lot, posting his bulls by memo and telephone. He looked at rushes of all the major films, dictating his wishes to producers and directors.

To Hal Wallis: "We must put brassieres on Joan Blondell and make her cover up her breasts because, otherwise, we are going to have these pictures stopped in a few places. I believe in showing their forms but, for Lord's sake, don't let those bulbs stick out."

To supervisor Sam Bischoff: "Be sure that Bette Davis has her bulbs wrapped up. If she doesn't do it, we are either going to retake, or put her out of the picture. And if you talk to her, you can tell her I said so."

Jack Warner could never be described as prude, but he was ever vigilant for anything that might let loose the dogs of censorship. Like all studio heads, he was also wary of any scandal that might cause censure of Hollywood, as did the sex and drug sensations of the 1920s.

In 1936 Mary Astor seemed on the verge of creating a major scandal. In a child custody suit, her former husband wanted to introduce as evidence Astor's diary, which reportedly detailed a flaming affair with George S. Kaufman. It was rumored that the diary also contained pornographic accounts of her liaisons with many top stars and directors. (She said the alleged document was a forgery.)

The powers of Hollywood were alarmed. Sam Goldwyn summoned Miss Astor and her attorney to attend a meeting with Jack Warner, Harry Cohn, Irving Thalberg, Louis B. Mayer, Jesse Lasky and other industry leaders.

"The scandal would give the industry a bad name," declared

Thalberg, urging the actress not to allow the diary as evidence. She rejected the pleas. As it turned out, the judge would not allow the diary to be introduced as evidence because pages had been torn out. Miss Astor's career survived the scandal. Within three years she was a Warner Bros. star.

When Hal Wallis proposed a biography of Louis Pasteur, Warner displayed little interest. Wallis persisted, and Warner said, "All right, go ahead. But don't let the sales department know what you're doing. They'll kill me when they find out." The Pasteur film, planned for Paul Muni, was hidden under the title *The Death Fighter*.

"What's this?" the head salesman exclaimed when J.L. presented the year's product at the sales meeting. "You're casting Muni as a pug? You'll ruin him."

"No, no," Warner replied quickly. "Muni plays the manager."

The Story of Louis Pasteur required no apologies when it was released in 1936. It won critical acclaim and good box office, and Muni was proclaimed best actor of the year by the Academy. The following year, *The Life of Emile Zola*, starring Muni, brought Warner Bros. its first Academy Award for best picture.

Jack Warner accepted the award with unexpected humility, expressing appreciation to Wallis, producer Henry Blanke, director William Dieterle, Muni and all others connected with the film. "They and they alone are entitled to the glory of having created the masterpiece this industry has so highly honored," he said.

Despite the periodic bloodlettings and contractual wrangles, Warner Bros. studio retained a curious air of bonhomie in the late 1930s. Actors, producers and especially writers railed against the unreasoned tyrannies of Jack Warner, but most of them took a grudging pride in the fact that Warner Bros. was the most exciting studio in town. Much of the year's product was routine, particularly Brynie Foy's mind-numbing B pictures. But each year brought fresh achievements, films that shed new light on history and examined America's social ills. No other studio did that so consistently.

As the only major studio in the valley—Universal's main asset was Deanna Durbin; Disney made only cartoons—Warner Bros.

had a geographical isolation that promoted an us-against-them attitude among employees. Crafts workers, many of whom held lifetime jobs, were especially loyal.

Ronald Reagan recalls: "In those days of contract players, directors and everything, there was a kind of family relationship. There was always a good morale about Warner Brothers. Every year the studio gave a banquet for all the employees. Even the back-lot fellows could go into the wardrobe department and come out with tuxedos to wear to the dinner.

"It was just a Warner Brothers family meeting. That was the affair that a lot of outsiders would have loved to attend. Because every year they would show the bloopers. Everybody waited for that."

Jack Warner ordered the bloopers—actors blowing their lines and other on-camera mishaps—saved by the cutting department through the year. They were assembled and screened at the banquet to a delighted response, especially when the butt of the joke was a serious actor like Paul Muni or Bette Davis. The clips were inevitably bootlegged out of the studio, and they turned up forty years later on television network blooper shows.

While Hal Wallis supervised Warner Bros.' major films, Bryan Foy, the ex-vaudevillian who made the first all-talkie, presided as keeper of the B's. In 1936 he produced twenty-nine movies at an average of $100,000 apiece, all of them destined for the lower half of a double bill. Foy became notorious as a plot switcher. Once he was instructed to start a movie starring Humphrey Bogart and the Dead End kids the following Monday. He borrowed bits and pieces from *Mayor of Hell*, *20,000 Years in Sing Sing*, *San Quentin* and *Road Gang*. The result was *Crime School*, which earned creditable reviews.

Foy once bragged that he had made eleven versions of *Tiger Shark*, in which Edward G. Robinson lost an arm.

"I followed the script of *Tiger Shark* scene for scene and made the same thing as *Lumberjack*, only this time the guy lost his leg instead of an arm," said Foy. "Then I made it as *Bengal Tiger*, exactly the same, scene for scene, only now he was a lion tamer with the circus and lost his arm. The writers protested that he had lost his arm in *Tiger Shark* and I told them he may have lost his arm in *Tiger Shark* too, but he's got two arms. Later I did *Tiger Shark* over again in Africa with a big-game hunter."

Foy's wide acquaintance included bookies, con men and underworld figures. He used them as sources for his crime pictures, especially those set in prison. Brynie loved prison pictures. He could repeat the same plots and use the same set, merely changing the name of the prison.

Every year Foy altered the gender of the characters in the script and made a film about a women's prison. There was a reason for this. Brynie's underworld pals kept pestering him to put their girl-friends in the movies. Brynie solved the problem by filming a women's prison story. One year he was inundated by inquiries about the next one. He handed the messages to an assistant and muttered, "Parole 'em."

Foy managed to include a nightclub scene in almost every picture. This was a service for the higher-class hoodlums, whose girl-friends could work as extras in their fancy gowns. One year he noted that most of the girls were Mexican and other Latins. He telephoned the assistant director: "You know that Ritz nightclub set? Change it to La Golondrina."

Foy in later years made this blunt commentary on Jack Warner: "He'll shake your hand on Friday and tell you you're set for two years, then go to New York, call you on Monday and fire you. I know him well and I like him—don't get me wrong—but he has no guts. Warner would fire anybody. I was in and out seven times, but he was fearless about calling you up three months later and insisting you come back."

"I have another Robert Taylor sitting in my office," said the hyperbolic Hollywood agent, Bill Meiklejohn.

"God made only one Robert Taylor," Max Arnow, Warner Bros. casting director, replied over the telephone. But Arnow was willing to look at Meiklejohn's client from midwestern radio, Ronald Reagan.

Reagan was tested and signed to a seven-year contract, which the studio could cancel each year. His starting salary was $200 a week. Reagan didn't meet his new employer, Jack L. Warner. Instead he was introduced to Brynie Foy, who immediately cast him in *Love Is in the Air*. It was a 1937 remake of the 1934 *Hi Nellie*, with Reagan in the Paul Muni role.

The new actor continued in Foy retreads with an occasional third or fourth lead in major films. Still, Reagan never complained about his status.

"I always thought it was a pretty smart thing [the studio bosses] did," he now remarks. "They never pretended that *they* could make a star or know who was or was not a star. But by putting you to work in those second features on the bottom half of a double bill, they waited for the audience to tell them whether they had a star. A pretty sound practice."

Three years and twenty-one pictures after Reagan had arrived at Warner Bros., Jack Warner finally took notice of the young actor. At a preview of *Knute Rockne, All American*, Reagan had the audience sniffling at the death scene of football player George Gipp, "the Gipper." Warner instructed Wallis: "Put the kid in *Santa Fe Trail* with Flynn." Wallis protested: "But the picture starts shooting tomorrow!" Warner merely repeated his command.

Reagan was awakened at dawn and told to report to the studio for wardrobe fittings. He would be playing the young George Armstrong Custer to Errol Flynn's J. E. B. Stuart in a movie about the future Civil War generals during their years as young officers.

Arriving at the studio on time, Reagan detected a palpable difference in the way his fellow workers regarded him. Before, they had treated him as an amiable but insignificant contract player. Now he was being greeted by people who had never spoken to him before.

In the wardrobe department, he was met by a sweating, porcine tailor with an armload of uniforms which had been altered to Reagan's measurements during the night. The tailor hung the uniforms on a clothing rack and then took another set of uniforms from a rack and tossed them into a bin. Reagan happened to notice a tag: "Dennis Morgan—Lt. Custer." Realizing he had replaced Morgan in the role, Reagan learned a profound lesson in how studios manipulated actors' careers.

Working with Flynn also proved a revelation, as Reagan recalls:

"I thought Errol was great at the type of things they had him doing, using his physical ability in action things. What I always noticed about him was that, believe it or not, he had an inferiority complex about his acting. He surrounded himself with great character actors, never realizing that if anybody could steal a scene, they would do it.

"He was always leery about a costar or a second lead. In other words, a leading man type. He worried about those. So he'd go to the director and plead for help."

That happened during a campfire scene in *Santa Fe Trail* when the young officers gathered to watch an Indian woman tell their fortunes in the sand, predicting they would fight in a great war— on different sides. Reagan noticed Flynn conferring with the director, Mike Curtiz. When the scene was lined up, Reagan found himself standing behind two taller actors.

Reagan realized the futility of protesting. As Curtiz delivered his instructions to the actors and the cameraman, Reagan noticed he was standing in loose sand. He slowly began collecting the sand in a mound. After the final rehearsal, he stepped on the mound and delivered his single line in full view of the camera.

After *Santa Fe Trail* Reagan returned to Brynie's B's. Among them was *International Squadron*, for which the old Cagney-O'Brien *Ceiling Zero* plot was transformed to the Battle of Britain, with Reagan a Yank in the RAF. *King's Row* finally convinced Jack Warner of Reagan's potential as a star. He was offered a new contract at three times the salary he had been receiving.

"But I had seen what the studio's pattern had been," Reagan says. "As soon as an actor showed promise, he would be offered a new contract at more money, but the contract would be extended. I didn't think I wanted that. But Lew Wasserman, who was my agent at MCA, told me, 'Look, Ronnie, you're a reserve officer. You're going to be called up eventually, so you might as well get as much as you can *when* you can.' I went along with him, and I'm glad I did."

Reagan was filming the anti-Nazi *Desperate Journey* with Errol Flynn when he received a red-ink envelope telling him to report for active duty. Jack Warner had written the army on March 30, 1942, asking that Reagan's call-up be postponed until he could complete the "patriotic" movie. The request had been denied, and Reagan's close-ups were filmed in a hurry before his departure. The long-shots were done later with a double.

Money was Reagan's concern. He knew that Warner Bros. salaries terminated as soon as an employee entered the service. He wasn't worried about his wife, Jane Wyman, who would continue receiving her studio salary, but Reagan asked the studio if his mother could be paid $75 a week to answer his fan mail. "We can't start a precedent," Jack Warner declared. But he did allow Reagan a $3,900 loan, from which his mother would be paid $75 a week. Reagan would be required to repay the loan at the rate of $200 a week after the war. No interest would be charged.

Jack Warner could never resist a wisecrack. Mervyn Leroy was excited about a massive new novel, *Anthony Adverse*, and asked Jack by telegraph if he had read it. Warner wired back: "Read it? I can't even lift it." However, he bought the novel for Leroy to direct.

In 1938 a new Warner Bros. player reported to the studio. He was Jules Garfield, late of the Group Theater. Warner greeted him: "We expect great things of you, Jimmy." When Garfield looked puzzled, Warner added, "I understand we're going to be calling you James something or other."

The actor protested that he had already changed his name from Julius Garfinkle to Jules Garfield and he didn't want to make another change.

"What kind of a name is Garfield?" Warner asked. "It doesn't sound American to me."

"American enough to be the name of an American president."

"All right, all right, we'll call you James Garfield."

"But that was the president's name. You wouldn't call an actor Abe Lincoln, would you?"

As John Garfield, he made a sensational debut in *Four Sisters* and joined the roster of Warner stars.

Jack Warner lost a third brother in 1939.

The first had been Milton, the athlete who had died young. Milton had been a four-letter man at Rayen High School in Youngstown, and his pitching prowess brought an offer from the major leagues. Milton became an eighteen-year-old sensation of the Cleveland Indians, pitching two no-hitters in 1915. In that same year his appendix ruptured, and he died a few days later. Twelve years after that, Sam Warner died.

David Warner was the quiet brother. He had been that way almost from his birth in Ontario, the youngest of the family. At first his parents believed he was merely overwhelmed by his older brothers and sisters. But as time went on, David remained a silent observer, smiling his amusement but adding little to the ferment of the family scene. When his four older brothers embarked on their mutual enterprise, David remained at home.

David studied for a time at Western Reserve University, and then dropped out, married a Cleveland girl and had a daughter. He was working for a film exchange, not Warner Bros., when he was stricken in 1918 with what was diagnosed as a form of sleeping sickness. He was twenty-eight.

Virtually no one outside the family knew about David Warner. Jack never mentioned him. Whenever Jack went to New York, he disappeared for a day, traveling to Boston to visit David in a sanatorium. Finally in March 1939, David could not be roused from his sleep. Jack's grief was almost as great as when Sam had died a dozen years before, but he shared his sorrow with no one but Ann.

Chapter 9

War Clouds

"I'LL BET IT'S A PIP!"

That was Bette Davis's reaction when Jack Warner had tried to entice her with a property called *Gone with the Wind* in a futile effort to forestall her contract-breaking flight to Europe. She later learned about *Gone with the Wind*, and desperately wanted to play Scarlett O'Hara. But Warner, alarmed by what the movie would cost, dropped his option to buy the book. David Selznick quickly made a deal to pay Margaret Mitchell $50,000 for the screen rights.

Selznick sounded out Jack Warner about borrowing Bette Davis to play Scarlett and Errol Flynn for Rhett Butler. Surprisingly, Davis opposed the deal. Her decision centered on Flynn; she loathed him and believed he was poor casting for the role.

She then urged Warner to buy the Broadway play *Jezebel*. Warner argued that no one wanted to see a picture about a woman who wears a red dress to a traditionally white New Orleans ball. "Ten million women would," she answered. *Jezebel* was a box-office hit, winning an Oscar for Bette and infuriating Selznick. He fired off a letter to Harry Warner, protesting that Jack had been comparing *Jezebel* to *Gone with the Wind* and that Bette Davis was being called Scarlett on the Warner lot.

"May I remind you that the rights to *Jezebel* were repeatedly turned down by your studio, as by all other studios," Selznick stated, "until after the public's attention was directed to *Gone with the Wind?*"

While Selznick continued beating the publicity drums over the casting of the *Gone with the Wind* leads, Olivia de Havilland received a telephone call from George Cukor, whom she had never met. "I'm going to direct *Gone with the Wind*," he said. "Would you be interested in playing Melanie?" When she replied that she would be very interested, he asked her to make a secret visit to his office at the Selznick studio in Culver City.

Cukor was delighted with Olivia's reading of the script. He called Selznick immediately and said, "I think you should hear Miss de Havilland."

A date was set for three o'clock on Sunday at Selznick's home. At Cukor's suggestion, Olivia committed a scene to memory. As Selznick sat five feet away, she played Melanie to the Scarlett of squat, fat, bespectacled George Cukor. Selznick, who had been impressed by Olivia in *The Adventures of Robin Hood*, was captivated by her performance.

When Olivia confronted Jack Warner about playing the role, he snapped, "You don't want to be in *Gone with the Wind*. It's going to be the biggest bust in town."

"I don't care if it's going to be the biggest bust in town," she replied. "I want to be in it."

"Why would you want to play Melanie? Scarlett is the big part."

"Scarlett doesn't interest me. Melanie does. That's the part I want."

"The answer is no!"

Olivia was downcast but not defeated. How else to approach the problem? she pondered. Why, of course, through Ann!

She telephoned Mrs. Warner and asked her to tea at the Brown Derby in Beverly Hills. Olivia poured out her feelings about Melanie. "I know how you feel," Ann said sympathetically. "I used to be an actress myself."

Jack resisted his wife's persuasions, arguing that he would have no end of trouble from de Havilland if he allowed the loanout. "Think of the prestige for Warner Bros.," she said. "After all, you discovered her and made her into a star." With grave concern he gave in.

Selznick would be allowed to borrow Olivia de Havilland, Warner said, but he wanted something in return. Selznick agreed to trade his one-picture contract with James Stewart, who would make a Warner Bros. film, *No Time for Comedy*, with Rosalind Russell.

Before Olivia left for the Selznick studio, Warner said, "If I let you go, you're going to be difficult."

"Oh no, Mr. Warner, I won't be difficult," she promised.

He seemed to be testing her when she returned to Warner Bros. Her first role after *Gone with the Wind* was a minor one as Lady Penelope in *The Private Lives of Elizabeth and Essex*, starring Bette Davis and Errol Flynn. Olivia was hurt, because she had been Flynn's leading lady. But she vowed to maintain her promise to Jack Warner, and she endured the film without complaint.

Next Warner loaned her to Goldwyn for *Raffles* with David Niven. She knew that remakes never worked and that she was miscast as the sophisticated older woman. But she accepted the film, knowing that it would be a failure.

Next assignment: a third remake of *Saturday's Children*.

"I had to take a stand," she recalls. "I had been good twice in a row. There had to be a limit."

When she declined the role, Warner exclaimed, "Ah-ha! I knew she'd be difficult! She *did* get difficult. You can't trust actors."

Jack brought George Raft to Warner Bros. in 1939 so that he would have another star for gangster pictures when Cagney or Robinson was on suspension. What Warner didn't know was that George Raft didn't want to make gangster pictures. Raft had been embarrassed by recurring reports that he was closely tied with organized crime bosses. The reports were true, but Raft thought he could offset them by reforming his on-screen image.

A prison picture, *Invisible Stripes*, was Raft's first at Warner Bros.

The director, Lloyd Bacon, reported to Jack that Raft was upsetting Humphrey Bogart, William Holden and other actors by changing his lines so that he would appear less hard-bitten. "I wish there were some way to fade him right out of the picture," Bacon sighed.

Warner provided the solution: kill Raft off early by having a prison guard knock him down a flight of stairs. *Invisible Stripes* proceeded smoothly thereafter.

Raft rejected any other script that dealt with crime. Finally he agreed on a trucking melodrama, *They Drive by Night*, which proved to be his best Warner Bros. film. Humphrey Bogart was also in the cast, and his constant needling made Raft furious. Raft refused to work with Bogart in *Manpower*, and Warner assigned Eddie Robinson as substitute.

The costarring was destined for trouble. Robinson, the aesthete, took his acting seriously. The unschooled Raft played himself on the screen. Poles apart in personality, they had another conflict: both were infatuated with their costar Marlene Dietrich.

The first flare-up came when Raft insisted on changing Robinson's dialogue. "Look, George, you may think the line does not make any sense, but I have to speak it and it's all right with me," said Robinson. Raft then unleashed a burst of expletives at Robinson before the entire company. Filming was halted for hours until peace was restored.

For a week the two stars spoke to each other only while reading lines in scenes. One noon they were scheduled for a scene in which Raft was to stop a fight between Robinson and another character. Instead, Raft began pounding Eddie, pushing him around the set. "What the hell is this?" Robinson demanded between blows. Raft spouted more insults until the director, Raoul Walsh, and others separated them.

Raft and Robinson shook hands on the next day of filming, and *Manpower* resumed. In the climactic scene, Raft was supposed to be holding Robinson by his belt from the top of a tower and then release the belt so that Robinson would fall to his death.

"This will make me a heavy," Raft announced, refusing the

scene as written. A compromise was reached to make Robinson's fall seem like an accident.

Raft received an offer from Universal for a film with Rosalind Russell at a salary of $150,000. The actor couldn't get an answer from Warner Bros., so he flew to New York where he found Jack Warner in his Waldorf Astoria suite. Raft pleaded his case: the $150,000 would help him win a divorce from his long-estranged wife. Jack granted his permission.

"I left the Waldorf elated that I had Jack Warner's okay," Raft recalled. "I didn't have anything in writing, but who needed that when I had Jack Warner's word?" Raft had been naive. Warner reneged on his word.

The last of Raft's five films for Warner Bros. was *Background to Danger*, a spy adventure during which he slugged Peter Lorre for blowing smoke in his face during a scene. When the film was over, Raft told Jack Warner, "I want out of my contract."

Warner was relieved to hear the news. He offered to settle the contract for $10,000. Raft nodded and wrote a check for $10,000. Warner delighted in telling the story afterward. He had fully expected to pay Raft the $10,000.

Before leaving Warner Bros., George Raft provided his enemy Humphrey Bogart with two magnificent gifts. Among the films Raft rejected were *High Sierra* and *The Maltese Falcon*, both of which fell to Bogart.

Paul Muni had been the first to refuse *High Sierra*. He was unwilling to play another hoodlum after his string of biographies, and his association with Warner Bros. ended. Raft objected less about the character of Rick Blaine; he was concerned because the burned-out fugitive dies in the last reel. Raft was superstitious about such things.

Bogart grumbled about playing Rick Blaine; he had just appeared in another Raft reject, *All Through the Night*. But he accepted *High Sierra*, and the reviews provided the first recognition of his starring potential, despite the fact that Jack Warner had demoted him to second billing under Ida Lupino, a new and promising addition to the Warner Bros. contract list.

Warners had filmed *The Maltese Falcon* twice before, with Ricardo Cortez and Bebe Daniels in 1931 and Warren William and Bette Davis in 1936 (as *Satan Met a Lady*). After reading the script, George Raft wrote Jack Warner: "I strongly feel that *The Maltese Falcon*, which you want me to do, is not an important picture. . . . I must remind you again, before I signed the new contract with you, you promised me that you would not require me to perform in anything but important pictures. . . ." Raft also objected to the fact that *The Maltese Falcon* had been assigned to an untried director.

John Huston had arrived at Warner Bros. in 1937 at the age of thirty-one after a modest career as an actor, playwright and artist. He clashed immediately with the authoritarian Jack Warner.

"What kind of a racket do you think this is?" Warner demanded in a memo which castigated Huston for arriving late in the morning.

"I didn't know I was in a racket!" Huston wrote in reply. "This information comes as a considerable surprise to me. I don't associate with racketeers, but if such is the case, I terminate my contract here and now. . . ."

Warner forgave such insolence because of Huston's amazing productivity; he contributed to such screenplays as *Jezebel*, *Juarez*, *Dr. Ehrlich's Magic Bullet*, *High Sierra* and *Sergeant York*. When his contract was renegotiated, Huston was granted the right to direct the next script he wrote. To everyone's surprise, he chose the twice-failed *Maltese Falcon*.

Huston prepared meticulously, making sketches of each camera angle. Jack Warner was pleased when the film was completed in thirty-four days at $324,182, more than $50,000 under budget. The film was previewed several times, and although audiences were attentive, the comment cards indicated that they were confused by the plot. Jack Warner provided the solution: add a foreward that would help explain the forthcoming situation and insert a gloved hand firing a gun at the beginning of the film.

Warner was delighted when *The Maltese Falcon* played to a rapt audience at the next preview in Pasadena. To avoid comparisons to the earlier films, he proposed calling it *The Gent from Frisco*. Wallis convinced him to retain the original title.

"Don't call me back until you're not ready."

It was Michael Curtiz's parting remark after he and Jack Warner had ended a clash of wills. Warner scratched his head in puzzlement and added it to his ever-growing collection of Curtizisms.

No director at Warner Bros. was the object of more derision, scorn and praise than Michael Curtiz. He could make some of the studio's most sublime movies while simultaneously trashing the English language. Curtiz can seldom be found in critical works about directors because he was no *auteur*. He was a studio hand, a man who could direct comedies, dramas, musicals and westerns with equal skill. In thirty years at Warner Bros. he made a hundred films, including a handful of classics.

During one of his talent searches in Europe during the 1920s Harry Warner had discovered the voluble Hungarian who had earned a reputation for striking visual imagery in his films. Jack Warner liked Curtiz because he could shoot fast. His first major assignment was Warner Bros.' 1928 spectacular, *Noah's Ark*. Despite the mammoth production, including twosomes of every species obtainable, the film was a failure. Audiences were driven from theaters by the ear-splitting Niagaras, thunders and other sound effects that had been added to the film after *The Jazz Singer*.

Curtiz maintained an undistinguished course until *Captain Blood*, which he invested with a dashing excitement that made Errol Flynn a star. Flynn, who had a sadistic streak, delighted in tormenting Curtiz. The actor arrived late, hung over and blissfully unaware of his lines. Curtiz, who had directed Flynn's cadaverous debut in *The Case of the Curious Bride*, fumed: "I picked you up from a corpse and made you a hero. And now from a hero I'll put you back to a corpse and you'll be a bum again." During a dozen pictures together, Curtiz always referred to his star as "Earl Flint."

Humphrey Bogart was another Curtiz tormentor. Bogie and Peter Lorre shared a wicked sense of humor, and they were distressed to observe that Michael Curtiz was totally humorless. They decided to remedy that.

One morning Bogart recited a funny story to the blank-faced director. "Now ve shoot!" Curtiz announced. Bogart kept blowing his lines through take after take. Curtiz became increasingly perplexed and aggravated. Then Lorre told a joke to no reaction, and he stumbled through *his* dialogue. After two days of this treatment, Curtiz got the message: a laugh for a take. Shortly afterward, the two actors were approaching Curtiz on a studio street. As soon as Curtiz saw them, he burst out laughing.

Jack Warner loved to recite Curtizisms: "This scene vill make your blood curl"; "I'm at the pinochle of my career"; (to extras) "Stop standing around in bundles."

During a story conference for *Kid Galahad*, Curtiz turned to an underling and said, "No, I don't vant yes men. If you don't agree, say so even though I vill fire you."

Warner recalled a *Casablanca* conference when Curtiz remarked, "Vell, Jock, the scenario isn't the exact truth, but ve haff the facts to prove it."

One of Curtiz's actors in *The Charge of the Light Brigade* was a newcomer to Hollywood, David Niven. He witnessed an authentic Curtizism when the director called for a stampede of a hundred riderless chargers. Curtiz yelled, "Bring on the empty horses." It became the title for Niven's second book of reminiscences.

Jack Warner had been going to Europe every summer since the early 1930s. He and Ann spent a few weeks at their villa in the south of France, and he visited Warner Bros. exchanges in European capitals. With each trip, Warner became more alarmed at the growing might of Naziism. In 1938 he performed a mission for Michael Curtiz. The director feared for his mother and two brothers who were living near Budapest. Warner found them in comfortable surroundings but convinced them to leave Hungary for the United States.

Warner Bros. began producing patriotic short subjects, pleasing Harry immensely. He took more interest in the shorts than in most of the feature product. Jack was also proud of them and delighted in their by-product: awards. Jack adored awards. His biggest thrill came when the French gave him the Legion of Honor for the Pasteur and Zola films. He could also find elation in a plaque from an American Legion post for a short about the Bill of Rights. Warner Bros. won three Oscars in three years with *Declaration of Independence, Sons of Liberty* and *Teddy, The Rough Rider*.

Both Harry and Jack were fiercely anti-Nazi at a time when many Americans believed the country could coexist with Hitler. Other studio owners cautioned the Warners about hurting film sales in Germany. The Warners' answer: *Confessions of a Nazi Spy*. It was a replay of *My Four Years in Germany*, except that in 1939 the United States was not at war with Germany.

J. Edgar Hoover had suggested the project to Jack Warner. One of his FBI agents, Leon Turrou, had worked as an undercover agent and was writing a book about German espionage. Hal Wallis sent the scriptwriter, Milton Krims, to pose as a Nazi and attend German-American Bund meetings. The result was a strong script which was cast with Edward G. Robinson as Turrou and Francis Lederer, Paul Lukas and George Sanders as spies.

"The Warner brothers have declared war on Germany with this one," wrote critic Pare Lorentz. "There is no way any producer could argue against dramatizing any social or political theme on the grounds that he's afraid of domestic or foreign censorship. Everybody duck."

Cautious studios began following the Warner Bros. lead despite the vituperation aroused by *Confessions of a Nazi Spy*. The German ambassador protested to Secretary of State Cordell Hull. The German-American Bund sued for a half-million dollars. Hitler saw the movie at Berchtesgaden and frothed. Theaters were threatened with bombings, and the film's makers and actors received death threats.

Jack and Ann Warner received a bombing threat that included a detailed plan of their house and grounds.

Warner Bros. pressed on with other anti-Nazi subjects, *Underground* and *All Through the Night*, and produced shorts about London's survival of night bombings, narrated with cool realism by Quentin Reynolds. Jimmy Cagney flew for the Canadian Air Force in *Captain of the Clouds*, and Errol Flynn piloted for the U.S. Navy in *Dive Bomber*.

In 1940 a party of generals and admirals visited Jack Warner. War was inevitable, they said, but Americans remained apathetic about preparing for it. Would Warner Bros. produce some short films about the services? Of course, Jack replied.

Warner placed Owen Crump in charge. Crump had come out of radio to join Gordon Hollingshead's shorts department, and Warner knew him as a fast, competent worker. Crump toured bases and airfields throughout the country and produced stirring films that were popular in the theaters.

After the United States entered the war, Warner summoned Crump to his office. "We're going to Washington," Jack announced. "Hap Arnold wants to see us."

"What for?" Crump asked.

"He says he wants us to make some training films."

The commander of the Army Air Corps had more in mind. When Warner, Wallis and Crump entered his office, he explained that the air corps would soon become a separate entity. The Army Signal Corps had been making films for the air corps, and now Arnold wanted his own unit.

"Jack, you know how to make pictures," said General Arnold. "Can you do that for me?"

"Sure," Jack replied.

After a two-hour conference, Arnold said his visitors would need army commissions to assure their authority. Jack, aware that Darryl Zanuck had been made a full colonel in the army, half-seriously asked to become a general. He had to settle for lieutenant colonel. Wallis was offered a major's commission but declined it. Crump became a captain.

Jack returned to California and was fitted for a uniform by the studio wardrobe department (the cost was added to a movie's budget). His secretary, Bill Schaefer, read from an army manual about how an officer was supposed to behave, and Jack took notes. Every morning Crump saluted the boss and reported on the unit's activities.

Directives began pouring in from Washington, and Warner suddenly realized that being a lieutenant colonel was not simply an honorary title; now he had to produce films. And nobody had said anything about where the money would come from. He sent Crump to Washington to work out the details.

"I'll give you the Sunset Boulevard studio; you can make the pictures over there," Warner told Crump. The First Motion Picture Unit was established on the old lot where *The Jazz Singer* had been filmed. Stages became barracks with rows of cots, and a mess hall was installed. Trade paper ads attracted top professionals to man twelve film units; many of them were overage for military service and eager to serve. The outfit later moved to the Hal Roach studio in Culver City.

"We're in desperate need of pilots," Hap Arnold told Jack Warner. "We can't just draft 'em; we need college graduates. Can you make a recruiting film that can play in college towns in May, before graduation?"

Warner assured the general that he could, even though it was already late April. He gave Crump all of Warner Bros.' resources to complete the assignment. Crump borrowed stock footage from the air corps and the studio, and he began writing a script. He needed someone to narrate and appear in the film, and he asked for James Stewart, who was training as a pilot. Stewart flew his own plane from a northern California base to March Field, disgruntled because he thought he had been enlisted for a Warner Bros. publicity stunt. As soon as he learned the nature of the mission, he memorized his lines, delivered them and flew back an hour later.

Warner placed the studio on a twenty-four-hour basis to complete *Winning Your Wings*, and the final print was ready eleven days after General Arnold's request. Then Warner telephoned the heads of other studios to urge their theater chains to book the film. Arnold credited *Winning Your Wings* with helping recruit over 100,000 pilots, all that the air corps needed, and more. Another film, *Rear Gunner*, brought thousands of other recruits to complete manning of the aircraft.

The First Motion Picture Unit made six hundred training films as well as propaganda shorts. Jack Warner saw them all, even though some were too technical for any layman to understand. After a couple of years, he decided to resign his commission and devote himself full-time to the studio. He felt that he had done his duty for the national effort. A legacy of his service was the title he gloried in ever afterward: The Colonel.

Warner Bros. made more pictures about the war than any other studio. All the services were covered, as well as most of the allies. There were movies about the home front as well as patriotic musicals like *This Is the Army* and *Yankee Doodle Dandy*.

Nearing the end of his life, George M. Cohan had yearned for a film biography. He proposed the idea to Sam Goldwyn, who wanted Fred Astaire to star. But Astaire did not want to attempt an imitation of the famed song-and-dance man, and Goldwyn dropped the project.

Learning that Cohan was dying of cancer, Jack Warner visited him at his Fifth Avenue apartment in the spring of 1941. Cohan agreed to let Jack Warner make his life story. "Why not?" Cohan told Warner. "At heart you're a song-and-dance man like me." Cohan insisted on script approval, since he was touchy about his private life. He heartily approved of James Cagney as Cohan. Cagney welcomed the role. He had been the object of bad publicity from conservatives who called him a radical for his vocal support of Rooseveltian reforms. A piece of Americana like *Yankee Doodle Dandy* would repair his image.

But when Cagney read Robert Bruckner's script, he told Jack Warner: "It's no good, I won't touch it. But I'll tell you what I'll do. I'll give it a blanket okay now if you put the Epsteins on it to liven it up and inject some humor." Warner agreed to a rewrite by Philip and Julius Epstein, the bothersome, brilliant twins who had brightened many a Warner Bros. script.

Michael Curtiz directed *Yankee Doodle Dandy* with the customary speed that made him Warner's favorite. Cagney complained that he was being rushed from one musical number to another without enough time to memorize the dances so that they would seem effortless. Finally in the "Off the Record" number from *I'd Rather Be Right*, he drew a blank.

"Mike, I can't think of the next step when I get there," Cagney said wearily. "I'm tired." Ever mindful of the schedule, Curtiz said the number had to be finished so that the extras would not be required another day. Cagney remained firm, and Curtiz complained to Jack Warner.

"Cagney is stalling so the extras can get another day's work," Warner grumbled. Cagney was president of the Screen Actors Guild and a notorious "friend of the little guy." No amount of argument could persuade Cagney to continue the day's work.

Yankee Doodle Dandy proved a perfect blend of patriotism and entertainment that won a grateful audience and the Academy Award for Jimmy Cagney. George M. Cohan was immensely pleased with the film (which depicted only one of his two wives) and wanted it premiered on his birthday, the fourth of July. When it appeared he might not live that long, the opening was pushed up to May 29, 1942. Cohan died the following November.

"Paul von Henreid, I believe." Jack Warner rose from his desk chair with mock formality, clicking his heels.

"Delighted to meet you, Mr. Warner," replied the suave Viennese.

"You can call me Jack."

"In that case you should call me Paul."

"I intended to."

Warner had seen Henreid in his first American film, *Joan of*

Paris, and wanted him to appear with Bette Davis in *Now, Voyager*. Although the part was small, Henreid agreed to it. Then he discovered that Warner wanted him to be "a cross between Leslie Howard and George Brent."

Henreid was fitted with wide-shouldered suits, his hair was trimmed, and his face was plastered with makeup. When Davis saw his test, she exclaimed, "What did you do to that man? How can I act with him? He looks ghastly, like some floorwalker in a department store!" The actor was allowed to restore his own look and wear his Savile Row suits.

The cigarette scene: Casey Robinson had written it with Henreid lighting his own cigarette, taking Davis's from her mouth and replacing it with his, and then putting hers in his own mouth. Too much business, Henreid objected. He remembered something he and his wife Lisl had done while motoring in Europe—the passenger would light two cigarettes at once and then hand one to the driver.

"Sensational!" Bette Davis responded when he demonstrated the move. But the director, Irving Rapper, didn't like it. Bette immediately went over his head and sent for Hal Wallis. He not only approved Henreid's cigarette bit, he ordered it included two or three times in the script.

"Great piece of business," Jack Warner agreed when he saw the rushes the following day. A national fad was started, one that would haunt Henreid and Davis whenever they appeared in public. Ever the gentleman, he acceded to fans' requests to light two cigarettes. She responded in Bette Davis style: "Leave me alone. I don't know you and you don't know me."

Tennis became a ritual for Jack Warner. He was crazy about the game, and he built a tennis court a short distance from his Burbank office. During Darryl Zanuck's tenure at the studio, he and Jack often engaged in a spirited match. In later years Warner could look down from his office and see writers and messenger boys playing on the court. He ordered it padlocked.

One of Bill Schaefer's weekly duties was to prepare a list of possible players for weekend tennis at the Angelo Drive house. They included actors, directors and producers from Warner Bros. as well as other studios. A regular was Solly Biano, casting director for Warner Bros. He had been a tournament player, and he served as Warner's doubles partner, covering most of the court.

One Saturday Biano introduced a young player to Warner: "This is Bill Orr." Jack looked quizzically at the good-looking blond man with alert blue eyes. "Have you been up here before?" he asked. "No," replied Orr, "but I was under contract to your studio for two years."

Bill Orr was a graduate of Phillips Exeter Academy who astonished his social family by becoming an entertainer. He did imitations of Franklin Roosevelt and other prominent figures in a socially conscious revue, *Meet the People*, which became a huge hit in Hollywood. Sought by all the studios, he accepted a contract with Warner Bros. Before he signed, he insisted on meeting the boss. Orr's mother accompanied him.

"What do we want this kid for?" Jack Warner joked. "Why don't we sign the mother?" He devoted the meeting entirely to the attractive Mrs. Orr.

Orr continued appearing in *Meet the People*, declining his studio salary until the show ended. He had appeared in two loanouts to MGM before the war came. When he came to Jack Warner's house for tennis, he was serving with the First Motion Picture Unit.

On the tennis court Warner and Biano faced Orr and Steve Trilling, studio manager of Warner Bros. Starting a game, Warner delivered a serve that Orr could see was a foot outside the line. But Warner started to move to the advantage court, as if he had served an ace.

"Mr. Warner, your serve was out," said Orr.

"No, it was good," Warner said firmly. "Wasn't it good, Steve?" Trilling was unsure what to say; he certainly didn't want to contradict the boss.

"So you think it was out, kid?" Warner asked. When Orr responded positively, Warner shrugged and moved back to the deuce court to serve again. Orr had learned a salient lesson about this powerful man: call his bluff and he will retreat without complaint. But if you don't challenge him, he will walk all over you.

Shortly afterward, Ann Warner met Orr at a party and asked him to join a group at the house for a movie. There he met Joy Page, who had inherited her mother's dark beauty and had made a few appearances as an actress at Warner Bros. He met her again at tennis and when he asked for a date, she hesitated. "Oh, go on, Joy, you're not doing anything," said her stepfather.

The dates became frequent, and Hedda Hopper predicted wedding bells in her column. She had asked Jack Warner if the pair would marry, and he replied, "I don't know. I guess they will." After reading the item, Orr called Joy from his army post and said, "Just say yes, and we'll figure out the details later."

Ann didn't want a large wedding because of the quandary of whom to invite. Bill and Joy were married at the Fliers' Chapel of the Mission Inn in Riverside on April 10, 1945.

To the handful of wedding guests, Jack and Ann Warner seemed the customary picture of the joyful parents of the bride. But something had happened a few years before that had altered their relationship forever.

It was one of those scandals that everyone talked about but nobody could confirm. The story went that Ann Warner had been caught in a compromising situation with a Warner Bros. contract player and that he had fled the scene nude. The alleged incident quickly became a Hollywood legend that no one doubted, like Joan Crawford's blue movie, Walter Pidgeon's being caught in a plush brothel, and Anatole Litvak's descent under the nightclub table while in the company of Paulette Goddard at Ciro's. Those who tell the Warner story at this late date give three different locales: Jack Warner's own yacht, the actor's dressing room, a motel in Glendale.

The most reliable account of the incident came from someone close to the Warner family. After five years of playing the decorative consort to a Hollywood potentate, Ann Warner became restless and sought her own fulfillment. She took up painting, but concentration was impossible amid the obligations of managing a luxurious home. Jack grumblingly agreed to rent a small house in the hills for Ann to use as a studio.

Ann reveled in her newfound freedom and found she could shut out her frustration as Mrs. Jack Warner by painting in her quiet cottage. One of the few persons who took an interest in her art was a Warner Bros. contract player, Eddie Albert.

The studio's New York talent department had spotted Albert when he appeared in the hit comedy *Brother Rat* on Broadway. He came to Burbank to repeat his role as the hapless military school cadet Bing in the 1938 movie version. His cheerful personality made him an appealing figure in eleven Warner films, including *Four Mothers*, *The Wagons Roll at Night* and *On Your Toes*. He was an independent soul, an adventurer who welcomed the peril of making a play for the boss's wife.

Jack Warner discovered the liaison, and he was outraged. Albert had worked three days in a musical, *Navy Blues*. He was removed from the film and replaced by Herbert Anderson. No explanation was given, but by this time reports of the interrupted tryst—in various versions—had swept the studio. Warner kept Albert under contract, but the actor was assigned to no films, nor was he loaned to other studios. Warner was determined to starve Albert's career to death. Albert finally escaped by entering the military service.*

In April 1941, newspapers received the terse announcement: "Mr. and Mrs. Jack Warner of Beverly Hills have separated because of incompatibility." The notice was signed by his attorneys.

Reporters discovered that Warner still resided at the Angelo Drive house and his wife had left with their daughter Barbara to live with relatives.

A studio representative told the press: "The flat announcement of the separation came in reply to a flood of rumors, reports, cracks in gossip columns and other hearsay reports."

Five days later came another announcement: Jack L. Warner and his wife had reconciled and were on a trip to Santa Barbara.

*Eddie Albert did not return telephone calls requesting an interview.

The rift was over, and the Warners forever afterward maintained the semblance of their marriage, often displaying affection toward each other. Jack's wanderings from monogamy would become a matter of course. Never again would he consider divorce—not when California law granted half of the community property to the wife.

Chapter 10

Casablanca and the Wallis Defection

THERE IS NO REAL EVIDENCE that Ronald Reagan was ever considered for the role of Rick Blaine in *Casablanca*. Reagan himself says such a possibility was never mentioned to him by Jack Warner or anyone else. Press releases from the Warner Bros. publicity department declared that Reagan and Ann Sheridan would costar in the film, but he may have been considered for the role of Laszlow, played by Paul Henreid. Speculative casting was a common practice to attract publicity for a forthcoming movie.

The first name mentioned for the Rick Blaine role in the Warner Bros. archives is Humphrey Bogart. A month before filming, Jack Warner suggested casting George Raft—"He knows we are going to make this and is starting a campaign for it." Hal Wallis ignored his suggestion.

Ann Sheridan was first considered for the role of Rick's former lover, Ilse Lund. Warner then tried to borrow Hedy Lamarr from MGM, but Louis B. Mayer said no. Michele Morgan was tested for the role. Then the focus centered on Ingrid Bergman. Once more David Selznick acted the canny trader. He would lend Ingrid Bergman for eight weeks in return for the eight-week services of Olivia de Havilland.

Casablanca was a problem picture from the time the story was purchased as an unproduced play. Despite some discouraging reports about the project from underlings, Hal Wallis assigned the Epstein twins to write a script. Their work was interrupted when they left the studio to work with Frank Capra on the *Why We Fight* series for the government. Meanwhile, Wallis assigned Howard Koch to write another version.

Jack Warner grumbled because of the high prices paid to the actors Wallis cast in *Casablanca*. Conrad Veidt was borrowed from MGM, Peter Lorre from Universal, Dooley Wilson from Paramount. Although under contract to Warner Bros., Sydney Greenstreet and S. Z. Sakall demanded higher salaries for the film. Free-lancer Claude Raines jacked up his price to $4,000 a week. Paul Henreid, who had just signed a Warner Bros. contract, refused the role of Victor Laszlo because "I don't want to be the second lover in a film, second to Humphrey Bogart." Wallis convinced him that the Laszlo role would be more substantial in the Koch version of the script.

The script problems continued while Warner and Wallis fretted over Selznick's stop date on Bergman's services and Bogart's commitment to Columbia for *Sahara* in return for a Cary Grant commitment. Finally in May 1942, *Casablanca* began principal photography. Jack Warner sent a pep memo to Michael Curtiz: "These are turbulent days and I know you will finish *Casablanca* in tops seven weeks. I am depending on you to be the old Curtiz I know you to be, and I am positive you are going to make one great picture."

It didn't seem like one great picture in the making. Bogart and Curtiz were constantly at each other's throats, delaying production for hours. All the actors complained of receiving new script pages each morning. Max Steiner hated the song "As Time Goes By," and wanted it eliminated from the score. The industry censors demanded script changes ("The suggestion that Ilse was married all the time she was having her love affair with Rick in Paris seems unacceptable. . . .").

Finally *Casablanca* ended, eleven days over schedule. The budget amounted to $878,000, less than average for a major Warner Bros. film.

Then a piece of Warner luck occurred. In November the allied forces established a North African beachhead by landing at Casablanca. Afterward, Roosevelt, Churchill and Stalin held their summit meeting in Casablanca.

The jubilant Warner Bros. sales department in New York urged Jack Warner to add an epilogue to *Casablanca* depicting the news events. Warner wired back: "Will definitely not touch picture. Previewed it again last night and audience reaction beyond belief. From main title to the end there was applause and anxiety. . . . Ship your negatives and positives to all foreign countries. . . ."

From its release in January 1943, *Casablanca* was everything that Jack Warner hoped. A year later the Academy declared *Casablanca* the best motion picture of the year. In a masterpiece of irony, the award precipitated the final split between Jack Warner and Hal Wallis.

It was bound to come. With feverish intensity, Wallis had supervised all of Warner Bros.' major films for the ten years since Zanuck's departure. Warner and Zanuck were alike: both were heavy gamblers and persistent womanizers, and both reveled in the excitement of filmmaking. Wallis was equally ego-driven, but more introspective. A cold, distant man, he was admired for his acumen but he wasn't well-liked. He and his wife, the comedienne Louise Fazenda, were not major players in the Hollywood social scene. His relationship with Jack Warner was strictly on a business basis, not personal.

Warner fiercely defended his prerogatives as a founder of the company. Whenever a producer or director argued too long on an issue Jack disagreed with, he walked to his office window and pointed upward. "See the water tower?" he asked. "Whose name is on it?" End of argument.

Throughout Hollywood, Hal Wallis was being acknowledged as the brains behind Warner Bros.' great burst of creativity in the late 1930s and early 1940s. Such an impression seemed confirmed when the Academy presented Wallis with the Irving G. Thalberg award in 1938 and again in 1943. Jack Warner had not received one.

Warner became increasingly touchy about any publicity Wallis received. After reading an interview in the Los Angeles *Daily News*, Warner wired Wallis: "I resent and won't stand for your continuing to take all credit for *Watch on the Rhine, This Is the Army, God Is My Copilot, Princess O'Rourke*, and many other stories. I happened to be the one who saw these stories, read plays, bought and turned them over to you. . . . You certainly have changed and unnecessarily so."

Wallis tried to explain that he had given Warner credit in the interview but the reference was not included in the story. Jack would not be mollified. He threatened Wallis with legal action if Warner's contribution was not included in future interviews. Warner told his publicity chief to warn all producers to give proper credit in interviews to him as executive producer. "Sick, tired everyone taking all credit and I become small boy and doing most of work," he wired the publicity chief.

Warner had another reason for his antagonism toward Wallis. Although he was far from being a religious man, Jack Warner became a potent force in raising funds for Jewish causes. When Warner canvassed his executives for donations to a wartime Jewish fund, Wallis agreed to give $2,500. "You're making a big salary at this studio, Hal, you can afford to give more," Warner insisted. Grudgingly, Wallis agreed to double his donation. But he called the charity and said, "Look, officially I'm giving you five thousand dollars, but in reality I'm giving you twenty-five hundred." Warner was told about the subterfuge, and he was furious.

March 2, 1944. The audience in Grauman's Chinese Theater gasped when *Casablanca* was named best picture of 1943; it had not been considered a favorite. Hal Wallis was halfway out of his seat to accept the Oscar when he saw Jack Warner hurrying down the aisle.

Wallis was livid. Academy tradition dictated that the producer of the best-picture winner accept the award, not the studio head. But Jack Warner stood onstage beaming amid the applause while

Wallis, who had sweated through a thousand crises on *Casablanca*, remained in his seat.

Word circulated through the industry that Hal Wallis was considering a change. Most of the studios sought him, and later that year Wallis announced his new affiliation as an independent producer at Paramount. The departure went unmentioned in Jack Warner's autobiography, as did Wallis himself.

What was there about Warner Bros. that created such rebellious stars?

Partly it was because the studio attracted free-thinking actors to its vital, fast-tempo movies. But the major reason was Jack Warner's attitude toward them. At MGM whenever stars challenged Louis B. Mayer's will, he cried a little, explained the error of their ways and sent them back to the set with a dose of parental advice. That wasn't Jack Warner's style.

"Give an actor a break and he'll fuck you later," was his credo. He expected his employees to adhere to their contracts, an unrealistic attitude in the movie business. Yet Jack was old-fashioned enough to believe in the validity of contracts, and he felt betrayed whenever a star wanted more money or refused a role. He would rage against such wrongdoing and fire off his principal weapon, the suspension. It was a convenient way to express his displeasure, tidily executed by lawyers. Personal confrontation distressed him.

Bette Davis was causing problems on *Mr. Skeffington*. She disliked playing an older woman and found all kinds of reasons to dispute the director, Vincent Sherman, and the writer-producers, Julius and Philip Epstein. The Epsteins, who had been elevated to producers as a reward for *Casablanca*, told Bette that a retake was needed.

"I won't do it," she answered flatly. No amount of reasoning could convince her. The Epsteins reported the impasse to Jack Warner, who erupted predictably: "Why that goddamn bitch. Who the hell does she think she is? I'll fix her. Come with me."

The Epsteins followed Warner as he strode through the studio street ranting, "Who the hell does she think built these twenty-four stages? Bette Davis? No, goddamn it, I did!" Then he reached Davis's dressing room. "Bette, darling!" he smiled.

Davis did not do the retake, and the Epsteins abandoned producership, reasoning that the position was powerless.

James Cagney's long campaign against Jack Warner ended after *Yankee Doodle Dandy*, when he decided the studio was dealing from a loaded deck when figuring his percentage of the profits. He and Bill Cagney formed their own company.

A major star after the success of *Casablanca*, Humphrey Bogart conducted his own war with Jack Warner. Unlike Cagney, who fought over salary and roles only, Bogart devised elaborate schemes to bedevil the boss.

Errol Flynn was a constant problem, and he became more so in 1943 when he faced two charges of statutory rape. When two women under eighteen claimed to have had sexual intercourse with Flynn on different occasions, his career seemed ruined. With millions invested in Flynn's career, Jack Warner understandably did not exercise the morality clause that was included in all actors' contracts. Instead, he guaranteed the $40,000 fee of Jerry Geisler, the legendary defender who had rescued Busby Berkeley. When Flynn was acquitted, he became a bigger star than before, further popularizing the expression "in like Flynn."

Now comes demure Olivia de Havilland to ruin Jack Warner's suspension game.

Ever since his reluctant loanout for *Gone with the Wind*, Warner had appeared to stifle Olivia's career, relegating her to westerns with Errol Flynn and other unrewarding films. Even when Norman Krasna wrote *Princess O'Rourke* especially for her, Warner hesitated giving it to her. Finally in May 1943 her Warner Bros. contract had expired—except that she had accumulated six months in suspensions which had to be served out, like a prison sentence for bad behavior.

Although she didn't like the script, Olivia agreed to do *Government Girl* on loan to RKO. When she returned, Warner sent her to Columbia for a film about the pioneering woman doctor, Elizabeth

Blackwell. The script was unfinished, and the actress felt uncomfortable in the role. She turned it down.

Warner responded by sending 150 telegrams to producing companies, some of them defunct, warning them not to hire Olivia de Havilland. Her agent's attorney, Martin Gang, said that although employer contracts could not extend more than seven years, it wasn't clear whether that meant seven years of work or seven calendar years. Olivia decided to find out.

"They'll put you on the stand and try to paint you as a spoiled movie star," Gang warned. She remained resolute.

Olivia chose her courtroom wardrobe carefully: a black suit with thin pinstripes and a black hat with a veil. Accused by the Warner lawyer of having "willfully refused" film roles, she quietly answered, "I *declined*."

She won the case, but Warner again dispatched the warning telegrams, forbidding her employment pending appeal. The case went to the appellate and the state supreme court, and each confirmed Olivia's victory. She was free to guide her own career, and within five years had won two Academy Awards. Her fellow actors were forever free from contracts that could have kept them tied to studios indefinitely. The Screen Actors Guild later cited her for a historic contribution to the emancipation of actors.

Twenty years after her court victory, Olivia de Havilland was invited to speak at a dinner honoring Jack L. Warner.

"When I learned that I was invited to attend this dinner at which Jack Warner was to receive a humanitarian award, I decided to accept," she told the Beverly Hilton audience. "I'm all for encouraging humanitarianism, especially in Jack. (laughter)

"In spite of a history which led us through some historic court confrontations—and I may add, my victory—I will reveal something that you would not guess is the case and indeed has been a secret for many years." She addressed the guest of honor: "Jack, I want you to know that in spite of everything, I always liked you very much."

"Oh, I wasn't mean to you, Olivia," the flustered Warner declared. He seemed so distressed that she kissed him on both cheeks.

*   *   *

Mission to Moscow was the film Jack Warner wished he had never made. But how could he resist one of the great charmers of the twentieth century, especially when he was President of the United States?

Even though he and Harry had returned to their Republican allegiance after the 1932 election, Jack remained under Franklin Roosevelt's spell. The president often consulted him, and Roosevelt was impersonated in Warner Bros. films such as *Yankee Doodle Dandy*. During a wartime visit to Washington, Jack was surprised when Roosevelt called to invite him and Ann to dinner.

Roosevelt asked Jack if he had read *Mission to Moscow*, Joseph E. Davies' account of his years as ambassador to Russia. Warner, who rarely read a book, had read this one because Davies was a longtime friend.

"Jack, this picture *must* be made, and I am asking you to make it," Roosevelt said.

"I'll do it," Jack replied. "You have my word."

Roosevelt had his reasons. According to Warner, the president wanted American support for the Russian war effort, fearing that Stalin would again make a deal with Hitler if the Soviet forces lost a major battle.

Warner returned to Burbank in a quandary. He was determinedly anticommunist, but he had orders from his commander-in-chief. He bought the rights to *Mission to Moscow* and assigned Howard Koch to write the script and good old reliable Michael Curtiz to direct. The large cast was headed by Walter Huston as the ambassador and Ann Harding as Mrs. Davies.

Mission to Moscow opened in May 1943 to a wildly divergent reaction. Some critics hailed it as a brave and stirring account of recent history. Others found it stodgy and unconvincing. Wrote James Agee: "A mishmash of Stalinism with New Dealism with Hollywoodism with opportunism with shaky experimentalism with mesmerism with onanism, all mosaicked into a remarkable portrait of what the makers of the film think the Soviet Union is like—a great glad two-million-dollar bowl of canned borscht, eminently approvable by the Institute of Good Housekeeping."

American audiences wanted entertainment in wartime, and *Mission to Moscow* was a financial failure. It would haunt Jack Warner for years to come.

The right-wing cannonading began immediately after the film's release. The Republican National Committee called it "New Deal propaganda." Westbrook Pegler blasted it in his column. Trotskyites rose up in wrath, and *The New York Times* printed a letter defending the deposed Russian leader. The Hearst newspapers reprinted the letter on orders from the chief. When Warner protested to his old friend and onetime business partner, Hearst replied stiffly, addressing him as "Mr. Warner." It was the end of their friendship.

Four years later the Iron Curtain had descended, and Red baiters prowled the land. Republican Jack Warner was forced to defend himself before a congressional committee. He denied that any subversive propaganda had ever entered Warner Bros. pictures, including *Mission to Moscow*. Asked whether statements in the film were right or wrong, Warner replied, "I have never been in Russia. I don't know what Russia was like in 1937 or 1944 or 1947, so how can I tell you if it was right or wrong?"

Another longtime friendship ended during the war. Jack had known Charlie Chaplin since the early 1920s, and they often played tennis at each other's courts. Jack was both amused by the comedian's brilliance and appalled by his parsimony. He also couldn't understand Chaplin's pro-Russian politics.

In his autobiography Warner told of receiving a message from the White House: Roosevelt wanted him to persuade Chaplin not to make a scheduled speech at a New York rally calling for a second front in Europe.

After tennis one day, Warner explained to Chaplin that high government sources did not want him to make the Carnegie Hall speech because the Allies were not ready to invade the continent. Warner claimed that he extracted Chaplin's promise not to attend the rally. A few days later Chaplin appeared before the newsreel cameras at the New York meeting and made an emotional call for the second front.

In his own memoir, Chaplin recalled Jack Warner's admonition, "Let me tip you off, don't go." Chaplin wrote: "This had the opposite effect. It was a challenge. At that moment it needed little eloquence to ignite the sympathy of all America for a second front, for Russia had just won the battle of Stalingrad."

Charlie Chaplin and Jack Warner never saw each other again.

After Hal Wallis's departure, Jack Warner appointed Steve Trilling as his chief assistant. Trilling, who had emerged from Warner Bros. theaters, was an affable man and an effective executive, but he lacked the superior creativity of Wallis. Warner himself was calling the shots now, though relying on producers like Henry Blanke, Jerry Wald and Mark Hellinger. The quality of the Warner product declined in the postwar years; the films lacked the studio's daring of the 1930s and early 1940s. Formulas were reworked, old scripts remade. Warner Bros. had fewer films among the Academy's best-picture nominees or on critics' ten-best lists.

After Warner Bros. lost the Olivia de Havilland case, Harry Warner suggested that Jack give up the suspension weapon. Liberty and freedom were in the air, Harry noted, "and actors are getting to believe it." He proposed that if a star rejected one script, the studio should provide another—anything to keep the star working.

Jack agreed to skip handing out suspensions, but warned "all you have to do is let actors play parts they want to and you won't be in business very long." Most of the time they rejected scripts as a gambit to get more money or contract revisions, he said, adding that "we play ball with them but when people become ornery like Bogart, de Havilland, that type, you haven't any alternative."

Warner tried to conduct studio business as he had for twenty years—that is, with iron control—even while filmmakers returned from the war with yearnings for independence and freedom. John Huston reported back to Warner Bros. and embarked on *The Trea-*

The Warner brothers' first theater, the Cascade in New Castle,
Pennsylvania, 1903. Albert Warner stands at the entrance.
(*USC Cinema-Television Library*)

To the right of "This Week's Attractions": Sam and Jack Warner on tour
with *Dante's Inferno*, Atlantic City, 1910.   (*USC Cinema-Television Library*)

Warner Brothers studio rises from the weeds on Sunset Boulevard, circa 1920. *(USC Cinema-Television Library)*

Jack with his two greatest finds of the 1920s: Darryl Zanuck *(left)* and Rin-Tin-Tin. On the right is director Alan Crosland. The handwriting is Warner's. *(USC Cinema-Television Library)*

Jack Warner with some of his early stars, circa 1922. *(USC Cinema-Television Library)*

Jack *(far left)* and Sam *(far right)* ballyhoo their "Classics of the Screen," along with stars, directors, and producer Harry Rapf *(third from right)*, in 1923. *(USC Cinema-Television Library)*

The Jazz Singer, 1927. Warner Oland delivers the word to son Al Jolson, as mother Eugenie Besserer agonizes. *(Warner Bros.)*

Marilyn Miller prances through *Sunny* (1930) under the gaze of two of her lovers, Jack Warner and Florenz Ziegfeld *(right)*. *(USC Cinema-Television Library)*

The Warners, *père et fils. From left*: Jack, David, Albert, Ben, Harry, and Sam. *(USC Cinema-Television Library)*

The stars turn out for the first national broadcast from KFWB in 1932. *Left to right*: Evelyn Knapp, Joe E. Brown, Lloyd Bacon, "Leon Zuardo," Edward G. Robinson, Mervyn LeRoy, Bebe Daniels, Ken Murray, Paul Muni (in his *I Am a Fugitive* stripes), Glenda Farrell, and David Manners. *(USC Cinema-Television Library)*

Three generations of Warners aboard the 42nd Street Special. *Left to right*: Jack Jr., Ben, and Jack, 1932. *(USC Cinema-Television Library)*

Anything for a laugh. Jack Warner claims to be riding MGM's Leo the Lion, 1932. *(USC Cinema-Television Library)*

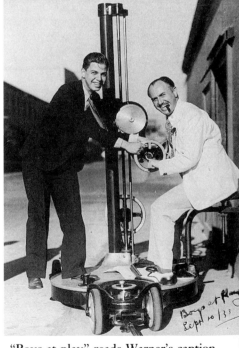

"Boys at play" reads Warner's caption for this shot. Jack Jr. and Jack with new studio equipment, 1933. *(USC Cinema-Television Library)*

A couple of clowns. Jack Warner
(left) and Al Jolson in 1934.
(USC Cinema-Television Library)

At the post-premiere party for *A Midsummer
Night's Dream*, 1935. *Left to right*: Max
Reinhardt, Marion Davies, and Jack Warner.
(USC Cinema-Television Library)

At the premiere of *The Story of Louis Pasteur*, 1935. *Seated, left to right*: Cecil
B. DeMille, Charlie Chaplin, and H. G. Wells. *Standing, left to right*: Jack
Warner, Paul Muni, William Dieterle, and Hal Wallis.
(USC Cinema-Television Library)

Ann and Jack on their honeymoon at Hialeah racetrack in Florida in 1936. *(AP/Wide World Photos)*

Lieutenant General H. H. Arnold and Lieutenant Colonel Jack L. Warner during the filming of *Under Those Wings*. *(USC Cinema-Television Library)*

The Warners on the town with Norma Shearer and Irving Thalberg, 1936. *(USC Cinema-Television Library)*

Howard Hughes, flanked by Jack Warner *(left)* and Edmund Goulding
on the set of *The Dawn Patrol*, 1938.   *(USC Cinema-Television Library)*

Jack Warner gets a light from his son, Major Jack Warner, Jr., at a military
nightclub in Wiesbaden, Germany, in July 1945.   *(AP/Wide World Photos)*

Jack Warner peruses a transcript during his disastrous appearance before the House Un-American Activities Committee in Washington, D.C., in 1947. At left is Paul V. McNutt, the film industry's lawyer. *(AP/Wide World Photos)*

Official photos of the Warner brothers. *Left to right*: Jack, Harry, and Albert, 1949.

Warner dances with Virginia Mayo at a charity ball.
(Virginia Mayo)

Vivien Leigh and Marlon Brando in the landmark *Streetcar
Named Desire*, 1951.   *(Warner Bros.)*

Alfred Hitchcock introduces his partner, Jack Warner, in 1948.   *(USC Cinema-Television Library)*

Field Marshal Montgomery visits Warner Bros. in 1954. *From left*: John Wayne, Greer Garson, Montgomery, Sam Goldwyn, Jack Warner, John Farrow, Mervyn LeRoy.   *(USC Cinema-Television Library)*

Jack Warner *(left)* meets Jack Kennedy at a dinner for the
President, November 18, 1961. *(USC Cinema-Television Library)*

Joan Crawford *(right)* manages a grim smile as Bette Davis
and their old boss Jack Warner celebrate the stars'
return in *Whatever Happened to Baby Jane?* in 1962.
(AP/Wide World Photos)

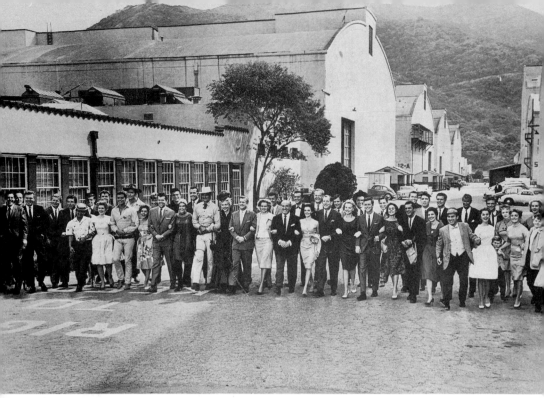

Jack Warner *(center)*, flanked by his television stars.   *(William T. Orr)*

At the premiere of *A Star is Born*. *From left*: Judy Garland, Sid Luft, Jack Warner, Liberace, Sophie Tucker.

On the set of *My Fair Lady* in 1964. *From left*: Wilfred Hyde-White, George Cukor, Jack Warner, Audrey Hepburn, and Rex Harrison. *(USC Cinema-Television Library)*

A peacemaking handshake after the 1965 Oscars. *Left to right*: Audrey Hepburn, Jack Warner, Gregory Peck, and Julie Andrews.   *(AP/Wide World Photos)*

An exuberant Jack Warner with Jackie Park at a post-premiere party in the early 1960s.

The *Virginia Woolf* team: Elizabeth Taylor, Ernest Lehman, Mike Nichols, and Richard Burton. *(Bob Willoughby)*

Still smiling after all those years. Warner on the set of *Dirty Little Billy* with director Stan Dragoti and his wife, Cheryl Tiegs, 1972. *(Columbia Pictures)*

sure of the Sierra Madre; he had hoped to film it before the war and had asked Henry Blanke to save it for him.

Huston completed the script and told Warner that he wanted to film it entirely in Mexico. Impossible, Warner said. The studio had never made a movie on a foreign location. Having Huston so distant would place him outside Jack Warner's control, and Jack feared Huston's capriciousness, like the time he left Bogart in an inescapable trap.

The picture was *Across the Pacific*. Bogart had been captured by the Japanese and their spy Sydney Greenstreet in a shack near the Panama Canal, which they planned to destroy. Huston was close to being commissioned in the signal corps, and he had directed the film up to Bogart's capture. He had Bogart tied to a chair, surrounded by a small army of Japanese with machine guns. Then he called Jack Warner and said, "Jack, I'm on my way. I'm in the army. Bogie will know how to get out." Vincent Sherman replaced Huston as director, and his only solution was to have one of the soldiers go berserk.

Henry Blanke finally persuaded Warner to allow the Mexican location. Warner quickly regretted his decision. *The Treasure of the Sierra Madre* fell behind schedule, and there was nothing he could do about it. Besides, he hated the rushes that were flown to Burbank. "Can't you get those guys to shave?" he messaged Huston.

Warner had different feelings when he saw the film assembled. He wired his general sales manager, Ben Kalmenson: "This is definitely the greatest motion picture we have ever made. It is really one we have always wished for."

The Treasure of the Sierra Madre won Academy Awards for John Huston's direction and writing and for Walter Huston's supporting performance. The film's success had no effect on Warner's resistance to change. Why alter the studio's ways? Warner Bros. profits zoomed to an all-time high of $21.1 million in 1947.

The Warner Bros. regulars—Davis, Flynn, Bogart, Garfield, Ann Sheridan, Dennis Morgan—continued to draw at the box office. Only a few personalities had been added to the star list, notably Bogart's new wife, Lauren Bacall.

At first Bacall had little contact with Jack Warner. Howard Hawks had discovered and trained her, and he brought her to Warner Bros. to costar with Humphrey Bogart in *To Have and Have Not*. Warner occasionally paid visits to the set, usually to urge Hawks to shoot faster. Whenever Jack arrived, the imperious Hawks stopped filming. He resumed only when the stage door shut behind his unwanted visitor.

Hawks was contemptuous of all studio bosses, and especially Jack Warner. The director delighted in showing Warner's memos to Bogart and Bacall, including one that said, "I hear you're having fun on the set. This must stop!"

Bacall's debut in *To Have and Have Not* proved one of the most sensational in film history, and she expected to be rewarded with important films. Instead, she was cast in *Confidential Agent*, a murky melodrama based on a Graham Greene novel. Her reviews were devastating.

Thereafter Bacall took suspension after suspension rather than work in inferior films.

"Jack never had any sense of wanting to protect me, to pick things that were good for me to sustain my career," she recalls. "He put me in *Confidential Agent*, which was a disaster and almost ruined me. I had to spend the next twenty years of my life trying to prove that I was legitimate enough to have my name over the title. He not only made my life hell professionally, he never had any vision, any sense of protecting anyone. He became the enemy in that sense. Because I allowed him to make that choice [*Confidential Agent*] for me, I never allowed him to make another choice."

Few young actors were being developed at Warner Bros. Instead, Warner relied on long-established stars like Barbara Stanwyck, who appeared in five Warner Bros. films. Another addition was Joan Crawford.

After eighteen years at MGM, Joan Crawford's career seemed to be over. She left the studio in 1943 after a series of flops, and only one studio sought her services. Jack Warner wanted to add the class of an MGM star to Warner Bros. Also, Crawford could provide him with a threat to his ever-contentious star, Bette Davis. Crawford agreed to a contract calling for $500,000 for three pictures.

For two years Crawford played only one role, a walk-on as herself in *Hollywood Canteen*. Warner proposed her as Cagney's wife in *Yankee Doodle Dandy*, but she said, "I'm too old. Give it to Joan Leslie."

She continued rejecting scripts until Warner sent off an angry memo reminding her that Warner Bros. was not MGM and that he expected his actors to earn the huge salaries he paid them. Joan appeared at his office and asked to see him. Warner was panic-stricken by the thought of confrontation. "Don't tell her I'm here," he instructed the secretary, and he scurried out the back door. The actress left the message: he was right that actors should not be paid for doing nothing; therefore she wanted to be taken off salary until they agreed on a vehicle.

"That broad must be crazy," said the astonished Warner.

The studio had bought the James Cain novel *Mildred Pierce* as a vehicle for Bette Davis, but she declined it. Seven writers worked on scripts, but none could pass the Breen office censors. Finally Ranald McDougall devised a way: by telling the story in flashback. Crawford accepted the script, and Warner told the producer, Jerry Wald, that he wanted Mike Curtiz to direct.

"Me direct that temperamental bitch? Not on your goddamn life!" replied Curtiz. "She comes over here with her high-hat airs and her goddamn shoulder pads. I won't work with her. She's through, washed up. Why should I waste my time directing a has-been?"

Crawford volunteered to appear in a test for Curtiz, and afterward he said, "Okay, I work with her. But she better know who's boss."

The first days of filming were catastrophic, and at one point Curtiz exclaimed, "You and your damned Adrian shoulder pads!" He began tearing them from her dress until she disclosed that she had bought the dress at Sears, Roebuck.

Curtiz gradually learned to work with Crawford, and her performance won her the Oscar as best actress of 1945. Jack Warner had a new-old star for his contract list.

Bette Davis was undeterred by the new threat to her status as queen of Warner Bros. She continued making her opinions heard. She was incensed when she picked up a newspaper and saw herself in a skimpy gown in an ad for *The Corn Is Green*. Faced with a talky drama about a Welsh schoolteacher and her coal miner protégé, the Warner Bros. ad department had tried to spice it up as a romance.

Davis immediately called her agent, Lew Wasserman. "I'll set up a date with Jack Warner," he said.

Barging into Warner's office, Bette waved the ad and began ranting, "This is not the picture we made. . . ." Warner held up his hand and said, "Okay, we'll pull the ads."

Despite all their disputes, boss and star developed a mutual respect. When Miss Davis had a difficult pregnancy and birth of her daughter Barbara, Jack told her to take her time about returning to the studio. He sent three pearls on a gold necklace for the baby, and he added pearls on her birthday for years afterward.

Errol Flynn became an increasing problem. His sexual escapades and his constant drinking on movie sets created endless trouble. Warner constantly reproved him, to no avail. During one grievance session, Warner recited a list of Flynn's transgressions, directing his ire at the actor's agent, Lew Wasserman. "You can't talk to my agent like that!" Flynn exclaimed, and he stormed out of the office.

The nadir of Flynn's behavior was reached on *Silver River*, a 1947 western. Both he and Ann Sheridan were seeking better contracts, and they seemed hell-bent on sabotaging the movie so that Warner would be forced to come to terms. Flynn spent long, wet lunches at the nearby Lakeside Country Club with his pals, and Sheridan was so drunk by two o'clock that she couldn't do close-ups.

Flynn displayed his meanness with an extra who had a reputation as an easy lay. He invited her to his dressing room for a lunch hour of vigorous sex, during which she discussed her various techniques. Later that day, Flynn quieted the cast and crew and announced he had something unique for them to hear. He had recorded the lunch-hour tryst, and he played it on the loudspeaker. The extra fled from the stage.

After fuming over Flynn's two-hour lunches, Warner told the producer, Owen Crump, "If he isn't back by one-thirty, have him call me as soon as he gets to the set."

The gambling saloon set was filled with extras, and they waited until 2:30 when Flynn sauntered onto the set, rakish in gambler's costume with high-topped hat. Crump gave him Warner's message, and Flynn called for a telephone stand to be wheeled onto the middle of the set.

"Mr. Warner's office, please," he said as the western extras and the film crew quieted. After a pause, he said, "Is this Jack? Well, what do you want, you _____?" Warner's raging voice could be heard on the receiver. Flynn made a few curt comments and hung up. He knew he couldn't be fired; too much of the movie had already been filmed.

One day Arthur Park, who had become Flynn's agent at MCA, received an urgent call to report to Jack Warner's office at Warner Bros. When he arrived, Warner was vomiting in his private bathroom, and his executives huddled outside in great agitation.

"That goddamn Flynn, I oughta kill him! I oughta kill him!" Warner yelled. "He called up and said he was gonna kill me! He threatened my life!"

Park calmed everyone and asked for an explanation. On the *Silver River* location there had been an argument between Flynn's wife, Nora Eddington, and the wife of the director, Raoul Walsh. Both were barred from the set. Flynn was so incensed by the discourtesy to his wife that he decided Warner would pay for it.

"Well, he hasn't killed you yet," Park said, trying to lighten the atmosphere.

"That was a terrible thing to say to me!" Warner replied.

Park offered to mediate. He found Flynn on the movie set and listened to the affair of the two wives. Flynn agreed to meet with Warner after the day's work.

The two men greeted each other cordially, and Jack brought

out some of his private-stock Scotch. Over drinks and cigars, Flynn and Warner discussed their mutual problems. Flynn left the meeting with two bottles of Scotch, a handful of Havana cigars and Warner's promise to buy his book of South Sea adventures for a movie.

Jack Warner's relationship with writers was curious. He realized their value to the studio product, yet he seemed to resent his dependence on them. He seldom read scripts, preferring to scan a synopsis or have the story told to him. He had little patience with story conferences, and often ended them with snap decisions. His day-to-day dealings were largely with producers (who were called "supervisors" until the mid-thirties). As the role of directors ascended in postwar years, Warner included them in conferences, though reluctantly. Writers seldom appeared in Warner's office.

The boss expected writers to adhere to the studio's office hours, just like normal employees. That led to difficulties, given the nature of the writing breed.

Philip and Julius Epstein were especially resistant to regimentation. They would sometimes work on a script for twenty-four hours. Afterward they would arrive at ten or eleven in the morning and spend a couple of hours at the writers' table in the commissary. One day they encountered Warner outside the administration building.

"Goddamn it, bank presidents go to work at nine!" he ranted. "Railroad presidents get in at nine. Read your contract. You're coming in at nine."

The Epsteins replied by sending him a script that was half-written. "Have the bank president finish it," they said.

The brothers always wrote as a team, except when Julius was in military service during the war. Warner asked Philip to write a badly needed scene. After reading it, Warner complained, "This is the worst scene I've ever read in my life!"

"How is that possible?" Epstein replied. "I wrote it at nine o'clock."

"You've cheated me," Warner protested. "I want my money back."

"I would love to give your money back, but I built a swimming pool with it. However, if you're ever in the neighborhood and feel like a swim, feel free to drop over."

It was inevitable that William Faulkner could not conform to Warner Bros. regulations. He had been brought to Hollywood by Howard Hawks, who claimed to have discovered the author's works while Faulkner was working as a clerk in Macy's basement in New York. Starting in 1942, Faulkner contributed to seventeen films, most notably Hawks' *Air Force*, *To Have and Have Not* and *The Big Sleep*.

Jack Warner had been briefed about Faulkner's growing literary eminence, and he treated the Mississippian with more respect than he gave to other writers. When Faulkner said he preferred not to work in an office, Warner grandly allowed him to write at home. Faulkner went home—to Oxford, Mississippi. That was not what Jack Warner had in mind.

Faulkner suffered the chores of writing lines for Lauren Bacall and Joan Crawford (he was one of the many rewriters of *Mildred Pierce*). In October 1945 he left the studio and returned to Oxford, refusing to sign a suspension agreement despite a threat that Warner Bros. would prevent him from selling his work to any publisher.

He sent an impassioned plea to Jack Warner for release from his contract, declaring that he "had made a bust of motion picture writing."

"I have spent three years doing work (trying to do it) which was not my forte and which I was not equipped to do," Faulkner wrote, "and therefore I have misspent time which as a 47-year-old novelist I could not afford to spend. And I don't dare misspend any more of it."

The request was denied, and Faulkner spent four more years at Warner Bros.

Chapter 11

The Clown Prince
in Action

"JACK WARNER WOULD RATHER tell a bad joke than make a good movie." Jack Benny's oft-quoted remark was only partly true. Benny certainly made capital of the bad movie he starred in for Warner, *The Horn Blows at Midnight*, in which he played a trumpet player who falls asleep and dreams he is an angel returned to earth to preach Armageddon. For years the failure of *The Horn Blows at Midnight* served as a running gag on Benny's radio show.

Decades after his season on the Gus Sun circuit with jokes cribbed from Madison's Budget, Jack still considered himself a comedian. Once he enlisted Pat Buttram to appear at a political dinner. "I need you," said the president of Warner Bros. "You and I will be the only comedians on the dais."

Jack developed a slicker's patter that his associates heard over and over. If someone asked "How are ya?" he replied, "Honolulu." A farewell greeting of "Arrivederci" would be answered with "And a dirty river to you, too." If an employee pleaded for a salary increase, he replied, "Go to the crafts building and get a raise." Explanation: the crafts building had the only elevator on the lot.

Sometimes he fed a straight line to an employee: "Do you know anything about the real estate business?" The proper answer: "A lot." He was full of aphorisms such as: "Uneasy lies the head that wears the toilet seat." The meaning was clouded, as was a favorite phrase: "I want to get this off my sleeve." Most people said "chest."

Like all would-be comedians, Warner did not like to be topped. After Rudi Fehr was hired as an editor in the 1930s, Warner's favorite greeting was: "Hello, Rudi, is everything Fehr?" When the editor replied, "Yes, Fehr and Warner," Jack stopped asking the question.

When visitors were in his office, he often opened a desk drawer, pulled out a business card and handed it to them. It read:

JACK L. WARNER, PRESIDENT
BON TON WOOLEN COMPANY
YOUNGSTOWN, OHIO

When asked the significance of the card, he replied, "You can't pull the wool over my eyes."

Warner delighted in entertaining visiting heads of state and other dignitaries at the studio. During the war Madame Chiang Kai-shek came to America to enlist support for China's fight against Japan. At a luncheon attended by studio heads and stars, she made an impassioned speech. During a brief pause, Jack Warner muttered in a voice all could hear: "Jeezus, that reminds me. I forgot to send out my laundry."

When he was presented with the Legion of Honor, Warner presided over a studio luncheon attended by Warner Bros. stars. Warner introduced Bette Davis, Robert Alda, Alexis Smith, and other stars to the French officials. When he came to Paul Henreid, who had sung "La Marseillaise" in *Casablanca*, Warner said, "This is the man who sang your song: Paul Hemaroid."

At a postwar dinner for Field Marshall Montgomery, Samuel Goldwyn stumbled through his prepared speech and concluded: "I would like you to rise and join in a toast to our honored guest, Marshall Field Montgomery."

A giggle danced through the formal crowd, and Jack Warner spoke out: "Sam's got it wrong. What he meant to say was Marshall Field Montgomery Ward."

During a political campaign of Nelson Rockefeller, Warner agreed to host a banquet on a studio stage. He inveigled the handful of his stars who were Republicans to attend, and he restrained himself from attempts at humor in introducing the New York governor. After the speeches, Warner cautioned Mrs. Rockefeller about the steps leading off the platform: "Be careful, Mrs. Governor, don't fall on your ass."

Warner underlings shared one moment of certain terror: when the boss threw away his prepared speech and launched into his own ad libs. Max Bercutt, who was Warner Bros.' publicity chief in postwar years, recalls his worst experience. The San Francisco Press Club was presenting an award to Warner, and Bercutt accompanied him to the event.

After a series of speeches extolling him as a film pioneer, daring producer and devoted patriot, Warner took the floor. He tossed aside his printed speech and reminisced about his years as a young film salesman in San Francisco. "I love this town," he mused. "San Francisco is where I got my first dose of clap."

Lord Mountbatten came to Hollywood after the war, and he was the guest of honor at a formal dinner attended by a host of British and American admirals. Warner began reading his speech, and then looked up at the audience and pushed the pages aside. "Milords," he said, "this is a lot of shit that they've written for me."

Warner's rambling, unfunny speeches became a minor Hollywood scandal, and banquet audiences groaned when he was introduced. Yet his eminence in the community necessitated the invitation for him to appear, and often he insisted on it. After one of Warner's windy effusions of non sequiturs at a Friars Roast, the emcee George Jessel questioned the audience: "How did this man become the head of a big studio?"

Such barbs never wounded Jack. *He* thought he was funny. The trouble was that he was marching to a different rim-shot drummer. He could take a perfectly valid joke and mangle the punch line so that it made no sense.

Meetings of the Association of Motion Picture Producers provided a splendid forum for Warner's wisecracks. He enjoyed the give-and-take with his fellow studio heads, but his attitude was different when he had to deal individually with his competitors in business deals. He believed, not without reason, that they were out to swindle him.

Socially, Jack was amused by Sam Goldwyn, whose malapropisms ("The major studios will soon be dead as a doughnut") he collected. But doing business with Sam was another matter. There was the matter of the Gary Cooper–Bette Davis swap.

Jesse Lasky, down on his luck, had long sought a studio to finance a biography of the great World War I hero, Alvin C. York. Finally in 1941 he appealed to Harry Warner's patriotism, and Warner Bros. accepted the project. Lasky needed Gary Cooper to lend the film importance, but Cooper was under contract to Lasky's onetime partner and brother-in-law, Samuel Goldwyn, and the two despised each other. The desperate Lasky decided to make a plea to Goldwyn, who surprisingly gave his assent.

"Jesse just told me you're loaning us Coop," Jack said on the telephone.

"That's right," confirmed Sam Goldwyn.

"Well, Sam, I just don't know how to express my appreciation."

"Don't express it. Just loan me Bette Davis for *The Little Foxes.*"

Jack exploded. Davis was Warner Bros.' biggest star. He didn't lend her to anybody. Then Goldwyn played his trump card. He sent a note to Warner reminding him that he had incurred a $425,000 gambling debt. Warner panicked. He had tried to hide his heavy gambling from Harry, who would be furious if he knew. Jack wrote back that he would like to settle the debt for $250,000. The exchange of Cooper for Davis was consummated.

Harry Cohn was Jack's particular bête noire.

The mutual antipathy dated back to Sam Warner's funeral in 1927. As president of Columbia Pictures, Cohn occupied a privileged position among the mourners. Cohn had also acquired a large block of Warner Bros. stock, not for any ulterior motive but because he thought talkies would raise the price.

Cohn found himself seated behind two of the Warner sisters. One of them told the other: "We're all selling our stock, and you should, too. Harry says that will push the stock down, then we can buy back at a lower price." Without waiting to see Sam Warner lowered into the ground, Cohn left the funeral and telephoned his broker to sell his Warner Bros. stock.

(In 1932 Harry Warner was called before a U.S. Senate committee to explain why he, Jack and Albert had sold large amounts of their stock using other names, and then had later bought the stock back at a lower price. Harry said that they hadn't used their own names for fear of influencing others to sell and that they had lent the company their proceeds so that it could stay afloat. The Senate counsel claimed the Warners had made $9 million by the transactions, but no breach of law was found.)

Warner and Cohn feuded over the years, but occasionally they were forced to do business together. When Warner needed Cary Grant for *Arsenic and Old Lace*, Cohn agreed to a loan; in return Columbia got Bogart for *Sahara*. But when Cohn wanted John Garfield for *Golden Boy*, Warner refused, thus facilitating the stardom of young William Holden.

Cohn's greatest revenge against Jack Warner came with *The Jolson Story*.

By the mid-forties the luster of *The Jazz Singer* and *The Singing Fool* had faded, and Al Jolson was a neglected name in Hollywood. Sidney Skolsky, a movie columnist, thought the old-time magic might capture a new generation if the Jolson saga could be told on the screen with a younger actor playing the role, pantomiming to Jolson's singing voice. While still writing his column, Skolsky was working at Warner Bros. as assistant to Mark Hellinger, and he proposed the idea to Jack Warner.

"Forget it," Jack said. "We had Jolson when he was hot. *The Jazz Singer*. Today he doesn't mean a thing."

So it seemed. Jolson had been replaced on radio by hillbilly Judy Canova. When his own country club, Hillcrest, presented a benefit program, Jolson wasn't asked to entertain.

One night Skolsky encountered Harry Cohn as he was rushing into Schwab's drugstore to buy condoms. Skolsky unloaded his Jolson idea. Cohn was immediately receptive. Like Jack Warner, he idolized Jolson, who was the king of Broadway when Cohn was a songplugger. Cohn said that Columbia Pictures would make *The Jolson Story*.

After the announcement had been made, Jack Warner met Jolson on the Superchief train. Hoping to outfox Harry Cohn, Warner made a counteroffer: $200,000 for the story rights, the Epstein twins to write the script, Mike Curtiz to direct, and Jolson could play himself. "After all, you're a major stockholder in Warner Bros., Al," Jack argued. "Charity begins at home."

Jolson was receptive. He told Skolsky, "What are we doing at a crappy studio like Columbia?" Cohn couldn't match Warner's offer, but Skolsky convinced Cohn to give Jolson fifty percent of the profits. *The Jolson Story* and the sequel *Jolson Sings Again* made millions for the mammysinger and Columbia, as Harry Cohn delighted in reminding Jack Warner.

For twenty-five years an invitation to a party at Ann and Jack Warner's house on Angelo Drive was, in Hollywood terms, the equivalent of a bid to dine at the White House or Buckingham Palace. Except that the host was neither presidential nor royal but a much-feared, often-ridiculed ruler of an industry.

The Warner mansion offered a magnificent setting for social gatherings. The two large swimming pools were surrounded by acres of delicately landscaped greenery. The chateaulike house contained room after ornate room of marble, tapestries, burnished leather and silken draperies. Ann Warner planned each party with style and grace. Dinners were prepared by French chefs and served with silent skill by a host of uniformed waiters.

"I remember one New Year's Eve party in 1939 or 1940," says Olivia de Havilland. "All the men were glorious in white tie. Errol Flynn was behind the bar, Howard Hughes was my date, and Jimmy Stewart was seated on a stool. Just the four of us having our first drink of the evening. All those beautiful women dressed in wonderful elegance. Dolores Del Rio in a white satin gown that contrasted her dark hair and dark eyes. Ann Warner, herself a striking presence. Those beautiful women, looking marvelous in this wonderful setting."

Paul Henreid remembers another party a few years later. Jack Warner had commissioned Salvador Dali to paint a portrait of his wife, and he and Ann invited three hundred of Hollywood's uppercrust for the unveiling. Tables adorned with fine china and silver and floral sprays sat under brightly colored umbrellas on the terrace. Through the trees could be seen the sparkling lights of Los Angeles.

Jack Warner greeted the arrivals with quips and banter. Ann Warner drifted among the guests, giving each a warm welcome. Dali himself commanded attention with his ice-pick mustache and wild eyes. After dinner the shrouded portrait was brought to the terrace, and Jack made a speech about the great surrealist "who has graciously consented to paint my beautiful wife."

Jack pulled a string and the cloth fell from the portrait. A gasp, then a chorus of "aaahhhhs," followed by polite applause. The picture of Ann was almost a photographic likeness, portraying her beauty as well as a hint of decadence. Behind her figure was a desolate Dali expanse and then a green oasis. A cage hung from a tree and captured inside was a monkey, bearing an eerie likeness to Jack Warner.

Jack gulped and cracked, "I'm so glad I was included."

Later that evening, Henreid recalls, he was standing in the Warner library conversing with Errol Flynn when Tallulah Bankhead made one of her distinctive entrances. She rushed to Flynn, fell to her knees and buried her face in his crotch. "Errol, dahling, it's going to be a *wonderful* night!" she exclaimed.

Still later, Henreid and his wife Lisl talked over brandy with Cary Grant and his wife, Barbara Hutton. The Grants left, and Lillian Gish peered inside the library in search of the bathroom. Tallulah, who was necking with a young actor in a corner, looked up and greeted Lillian warmly. With a fixed smile, Tallulah remarked, "Dear Lillian, here we are, surviving after all these years, you with your face lifted and your vagina dropped, and me with my vagina lifted and my face dropped."

Lillian giggled and left the room with a flutter of her white-gloved hand.

"Combining good citizenship with good picture making."—*The New York Times*.

The slogan was trumpeted on the billboard in the traffic island opposite Warner Bros. studio, and it was emblazoned in newspaper ads for the company's movies. The quote was bona fide; it had been lifted from *The New York Times*' review of a Warner anti-Nazi film of the early forties. (With a stroke of supreme irony, the critic later became a screenwriter and was blacklisted for his liberal associations.)

In September 1946, Warner Bros. was one of the studios being struck as a result of a violent battle between two opposing unions. A thousand pickets marched in front of the studio's main auto gate on Olive Avenue. Members of the rival union tried to enter the studio, and a melee ensued, with chains, rocks, bottles and two-by-fours as weapons. Three cars were overturned. Police ended the "battle of Warner Bros." with tear gas. Onlookers noticed guards armed with rifles atop the sound stages overlooking Olive Avenue. Julius Epstein quipped, "That's Warner Bros.: Combining good citizenship with good marksmanship."

The strike was a devastating event that deepened Jack Warner's conservatism and distrust of unions. Ten years before, he had done everything possible to prevent unionization of the studios. He had called a meeting of writers at the studio and had declared: "We're not going to use coercion or threats, but if any son of a bitch is a member of the Guild, by tomorrow he'll be out of a job."

Warner tried to continue filming during the 1946 strike. Always fearful of his personal safety, he never ventured outside the studio gates, and he urged his key personnel to do the same. *Silver River* was the only film in production at the time, and he instructed the producer, Owen Crump: "Keep that picture going!" Crump, as well as Errol Flynn and Ann Sheridan, slept at the studio, and filming continued.

163

Joan Crawford was scheduled to start a new film, and she was needed at the studio for wardrobe tests. Her agent, Arthur Park, called Warner to make sure his client would be able to enter the studio. "Certainly," Warner assured. "We've got guards at every entrance. Tell her to come ahead." Park relayed the information to Crawford, who said, "You go first." Park started to drive through the picket line, and the strikers broke his windshield, dented his fenders and threw a liquid in his face; he feared it was acid but it wasn't. Crawford saw what happened to him and drove away. "I'm not going to risk *this* face," she said.

Jack Warner went to Washington in 1947 and made a public clown of himself, in the most pernicious way.

It was the "time of the toad." Dalton Trumbo, one of its principal victims, gave it that term, drawing from Emile Zola's 1890 screed against the excesses of the press. By 1947, the euphoria of the war's end had passed into the hard chill of the cold war. Headline-hungry congressmen trod the land in search of Reds, liberals or "fellow travelers." Hollywood provided ideal hunting grounds.

In the fall of 1947, studio heads, producers, directors and stars trooped to Washington and testified of the industry's good character, despite a few bad apples. Warner Bros. had been under attack for having produced *Mission to Moscow*. Jack Warner defended it before the House Un-American Activities Committee on October 20.

"That picture was made when our country was fighting for its existence, with Russia as one of our allies," Warner declared. "It was made to fulfill the same wartime purpose for which we made such other pictures as *Air Force, This Is the Army, Objective Burma, Destination Tokyo, Action in the North Atlantic* and a great many more."

He rambled on, citing the "ideological termites" that had infested America, volunteering, "My brothers and I will be happy to subscribe generously to a pest-removal fund. We are willing to establish such a fund to ship to Russia the people who don't like our American system of government and prefer the communistic system to ours."

Without being asked, Warner named a dozen screenwriters he had detected and fired for being "communists." Thus he destroyed the filmwriting careers of the men, some of whom had no communist ties whatsoever.

Warner's colleagues were appalled. Eric Johnston, who had succeeded Will Hays as head of the producers' association, admitted privately that Jack Warner had "made a stupid ass of himself." Paul McNutt, a former high-ranking New Deal official who had been hired as front man for the producers, said, "I have spent all day reviewing his testimony in an effort to have Warner appear in a less idiotic light."

Warner made no apologies for his Washington performance. He was furious when Humphrey Bogart, Lauren Bacall, Paul Henreid and John Huston joined other members of the stellar Committee for the First Amendment in a flight to Washington to preach against the threat to free expression.

The resolve of the noncommunist liberals melted under the heat of studio pressure and the demagoguery of the politicians. After the Hollywood Ten had been indicted for contempt of congress, Eric Johnston called a meeting of film industry powers at the Waldorf Astoria Hotel in New York on November 24, 1947.

Alarmed by the onslaught of bad publicity, Johnston declared that the industry needed to take action. He was supported by other studio heads, including Jack Warner. Only Sam Goldwyn, Walter Wanger and Dore Schary advised caution. Schary argued that it wasn't unlawful to be a communist and there was no proof the Unfriendly Ten had tried to overthrow the government. Besides, no harm had been done, since the studios claimed they had been uninfected by Red propaganda.

The hardliners prevailed. The producers issued the infamous Waldorf manifesto which fired the Ten and declared: "We will not knowingly employ a communist or a member of any party or group which advocates the overthrow of the government. . . ." The blacklist had been made official.

*　　　*　　　*

During his acquisitive sweep of the late 1920s and early 1930s Harry had neglected one kind of subsidiary: the newsreel. Paramount, Fox, MGM and Universal serviced newsreels along with other short subjects; Warner Bros. did not. That omission was remedied in August 1947.

Charles Pathe had invented the newsreel in 1910, and over the years Pathe News became an institution on movie bills around the world. Having suffered bad times during World War II, the Pathe company sold its newsreel to Warner Bros.

"Now we gotta get rid of that goddamn rooster with his coo-coo-coo," Jack Warner declared, referring to the symbol that had introduced the Pathe newsreel for decades.

"That's too valuable a trademark to discard," reasoned Art Silver, who supervised the newsreel as head of the shorts department. "But we can do something new with it, maybe put the Warner Brothers' shield behind it. I'll have the art department work on it."

"All right, all right," Warner said impatiently. "But you gotta get rid of that old rooster. The sound is bad, and it looks dated. Get a new rooster, a bigger one, and reshoot the whole logo. I don't care if we spend a few bucks. We gotta do it."

Silver held a conference in the shorts department, and the idea was proposed: "Why not have a contest to choose the best rooster?" The publicity department went to work on the scheme, and poultry farms all over the country submitted contestants. The winner was a strutting specimen the size of a bald eagle.

A camera crew gathered on the back lot, and the rooster was positioned against the sky. "All right, make him crow," Art Silver told the fowl's owner.

The owner did everything possible to coax the rooster, but not a sound emerged. "I don't understand it," the owner said. "He crows all the time in the barnyard."

"He's gotta have something to crow about," suggested a crew member. "Get him a hen."

A cage of spare chickens was nearby, and a hen was placed

within the rooster's eyesight. Nothing happened. The rooster simply ignored the hen's clucking. The afternoon sunlight was beginning to fade, and not a foot of film had been exposed. "What the hell's going on down there?" Warner inquired by telephone. Silver explained the problem and promised to complete the assignment before nightfall.

The crew members contemplated the silent rooster. One of them suggested: "Maybe if we put another rooster in front of him, he'll get mad as hell."

"Let's try it," said the desperate Silver. At the sight of a rival, the rooster loosed a mighty crow that almost deafened the film crew. "Cut! Print!" Silver ordered. "Strike the set."

The following morning, Silver received a memo from J. L. Warner: "The next time you do anything like this, don't get me a fag rooster."

During the eight years following her arrival at Warner Bros. in 1936, Jane Wyman appeared in forty films, most of them second or third leads in B pictures. Like Bette Davis and Olivia de Havilland, she had to prove her acting talent at another studio. With *The Lost Weekend* in 1945, critics took her seriously as an actress. An Academy nomination for *The Yearling* in 1947 finally convinced Jack Warner that he had another dramatic star under contract.

Johnny Belinda had been bought by Warner Bros. after its mediocre success as a Broadway play. It seemed like a forbidding subject for the screen—a deaf, mute girl in a fishing town who is raped, bears a child and kills the rapist. Jerry Wald ordered a succession of scripts until he got one that seemed dramatic enough and passable by the Production Code. Jane Wyman was the leader among several actresses being considered for the lead. For the sympathetic doctor, Wald and the director, Jean Negulesco, favored a young actor the studio had screen-tested in New York. He was Marlon Brando, who had astounded Broadway in *A Streetcar Named Desire*.

Jack Warner decreed the casting as he left for his annual vacation at his Cap d'Antibes villa: "Jane Wyman for the girl. Forget that New York guy; he doesn't talk, he mumbles. Get the young actor who plays Dr. Kildare." He was referring to Lew Ayres, who had appeared in Warner Bros. films in the early thirties.

Wald purposely chose to film *Johnny Belinda* entirely at remote Fort Bragg in northern California, far from studio interference. The rushes continued flowing back to Burbank, and studio executives complained that Negulesco was photographing too many scenic shots. When Warner returned from France and saw Jane Wyman in the rushes, he was incensed.

"Look at that ugly dame!" he ranted. "She's gonna ruin the studio! I can't stand to look at her." He turned to Wald. "Jerry, call that Romanian son of a bitch and tell him to put some makeup on her."

"I will, Jack," Wald lied.

Warner next viewed rushes of Ann Sheridan in a western, her perfectly coiffed hair a bright red, her makeup in Technicolor perfection. "Now that's the way a star should look," Warner told the producer, Owen Crump.

After Warner saw the rough cut of *Johnny Belinda*, he pointed an accusing finger at Wald and Negulesco. "We invented talking pictures, and you two make a picture about a deaf and dumb girl," he grumbled. "Only one thing can save it: put some narration over her close-ups to tell the public what she is thinking." Wald and Negulesco groaned, and Warner did not pursue the idea. *Johnny Belinda* became Warner Bros.' biggest money-maker in 1948.

When the Academy Award nominations were announced, a jubilant Jack Warner telephoned Jean Negulesco: "Kid, we did it! We got twelve nominations. Next time we'll get thirteen." The director, who had left Warner Bros. for a contract at Fox, reminded him that any picture was only eligible for twelve categories. "We'll invent one extra," Warner replied.

Jane Wyman was the only winner among the *Johnny Belinda* nominees. After the ceremonies Jack Warner hosted a party for her at the Mocambo nightclub, where he basked in praise as a fearless producer of quality films.

Like other founder-rulers of motion picture empires, Jack Warner never considered grooming a successor. In 1947 he had reached his fifty-fifth year with no diminution of vigor. He had one of the greatest jobs in the world, and he saw no prospect of being forced to relinquish it. The stockholders were quiescent, and Harry, now sixty-six, was gradually losing the strength to challenge his impulsive kid brother.

Jack's relations with his son remained the same: distant. In Warner's view, young Jack was part of the hard-nosed family faction that had decried the divorce from Irma and had snubbed Ann, labeling her a harlot. Jack Jr. had grown up under the influence of his mother, who had married another producer, Al Rogell. Warner was certain that his former wife had poisoned their son's mind against him. He could never feel comfortable with Jack Jr., who was that rarity in the Warner family, a college graduate.

After Jack's graduation from USC, Harry had taught him the business side of Warner Bros. in New York. In 1938 Jack Jr. started work at the studio as an assistant to Mike Curtiz. After his wartime service, Jack Jr. returned to the studio. His father sent him to England where Warner Bros. was producing films with funds that had been frozen by the British.

Jack Warner always enjoyed the companionship of Bill Orr. Not only was Bill a son-in-law, he was delightful company. Showwise without being arrogant about it, he could perceive the humor in most situations. Orr did not even object when Warner introduced him at the first postwar Warner Club dinner with the comment: "My half-assed son-in-law is going to be your emcee. C'mon, sonny boy." Jack often used the "half-assed" reference on the grounds that Joy was his stepdaughter.

While Orr was on terminal leave from the army, Warner told him, "I want you to come back to the studio."

"I've been at your studio," Orr replied.

"I mean I want you to work behind the scenes."

"You mean not be an actor anymore?"

"You get the picture."

Orr was in a quandary. The Leland Hayward agency had submitted him for three roles at other studios, and he still wanted to act. He feared that Warner had offered the job because he didn't want Joy married to a ne'er-do-well actor. Orr was wary of the "son-in-law also rises" jokes that had been affixed to Milton Sperling, the Warner Bros. producer who had married Harry's daughter.

"Think about it," Jack Warner told Orr. "Meanwhile, read this script and tell me what you think. It starts in two weeks."

It was a *Two Guys* script designed for Dennis Morgan and Jack Carson. Orr thought it was awful. When pressed by Warner, Orr admitted, "I think it could be a lot better."

"You don't like it, then?" Warner demanded.

"No, I don't."

"Neither do I. We're calling it off."

Orr's acting jobs did not develop, and he agreed to work at the studio. Warner's instructions: "I want you to get there at seven-thirty in the morning and see if the actors have shown up. Find out if Flynn is sober, if Bogart is acting up, if Davis is fighting with her director."

Orr did none of those things. "Just what I need," he said privately, "for the half-assed son-in-law to be a fink for the chief." He continued at the studio for eight months until he was invited to perform at a Palm Springs benefit. His comedy style proved as sharp as before, and the audience's reaction persuaded him to revive his career as an entertainer. But after an unrewarding year, he returned to the studio.

Jack Warner was pleased. He told Orr: "I remember what my brother Sam told me when I came back from playing the Gus Sun circuit. Sam said, 'Get out front where they pay the actors. That's where the money is.' "

Chapter 12

Changing Times

THE BIG SLIDE BEGAN IN 1947. The wartime boom was over, and movie attendance began to falter. Americans became bored with the same bland formulas offered by the Hollywood studios, and more and more of them turned to something new and exciting: television. Warner Bros.' income reflected the shift in the country's entertainment habits. The company's profit in 1948 dropped to $11.8 million, almost half of the amount in the previous year.

Warner Bros. suffered a punishing blow in 1949. After years of pursuing the major film companies, the federal government finally enforced a consent decree under which the companies had to choose two of their three areas of operation: production, distribution, exhibition. The majors reluctantly opted to sell off their theaters. This proved devastating to their profit margins. Not only were theaters a sure source of revenue; they also provided a ready showplace for the studio's movies, good, bad or routine. Now the majors would be forced to sell their product on the open market.

Harry Warner constantly nagged his brother Jack to economize, economize, economize. No matter that the Burbank studio had always been and still remained the most tightly operated in Hollywood. J. L. himself reviewed the budgets of every department, and his eagle eye detected any padding.

Despite Warner's haggling over contracts, star salaries had ballooned. In 1947 he found himself in the embarrassing position of being the employer who paid the highest salaries in America for a man and woman: $467,361 for Humphrey Bogart and $328,000 for Bette Davis.

"You're paying too much for those goddamn actors," Harry told Jack.

Jack didn't exactly hate all actors, but he detested their agents. Throughout most of his career, he had tried to have as little to do with them as possible. But after the war, he discovered that agents, particularly those of the aggressive MCA, insisted on an active part in negotiations. And they were making more demands, not only for money but for such things as billing, dressing rooms and other perquisites.

Warner vigorously protected his power. Bette Davis once came to a grievance meeting with her MCA agent, Lew Wasserman. The matter was quickly settled, and then Davis launched into a critique of her current script. "Wait a minute," Warner interrupted, holding up his hand. "Is this going to be a story session?" When Davis said it was, Warner said, "Lew?" Wasserman waited for a question, and Warner repeated, "Lew?" "Oh, you want me to leave," said the agent, and he did.

The process of eliminating the high-paid stars began. In 1948, Barbara Stanwyck complained that she had brought *The Fountainhead* to the studio's attention and had assumed that it was being written for her. She was shocked to read that a newcomer from Broadway, Patricia Neal, had been given the role of Dominique. Declaring that she was "bitterly disappointed," she asked Warner to end her contract. He gratefully assented.

Errol Flynn continued to be a thorn in Jack Warner's side. Flynn's behavior on *The Adventures of Don Juan* was so erratic that Warner hired detectives in an attempt to keep him out of trouble. Filming had to be suspended for weeks while the actor engaged in a monumental bender. After one more film, Warner did not renew Flynn's contract.

Ann Sheridan had to buy her way out of Warner Bros. Weary of being forever cast as the "Oomph Girl," she settled her contract in 1949 by paying the studio $35,000.

Paul Henreid was offered a role opposite Katharine Hepburn in *Song of Love* at MGM. He was worried that Jack Warner would not release him for the plum assignment, so Henreid bought the remainder of his contract for $75,000.

After his extraordinary success with *Champion*, Kirk Douglas was courted by all the major studios. Jack Warner offered what appeared to be an ideal contract: a picture a year for eight years at a handsome salary. Douglas was reluctant to ally himself with a big studio, but he acceded to the persuasions of his agent, Charles Feldman.

Douglas made two disappointing films at Warner Bros., and then was cast in a western, *Along the Great Divide*. He hated it. "I want out of the contract," Douglas told Feldman. The agent argued that Jack Warner would never agree to end the contract. "Oh yes, he will, when he hears my offer," said Douglas.

His proposal: he would make the next picture under his contract for no salary, in return for his freedom. Warner jumped at the opportunity, commenting, "The guy must be nuts." Douglas's gratis film was *The Big Trees*, the fourth version of *Valley of the Giants*.

After three years at MGM, Stanley Morner had done little but sing "A Pretty Girl Is Like Melody" in *The Great Ziegfeld*. In 1939 he came to Warner Bros., changed his name to Dennis Morgan and became the studio's most serviceable leading man, fully capable of musicals, comedies, westerns and military films. He could also play romantic leads opposite dramatic stars like Bette Davis, Ida Lupino and Barbara Stanwyck.

Morgan teamed successfully with Jack Carson in *Two Guys from Milwaukee* and *Two Guys from Texas*. Pleased with his own, more genteel version of Abbott and Costello, Jack Warner promised theaters another Two Guys movie for the fall of 1949. He summoned two of his most facile writers, Mel Shavelson and Jack Rose.

"Look, fellas, I gotta have a Two Guys script in three weeks," Warner said urgently. "It's already booked into the theaters, and if I don't deliver, I'm gonna look like a schmuck."

Shavelson and Rose returned to their office and started brainstorming. Their first two story lines proved unworkable; then they found the solution. They expounded their idea to David Butler, whom Warner had designated as director for the *Two Guys* film: "Since there's no time to build new sets, we'll have Morgan and Carson play themselves, making a movie at the studio. They discover Doris Day, who is a waitress in the commissary, and put her in the movie. We can have all the Warner Bros. stars do walk-ons."

"Sounds good, boys, now we gotta sell Dennis on the idea," said Butler.

"Okay, let's go tell him the story," Shavelson suggested.

"Can't do it. He's on suspension, and Jack has barred him from the lot."

"So we'll go see him off the lot."

"Yeah, but you know Jack won't allow writers to leave the studio during the day."

Butler devised a ruse: he drove his car out the studio gate with Shavelson hidden under a blanket in the backseat. They then traveled two blocks to the Lakeside Golf Club, where Morgan lunched with his studio cronies. Morgan approved Shavelson's story, and Butler drove back to the studio with his sequestered passenger.

Much relieved, Jack Warner proceeded with production plans for the film to be called *It's a Great Feeling*. Then the legal department discovered a catastrophe. While Dennis Morgan was on suspension, his contract had expired! Warner pleaded, cajoled and threatened, but Morgan's agents were unyielding. A new contract gave Morgan four times his previous salary.

By 1952, Dennis Morgan was by far the highest-paid Warner Bros. star. His contract was coming to an end, and Jack Warner hoped Morgan would spend his last weeks on suspension. Warner employed one of his standard strategies: presenting a script that the star couldn't possibly accept. It was thirty pages of a hackwork western called *Cattle Town*.

"You aren't going to do this picture, are you, Dennis?" the producer, Bryan Foy, inquired anxiously.

"Hell, yes," replied Morgan. "Do you think I'm going to pass up my salary?"

Cattle Town was undistinguished except for what may have been the longest cattle drive in film history. The town itself had been built on Stage 7, and the script called for herds of livestock to rampage through it. A hundred steers and cows were assembled in the street outside. The north stage door opened, and the cattle were raced through the western street and out the south door. Then the herd was directed around the stage and into the north door again. The cattle continued their loop until the set was almost demolished.

Bette Davis did not go gentle. Her battles with Warner raged incessantly, and she was reinforced by Lew Wasserman and MCA. Warner became so furious that he barred MCA from the lot. That added fuel to Bette's anger. During one acrimonious dispute, Davis came crashing into Warner's office, finding him seated on the toilet in his bathroom. She launched her tirade against the astonished Warner and then stalked out the door, slamming it behind her.

The breaking point came with *Beyond the Forest* in 1948. Davis considered the script mediocre and the leads miscast: herself and Joseph Cotten. She felt she was too strong a person to play Rosa, the small-town doctor's wife who endures a humdrum life until she meets a wealthy Chicagoan.

"If I was Rosa, I would get to Chicago a lot sooner," she told Warner. "You should get Virginia Mayo for the part."

She also argued that the novel had portrayed the husband as "a Gene Pallette type, a ghastly old man." Joe Cotten was much too attractive, she reasoned—"what woman would want to leave him?" Warner was deaf to her reasoning. "You will do the picture with Joseph Cotten," he decreed.

Now there was trouble with Joe Cotten. He considered his role too weak and balked at being loaned to Warner Bros. by David Selznick. King Vidor, who was to direct *Beyond the Forest*, had his own misgivings about the script, but he was prepared to go forward. He sent a telegram of encouragement to his close friend Cotten.

"What do you mean, that this is the greatest story ever written?" Cotten asked Vidor. The director had said no such thing in his telegram, and he puzzled over this. Then he learned that Jack Warner reviewed all telegrams emanating from the studio and had been known to edit and amend the messages.

Selznick declined to give Warner Bros. a start date for Cotten even though Selznick had already banked the payment. Warner gave Selznick an ultimatum: commit Cotten to the film or return the $100,000. Cotten was delivered.

The filming of *Beyond the Forest* was an ordeal for all concerned. Vidor did the best he could with the material, realizing that it represented a nadir in his distinguished career. Cotten struggled with an impossible role. Davis spawned hourly crises, objecting to the script, makeup, wardrobe, anything.

Three days before the end of filming, she issued the ultimatum: she would not complete *Beyond the Forest* unless her Warner Bros. contract was canceled. Jack Warner quickly agreed. Harry Warner was ecstatic.

Bette Davis remembers her last day after eighteen years and fifty-two pictures at Warner Bros.:

"There was no celebration. Henry Blanke and a cutter who had cut all my films and I sat on a bench on the back lot. We sat there all night, remembering and talking. Saw the dawn come up. I don't think Warner was in any mood to say goodbye. What could he do? He had to give me my release if he wanted to finish the film. He wasn't loving me very much.

"Funny thing. The last work I did on the lot was to dub a line. This is the last line I spoke for Warner Bros.: 'I can't stand it here anymore!' The engineer and all of us roared. It was the truth."

As dawn was lighting the Burbank sky, she drove out the Olive Avenue gate, tears in the Bette Davis eyes.

*   *   *

Amid all the departures from Warner Bros. there was a significant return: Jimmy Cagney.

After Ivan Goff and Ben Roberts had submitted the script for *White Heat*, a story of a hardened criminal with a mother complex, Jack Warner asked, "Who would you like to play the role?"

"There's only one actor in Hollywood who can do it justice," replied Goff. "That's James Cagney."

Warner exploded, "Why that son of a bitch! I wouldn't have him on the lot." He could never forgive the Yiddish taunts that Cagney had hurled during their many disputes.

But Warner relented, and the script was sent to Cagney. He liked the script but suggested more emphasis on making Cody Jarrett a psychotic and stressing his obsessive love for his mother. Cagney was pleased with the script changes but disheartened by Jack Warner's cheapness, which had intensified in the seven years since *Yankee Doodle Dandy*. Cagney later called *White Heat* "another cheapjack job. There was limited shooting time, and the studio put everybody in it they could get for six bits."

The pivotal scene of Cody's rage upon hearing of his mother's death was scheduled to take place in the prison mess hall. "Why build a mess hall set and fill it with a hundred prisoners?" Warner argued. "Shoot it somewhere else in the prison, say, the chapel."

"A guy like Cody Jarrett would never be in the chapel," said Goff. "We need to have him go berserk and cry in front of the other prisoners, so they can see the toughest guy in the prison break down."

Warner remained firm. Finally the director, Raoul Walsh, offered a compromise. He proposed converting the studio mill into a mess hall by putting cloths over the work tables. Only when he promised to begin shooting at eight and finish by noon did Warner grant permission. Without any preliminaries, Cagney performed his mad scene flawlessly, drawing on his boyhood memory of a visit to an insane asylum.

Cagney stayed on at Warner Bros. for a musical, *The West Point*

Story, appearing with the studio's new star, Doris Day. She had been a band singer with no acting experience when Michael Curtiz tested her for *Romance on the High Seas*. Curtiz, who had established his own production company at Warner Bros., had tried to cast Judy Garland or Betty Hutton for the film and had failed. After testing dozens of young singers, he chose Doris Day.

She proved to be Warner Bros.' biggest star in the postwar years. Her popularity led to a revival of musicals at the studio; she would appear in fifteen over seven years. But these were "cheapjack jobs," not the elaborate productions of the Busby Berkeley years. Doris once remarked to me that she yearned to appear in the big-time musicals at MGM. When her remark appeared in print, she caught hell from Jack Warner. "How can you bite the hand that feeds you?" he demanded. Doris didn't talk to me for years.

Ronald Reagan was discontented with the roles Jack Warner had given him after the war.

Reagan had returned from his army service, which he spent entirely on the West Coast, and resumed his $3,500-a-week salary which Lew Wasserman had negotiated four years before. (For Reagan's wartime appearance in *This Is the Army*, he received his first lieutenant's pay, $250 a month.) Months passed with no scripts, and he occupied himself with model boat-building and politics.

Finally a script arrived: *Stallion Road*, based on Stephen Longstreet's novel about a love triangle in horse country. Reagan was excited because he would costar with Humphrey Bogart, the studio's top-ranking star, in a Technicolor film about horses. A week before filming, Bogart refused *Stallion Road*, and Zachary Scott replaced him. Then Warner decided to shoot it in black-and-white.

Stallion Road was an inauspicious return to the screen for Reagan. *That Hagen Girl* was an accident he had tried to avoid. Shirley Temple had been cast in her first grown-up role as a small-town girl born on the wrong side of the sheet. Reagan was to be the man rumored to be her father, but in reality becomes her lover. "An impossible role," Reagan protested to Jack Warner. "Do it or else," Warner replied.

Warner had paid a half-million dollars for the Broadway hit, *The Voice of the Turtle*, and he wanted Cary Grant or Tyrone Power for the lead. Neither was available, so the role fell to Ronald Reagan. He was reluctant, because John Huston had offered him a role in *The Treasure of the Sierra Madre*, which would shoot at the same time. Reagan realized that if he refused *The Voice of the Turtle*, he would be denied *Sierra Madre* anyway. So he accepted the role of the lonely soldier on leave in New York, an out-of-date plot by 1948.

Reagan followed with another Broadway play, *John Loves Mary*, a melodrama, *Night unto Night*, and a comedy, *The Girl from Jones Beach*. Next came another hit play, *The Hasty Heart*.

Jack Warner scheduled the film, which takes place in an army hospital in the Burmese jungle, to be made in England in order to expend frozen funds. It was Reagan's first trip to Europe, but his excitement was tempered by distress over the end of his marriage to Jane Wyman. His costar, Patricia Neal, had been enmeshed in a love affair with Gary Cooper, who would not leave his wife. Reagan and Neal consoled each other over morose dinners in London, which was experiencing the worst winter in decades.

"Warner kept putting me in sophisticated Broadway plays," Reagan recalls. "I was just dying to do a western. He never outright said no. Finally one day I said to him, 'If you ever let me do a western, you'll make me the lawyer from the East.' He kicked me out of the office for it."

With three years remaining on Reagan's contract, Lew Wasserman negotiated a one-picture-a-year deal that cut his salary in half. Then the MCA agent arranged a five-year contract with Universal for $75,000 per film.

In early January 1950, I interviewed Reagan on the set of *Storm Warning*, an anti-Ku Klux Klan drama with Ginger Rogers and Doris Day. It was his first movie in almost a year; he had suffered a serious leg injury while clowning with George Tobias at a charity baseball game.

Reagan was in a feisty mood, and these were among his comments in the interview: "After spending most of last year in bed, I'm going to concentrate on my career in 1950. And there'll be some changes made. . . . I'm going to pick my own pictures. I have come to the conclusion that I could do as good a job of picking as the studio has done. At least I could do no worse. With the parts I've had, I could telephone my lines in, and it wouldn't make any difference. . . . Well, I can always go back to being a sports announcer."

After reading this story in the Los Angeles *Mirror*, Jack Warner immediately sent off a letter to Reagan: ". . . I am wondering if you did or did not give the enclosed interview to Bob Thomas, the AP correspondent. If in fact you did this interview I think it was very unfortunate of you to do so. . . .

"If you are not satisfied with the roles you have portrayed in the past, undoubtedly you will have the same attitude with respect to future roles. I would greatly appreciate your sending me a letter canceling our mutual contract obligations with respect to the two remaining pictures you are to do for this company. . . ."

The imbroglio was smoothed over by Lew Wasserman, but the relationship between Warner and Reagan remained cool. The actor made two more films at Warner Bros., *She's Working Her Way Through College*, a *Male Animal* remake with Virginia Mayo, and *The Winning Team*, a biography of baseball great Grover Cleveland Alexander. Then Reagan left Warner Bros., ending a fifteen-year association. Like Bette Davis, he departed without any official notice or even a note from Jack Warner.

By the time he reached his late sixties, the years of directing a complex corporation and a lifetime of contending with his brother Jack were beginning to show on Harry Warner. He looked grayer, both in hair and complexion, and the pursed-lipped undertaker's expression seemed permanent. His screeds against Jack's extravagances at the studio were beginning to lose their fire. He seemed to have only three interests: enjoying his family, racing his horses and fighting communism.

Harry became the grand dragon in the enforcement of the black-list. He was vigilant to expunge anyone suspected of leftist leanings from the studio payroll. At a meeting of industry leaders, Harry argued at great length for a loyalty oath to be signed by anyone who worked in the studios. Much as he loved his brother, he thundered, he would tie a rope around Jack's neck and lead him to the nearest police station if he was discovered to be a communist.

"Harry, that would be very uncomfortable," Jack quipped, drawing the only laugh of a rancorous evening. The industrywide loyalty oath failed to pass because of opposition of guild leaders and a few brave liberals. Shortly afterward, all Warner Bros. employees were issued a questionnaire by the studio police chief, Blayney Matthews. The questions included matters of religion, criminal record, and communist party membership. Because of a wave of resentment, the questionnaire was dropped.

In the 1930s, horse racing became for Harry Warner a passion akin to making money. He poured hundreds of thousands of dollars into building a first-class stable. When Santa Anita racetrack seemed like a gentleman's club for gentile stable owners, Harry provided the final money to build the rival Hollywood Park. He introduced his son-in-law, Mervyn LeRoy, to racing, and they formed the W-L Ranch, entering horses at the major tracks. Their horse Paper Boy won the Saratoga Cup. Harry even interested his brother in racing, and Jack served as president of Hollywood Park.

Harry had been buying west San Fernando Valley real estate since the mid-thirties, accumulating 1,100 acres for his Warner Ranch. There he built a 7,000-square-foot ranch house with a movie theater and stables. Harry joined with John Hertz, the U-drive tycoon, in a breeding farm that they hoped to turn into "Kentucky of the West." Harry even dreamed of building a racetrack on his property.

After the war, Harry moved the Warner Bros. head office from New York to Burbank, but it proved impractical, and the distribution and advertising executives returned to New York. Harry remained. He was spending more time in California, where he could enjoy his ranch and horses while keeping a closer eye on Jack. Harry's icy demeanor kept him from any familiarity with studio employees, and they enjoyed telling stories at his expense.

Harry took great pleasure in escorting dignitaries through the studio, displaying his realm like a grandee. He bragged to a visiting senator, "I have six thousand people working for me, and I know every one by name." At that moment, Wolfgang Reinhardt was passing by, and Harry saluted him with, "Hello, Gangwolf."

After twenty-five years as absolute monarch of Burbank, Jack resented Harry's presence at the studio. Jack was wary of any encroachment on his power by his oldest brother. Harry had befriended Christopher Nyby, who had worked as a carpenter at the ranch. When Nyby disclosed his ambition to be a film cutter, Harry arranged for a job through Hal McCord, head of the editing department.

Of all the studio departments, Jack considered editing his special province. He spent more time with editors than with anyone else and knew every one of them. When he saw an unfamiliar face in an editing room, he inquired of McCord, who explained Harry's intercession for Nyby.

"Fire the son of a bitch," Jack ordered. "I don't want him here." McCord followed his directions, and Nyby told Harry what had happened. "Put him back on," Harry instructed McCord. Nyby managed to stay out of Jack's view, and he later became a director.

One day Hugh Benson, a new producer at Warner Bros., dropped by the office of Milton Sperling, who had his own production company, United States Pictures. Sperling introduced his father-in-law, Harry Warner. Without a word of greeting, the old man demanded, "Young man, who runs this studio?" "Why, Jack Warner," Benson replied. Harry walked out the door without a word.

Harry resented the spectacle of Jack's holding court with his producers and executives, as he did every afternoon in the executive dining room. For a time the two brothers lunched at the same hour, Jack at the head of the table, Harry at the far end. Whenever Harry started pontificating about the Red menace or the dangers of Harry Truman's liberalism, Jack cut him off with a wisecrack. Soon Harry began arriving at noon, eating his lunch and vanishing before Jack's arrival.

Harry sometimes arrived after Jack's performance. Gil Golden, an advertising executive from the New York office, and his new assistant, Richard Lederer, came to the dining room for a mid-afternoon meal. They were startled to see a glowering Harry Warner sitting alone in the middle of the table. The flustered Golden introduced himself and gave Lederer a buildup to justify a junior staff member's presence in the dining room.

Harry raised a bony hand. "Stop," he ordered. "If you have to say so much about him, he must stink."

Golden quickly changed to Harry's favorite subject, horse racing. Harry's granite face suddenly transformed. He began a spirited dissertation on the sport of kings, concluding with: "You can trust horses. They're honest, they'll never lie to you. You can't say that about people. That's why I love horses."

Harry Warner continued as president of Warner Bros., while Jack remained Vice President in Charge of Production. While Harry spent more time in California, the power vacuum in the eastern office was filled by an improbable character named Ben Kalmenson.

He had spent the first ten years of his working life in the Crucible Steel mills of Pittsburgh, and his manner reflected it. He was completely unaffected by New York sophistication; his language was spattered with obscenities. A squat, muscular man, he reacted with the fury of a bantamweight fighter whenever threatened.

Ben Kalmenson enjoyed telling underlings how he entered the film business. By his mid-twenties he had worked his way out of the steel mill and was selling Buicks for a Pittsburgh dealer. The chief salesman for First National Pictures was passing through the city in 1927 and remembered that he had promised to buy his wife a car. He stopped at the Buick showroom.

The First National salesman was a heavy drinker, and later at his hotel he asked his companion, "How many cars did I buy?" The answer: "Two—one for yourself and one for your wife." "Who from?" "Some kid at the Buick place." "Get that son of a bitch on the phone. I want him to work for me."

Ben Kalmenson proved he could sell films as well as he sold Buicks. For First National and for Warner Bros. after the merger, he managed exchanges in Albany, Kansas City and Omaha, booked films for Warner Bros. theaters in Pennsylvania and became division manager of southern and western theaters. In 1941 he was elevated to general sales manager for all of Warner Bros.

In the arena of film selling, Kalmenson was absolute master, exacting the stiffest terms possible from buyers and ruling his staff with an iron fist. Outside of his element, his lack of education weighed on him. In California he never stayed at the fashionable westside hotels, preferring the Ambassador, which was owned by an old theater friend. Ben avoided the stylish restaurants of Beverly Hills, preferring the steak-and-potato menu of the Pacific Dining Car near downtown Los Angeles.

The relationship of Jack Warner and Ben Kalmenson fascinated their underlings. Ben seemed to have an almost hypnotic influence over Warner, who bowed to his head salesman's judgment on most matters. Again and again producers heard Warner tell them, "Ben says we can't sell this kind of picture. . . ." or, "Ben says [a star's name] is death at the box office. . . ."

When Warner came to the New York office, he was no longer the studio autocrat. He seemed almost meek, as if he had entered Ben Kalmenson's territory on a pass. Richard Lederer, then an advertising executive, recalls a Warner ritual in New York: "He would call me to his office every afternoon at four. 'I wanna read you something,' he said. He had copies of eight or so telexes that day, chewing out everyone in Burbank. He read them to me with relish. That seemed to resuscitate him. He wanted me to see that he was still the boss."

*   *   *

Having assisted at the birth of sound movies, Jack Warner in 1951 played a major role, perhaps inadvertently, in the first unraveling of the censorship bonds that had held American films captive for thirty years.

A Streetcar Named Desire had already revolutionized the American theater, both in terms of naturalistic acting and the boldness of Tennessee Williams' writing. The film industry's chief censor, Joe Breen, scared off the studios with warnings that the play could never be filmed without elimination of its themes of rape and homosexuality. Agent-turned-producer Charlie Feldman would not be intimidated. He bought the film rights and announced he would use the same Broadway team: Elia Kazan to direct; Williams to adapt the screenplay; Marlon Brando, Jessica Tandy, Karl Malden and Kim Hunter as actors.

Jack Warner agreed to the Feldman package with one exception: he insisted on a box-office name for the part of Blanche DuBois. The choice was obvious: Vivien Leigh, who had appeared in the London production of *Streetcar* directed by her husband Laurence Olivier.

Joe Breen continued his attack on the *Streetcar* script. He refused to permit profanity and rejected any hint of the homosexuality of Blanche's husband. And he vetoed Kowalski's rape of Blanche, the most important scene of the play.

Tennessee Williams pleaded with Breen in a letter: "*Streetcar* is an extremely and peculiarly moral play, in the deepest and truest sense of the term. . . . The rape of Blanche by Stanley is a pivotal, integral truth in the play, without which the play loses its meaning, which is the ravishment of the tender, the sensitive, the delicate, by the savage and brutal forces of modern society. . . ."

Breen relented on the rape, but decreed that Kowalski would have to pay for his lust: his wife Stella would tell her newborn baby that she was not returning to Stanley.

Elia Kazan, who had acted in *City for Conquest* and *Blues in the Night* at Warner Bros. in the early 1940s, filmed most of *Streetcar* in a single set on a studio stage. Vivien Leigh was the only outsider in the company, which included six supporting actors from the Broadway cast. At first she resisted Kazan's direction with the protest, "But that's not the way Larry did it in London." After a couple of weeks Kazan convinced her to follow his direction.

The preview in Santa Barbara was a shocker. The audience laughed at the pathetic Blanche. Charlie Feldman panicked; Jack Warner remained calm. He had seen a thousand previews and recalled that many films that had had disastrous previews had been turned into hits by judicious editing.

Kazan sensed where the problem lay. The audience had started laughing when Blanche went on the make for the Young Collector at the door. Kazan eliminated the young man's reactions so that he seemed almost like one of Blanche's apparitions. Feldman was convinced that massive cuts were needed. Jack Warner viewed Kazan's changes and approved. The director asked for Warner's promise that no further changes would be made.

The two men shook hands. "The picture will go to the theaters as it is now," Warner vowed. But he hadn't counted on the Catholics.

The Legion of Decency threatened to place *Streetcar* on its condemned list, making it a sin for Catholics to attend. The threat was removed only after the cutting of several lines in order to emphasize Stella's goodness, the meanness of Stanley and the waywardness of Blanche. Also gone was Alex North's music as Stella descended the stairs following a dispute with Stanley. The Catholics deemed it "too carnal."

Streetcar was a popular and critical hit, and it won Academy Awards for Leigh, Malden and Hunter but not for Brando. The Oscar went instead to Jack Warner's old sparring mate, Humphrey Bogart, for *The African Queen*.

Despite the cuts, *Streetcar* represented a milestone in the drive for creative freedom. For the first time, Hollywood had released a film that was not intended for the entire family and the subject of rape had been treated in a major film.

Said Geoffrey Shurlock, who succeeded Breen as head of the Production Code: "*Streetcar* broke the barrier. . . . The stage got a shock from Tennessee Williams. We got twice the shock. Now we know that a good deal of what we decide in censoring movies is not morality but taste. It began with *Streetcar*."

The ascendancy of the film director in the postwar years distressed Jack Warner, who preferred fast-working, unquestioning old studio hands like Raoul Walsh, Gordon Douglas and David Butler. But Warner also respected talent, and he brought Alfred Hitchcock, newly freed from a Selznick contract, to the studio.

Hitchcock's first Warner Bros. film was a failure. Ever seeking to relieve the boredom of shooting a picture, he devised a daring stunt for *Rope*. Based loosely on the Leopold-Loeb case, the London play had depicted two homosexuals in a thrill-killing of a friend. Hitchcock proposed to tell the story without interruption, filming eight ten-minute scenes that would add up to an eighty-minute movie. Total filming time would be eight days.

"It sounds nuts, but go ahead," said Warner.

Hitchcock wanted Cary Grant to play the two boys' sardonic schoolmaster, but Grant was unavailable, and James Stewart took the role. Hitchcock plotted all the camera moves and directions for the actors "with a blackboard-like football skull practice," he explained. Despite fifteen days of rehearsal, filming was chaotic. The actors were confused, the crew exasperated. Some of the ten-minute scenes required fifteen takes. *Rope* was finally completed in twenty-one days.

Perhaps anticipating the reception, Hitchcock did not attend the Santa Barbara preview. He was represented by his agent, Lew Wasserman. By the end of the screening, the only persons left in the theater were the visitors from Hollywood.

Warner held his usual postpreview meeting in the manager's office. He listened as his underlings offered suggestions on how to rescue *Rope*. Finally Wasserman spoke up: "Why don't you ship the print? There's nothing you can do about the picture." Warner agreed. The movie flopped, and Hitchcock later withdrew it forever from public view.

Hitchcock had planned to film his next Warner Bros. film, *Under Capricorn*, in the same method as *Rope*, but he changed his mind. After finishing *Under Capricorn*, Ingrid Bergman began her scandalous affair with Roberto Rossellini, and the resulting uproar hurt the film's box office.

Undaunted, Warner gave Hitchcock a four-picture, million-dollar contract which resulted in *Stage Fright*, *Strangers on a Train*, *I Confess* and *Dial M for Murder*. When Warner wanted a fifth film, Hitchcock said, "All right, I'll do it for nothing." He took a percentage only on *The Wrong Man*.

Remarkably, Warner only interfered with Hitchcock once. The director had imported a Swedish ice-blond, Anita Bjork, to appear with Montgomery Clift in *I Confess*. When Warner discovered that Bjork had arrived in Hollywood with an illegitimate child and a lover, he ordered, "Send her back where she came from. We don't need another Bergman scandal." She was replaced by Anne Baxter.

Gregory Peck had been accustomed to making first-class productions for Selznick, MGM and Fox, with whom he had contracts. One day in 1950 he was told by David Selznick's chief executive, Daniel O'Shea, to report to Warner Bros. on Tuesday for wardrobe tests. The following Monday he would be starting a western, *Only the Valiant*.

"Wait a minute," Peck said. "That's not the way my deal works. I have a nonexclusive contract."

"Yes, but David has one commitment left under your contract," O'Shea said, "and he's sold it to Jack Warner. He needs the money. He's committed to pay you sixty thousand, and Warner is paying a hundred and fifty. So David made a quick profit of ninety thousand."

Feeling sorry for Selznick, Peck agreed to report to Warner Bros. for a film that was destined to be a potboiler. After Jack Warner greeted him cheerfully, Peck said, "You know, I don't want to do this picture."

"But I've already sent David the check," Warner answered. "What do you want to do—break your contract?"

"No, I don't want to do that."

"Then you'd better get down to wardrobe."

The disheartened actor went to the wardrobe department, where he was fitted with a cavalry officer's uniform. As he pulled on the trousers, he noted a label that read "Rod Cameron." Throughout the filming of *Only the Valiant* he wore Rod Cameron's pants.

Peck returned to Warner Bros. in the same year for *Captain Horatio Hornblower, R.N.* The script concerned a young naval captain who was transporting an aristocratic English lady, an admiral's widow, from central America to England. In the course of the voyage, the lady falls in love with the captain. Peck told the director, the hardy, one-eyed Raoul Walsh, "I know an English actress who would be perfect for the role. She is beautiful, aristocratic, and a fine actress. Her name is Margaret Leighton."

"Okay, kid, I'll talk to Jack about it," Walsh replied.

Peck heard nothing from Walsh until they met one day on a studio street. "What about my suggestion of Margaret Leighton?" Peck asked.

"Sorry, kid, it's no deal," the director said.

"Why not?"

"Jack told me, 'No tits.' "

Virginia Mayo played the role of the admiral's widow.

Chapter 13

Television

Jack Warner hated television. Whenever he arrived home at night, he found Ann seated in front of the flickering box. "Turn off that box!" he ordered. "You can't see anything on that little screen."

Warner had declared war on television. He would allow no television sets at the studio. Although millions of Americans now watched television, no living room in a Warner Bros. movie had one. Television was never mentioned in dialogue. When Sammy Fain and Paul Francis Webster were writing songs for a Warner Bros. musical, they thought they had a bright idea with "I'm in Love with the Girl on Channel 9." When they played it for Mel Shavelson, he predicted, "Jack Warner will never approve it." He was right.

But television would not go away. It continued eroding theater attendance, and by 1953 the Warner Bros. profit had fallen to $2.9 million.

Jack Warner believed he had discovered a cure for the ailing box office: three-dimensional movies.

Warners launched three films in 3-D, *House of Wax*, *The Charge at Feather River* and *The Moonlighter*. The first two were hits; the other flopped. Two big-budget films, *Dial M for Murder* and *Hondo*, prospered in 3-D, but the novelty soon died as theater patrons complained that the glasses gave them headaches.

The next tampering with the screen concerned wide screens. Mike Todd started it with *This Is Cinerama* in 1952. Next, Twentieth Century-Fox introduced CinemaScope. Like talkies, the wide-screen process required conversion of the nation's theaters; hence Darryl Zanuck tried to convince other studio heads to use his company's anamorphic lenses. The fee was $25,000.

Zanuck arranged a private screening of CinemaScope tests for his old boss, Jack Warner. Warner was impressed, but he made no commitment. His 3-D movies had not yet run their course, and, most importantly, it would rankle him to pay tribute to another studio for a film innovation.

Warner tinkered with his own system, which he called WarnerScope. A print of the Cole Porter biography, *Night and Day*, was spread like butter across an immense screen. But the process lost almost half of the image at the top and bottom. Warner sent the lens makers back to the lab.

Fox launched a massive media campaign for the first movie in CinemaScope, *The Robe*, which was enthusiastically received by the press and the public. Among those who were impressed was Albert Warner.

"You should see those lines around the Roxy, day and night," Albert told his brothers. "Maybe we oughta give up on this WarnerScope thing and go along with Fox."

Since Albert seldom raised his voice on company matters, Harry listened. But Jack was hell-bent on having his own process so that he could thumb his nose at Zanuck. When the new WarnerScope lenses arrived from Germany, tests revealed fuzziness and distortion at the sides of the screen. Jack telephoned Harry and Albert in New York, and all agreed to go along with CinemaScope.

The first Warner Bros. film in CinemaScope was *The Command* in 1953. It was a routine western starring Guy Madison, and the size of the screen only magnified the script's shortcomings. Another CinemaScope film that year, *The High and the Mighty*, was highly successful. Unlike 3-D, wide-screen processes did not disappear after the novelty had passed. But producers came to realize that what mattered to audiences was not the size of the screen but what appeared on it.

Like most of the studio heads, Warner had resisted the siren calls of the television networks and advertisers who eagerly sought the quality programming only the movie companies could provide. Only Warner's enemy, Harry Cohn, had broken ranks. Columbia's subsidiary Screen Gems had contracted with the Ford Motor Company to provide thirty-nine half-hour dramas for $25,000 apiece.

"We gotta get into television," Ben Kalmenson kept preaching to Warner. Bill Orr, who had become Jack Warner's special assistant, was also convinced that the studio should join forces with the new medium. Orr had returned from an eastern trip, and he told Warner of seeing thousands of television antennas atop Chicago slums. "I think we should take advantage of TV, colonel, before it passes us by," said Orr.

Warner was impressed with the deal Walt Disney had made with the ABC network: Disney would provide a one-hour show, *Disneyland*, which would feature ample plugs for Disney's theater product; in return, ABC would partially finance Disney's proposed pleasure park in Anaheim, California.

In 1954 Warner agreed to provide ABC with a one-hour weekly show, *Warner Bros. Presents*, with rotating segments based on three old movies, *Casablanca*, *King's Row* and *Cheyenne*. Warner Bros. would be paid $75,000 per hour plus $37,500 for reruns. Each hour would include a ten-minute commercial for Warner Bros. movies, "Behind the Camera."

After the deal had been consummated, Warner invited ABC and advertising agency executives to the studio. They were greeted by Harry Warner, who delivered one of his rambling speeches. Afterward Jack said, "I apologize for my senile brother," and he regaled his visitors with his usual line of jokes and non sequiturs.

Jack always maintained a jovial attitude toward his new business partners, but he drew the line whenever network or advertising people tried to advise on scripts. "They're going to tell *us* how to make movies?" he said.

To head Warner Bros. Television Warner chose an outspoken young man from the publicity department, Gary Stevens. He had come from New York advertising and publicity and had been brought to the studio to handle radio and television publicity for Warner Bros. Stevens was among three dozen employees from all departments called to a crisis meeting in Jack Warner's office. The boss asked for suggestions on how to stop the studio's profit slide, and Stevens brashly raised his hand.

"It's two-thirty on Friday afternoon, and I may not be here Monday morning," he said, launching into arguments about why the studio should join television instead of fighting it.

"Keep talking, kid. You'll be here Monday morning," Warner assured.

They had first met, though Warner didn't remember it, when Stevens was underneath a table. Warner had come to New York for one of his favorite missions: to receive an award. The National Conference of Christians and Jews was scheduled to present him with a citation in Albert Warner's office. As publicity contact for radio, Gary Stevens was under pressure to supply network coverage. He was turned down everywhere. Desperate, Stevens borrowed microphones from friends at ABC, NBC and CBS, and he was under a table concealing the unplugged cords when Jack Warner entered Albert's office. The ceremony was conducted, photos were taken, and afterward Jack's flunkies told him how great he sounded on radio.

Warner Bros. Presents proved only a partial success in its first season. *Cheyenne* became an immediate hit with viewers; *Casablanca* and *King's Row* did not. The ten-minute trailer for the Warner Bros. product was dropped because ABC research showed that people used the time to go to the bathroom or the refrigerator.

Stevens lasted twenty months as executive producer and general manager of Warner Bros. Television. His tenure became perilous after he joined Warner and other executives in a screening of the recently finished *Sincerely Yours*, starring Liberace. The executives praised the film; Stevens predicted it would bomb.

"Look, I'm not president of some woolen company, you know," Warner shot back. "What the fuck do you know?"

Shortly afterward, Warner left for his Riviera vacation. Each day he was sent studio reports as well as newspaper clippings. Included one day was an interview Stevens had given to Cecil Smith of the Los Angeles *Times*. Stevens was quoted: "If Warner Bros. can't make better television than anyone else, they should turn this place into a parking lot." Smith added a comment that "I'd hate to see J. L. Warner in a jump suit handing out parking stubs."

Warner executives gathered nervously in Steve Trilling's office for the boss's daily telephone call from France. "Did you read that *Times* interview with Stevens?" he asked. When his listeners claimed they hadn't, he read the offending passage.

"Get that son of a bitch off the lot—*now*," Warner ordered. He asked about a possible replacement. Trilling had no ideas, but he reminded Warner that Bill Orr had been serving as liaison to the television department.

"Fine," said Warner. "Put Bill in charge."

Television meant Siberia to Bill Orr, who had been happy working as assistant to Jack Warner. The colonel still held television in low regard, and the department wasn't even located on the lot; it occupied offices above the drugstore across Warner Boulevard.

Warner insisted that the shows be made for the fee that ABC was paying—none of the deficit financing that later became prevalent in the television industry. *Cheyenne* was filmed on a five-day budget, which meant that the show had to be filled with stock footage from old Warner features. The Hollywood gag went: "If you see more than two characters in a Warners TV show, it's stock footage."

The ratings success of *Cheyenne* spawned *Maverick, Bronco, Sugarfoot, Colt 45, Lawman* and other Warner Bros. westerns. I once lunched with Boris Karloff in the studio's Green Room, which was filled with young actors in buckskin. "I hope these cowboys are saving their money," said Karloff.

Next, Warner Bros. Television moved into the detective genre. Says Hugh Benson, who was Orr's executive assistant: "We had four shows that were just alike—*77 Sunset Strip*, *Bourbon Street Beat*, *Hawaiian Eye* and *Surfside 6*. We changed names, switched locales, and used the same script."

Warner Bros. Television proved to be a profit-maker, earning between four and five million dollars a year, enough to offset the losses in feature production. Jack Warner retained his tight hold on the purse strings. None of the talent was allowed a percentage of the profits. Since the talent guilds had not yet discovered the gold to be found in residual payments, all returns from network reruns, foreign sales and syndication belonged to Warner Bros.

Jack Warner treated television actors the same as he had feature stars. He never revised contracts to reward a star's popularity; if they wanted more money, they could wait until the automatic raise at option time. He even claimed the money stars made on personal appearances, applying it against their salaries. When Connie Stevens of *Hawaiian Eye* went to Australia for a singing engagement, the long arm of Warner Bros. reached her with a cable forbidding her to appear. She defied the studio, and her singing fee was deducted from her salary.

Predictably, the television actors rebelled. Wayde Preston quit his starring role in *Colt 45*, declaring his contract was "about as equitable as a lynching party"; Donald May was cast in the role. Edd Byrnes announced he would not report to *77 Sunset Strip* until he received an improvement of his $284 take-home paycheck. Will Hutchins (*Sugarfoot*) said he felt "like a peon actor," and Peter Brown (*Lawman*) pleaded for a new contract.

Bill Orr issued a statement in response to the uprising: "Warner Bros. contracts have made it possible for many players to develop from complete unknowns in a brief time. These contracts, signed in good faith by both parties, have opened the door to opportunity and advancement. . . . The studio has every rightful reason to expect players to respect their contractual obligations."

The Screen Actors Guild took note of the complaints of the Warner Bros. cowpokes and gumshoes. All of them attended a meeting at the home of a Guild officer, Jimmy Lydon, and they recited their grievances far into the night. The Guild sent a long list of contract infractions to Jack Warner, warning that actors would be barred from working at the studio unless the fines and penalties were paid. Warner paid immediately. Working conditions improved; salaries did not.

Star rebellions became so common that all new shows were planned with two or more leading actors; if one became difficult, he could be replaced by someone else in the cast.

Efrem Zimbalist Jr. was the single Warner Bros. television star who had no complaint with Jack Warner, though he might have had reason. He came to the studio in 1957 and made a couple of features, and then was ordered to report for a television series pilot. "Oh, no, you're quite wrong," he told Bill Orr. "My contract calls for features." A rereading of the contract showed that Zimbalist was indeed committed to appear in television.

Zimbalist's first pilot failed; a second sold to ABC. It was a private-eye series, *77 Sunset Strip*, which continued for seven years. During one of the late seasons, Zimbalist was devastated by the death of his wife. He told Orr: "Bill, I have got to get out of here for six to eight weeks." Orr pleaded for time to film a few shows, after which the costar, Roger Smith, could carry the series load. Zimbalist replied: "Bill, I'd love to do it, but I must leave tonight. There is no other way. I can't live if I don't."

The consequence seemed obvious: Zimbalist would be placed on suspension. To everyone's astonishment, Jack Warner said, "No. The guy's in trouble. Let's show him who his friends are."

Of all Jack Warner's mutinous television stars, James Garner was the most troublesome.

With little more experience than playing a silent role as a judge in *The Caine Mutiny Court Martial* on the stage, Garner had been signed to a Warner Bros. contract in 1957 at $175 a week. After minor roles in three films, he was chosen to play Marlon Brando's buddy in *Sayonara*. When Garner returned from the locations in Japan, he made the pilot for a western television series to be called *Maverick*.

At 5:30 on a Friday afternoon, Garner was called to the television department and offered a salary raise from $250 to $350 a week, provided he added a year and a half to his seven-year contract. He declined. The ante was raised to $500. Since his wife was pregnant and their young daughter was recovering from polio, he accepted. On the following Monday Garner learned he was replacing Charlton Heston in *Darby's Rangers*.

"If *Maverick* works and the movie goes, they'll rewrite the contract because they know how inequitable it is," Garner reasoned faultily.

Maverick worked brilliantly, burying *The Ed Sullivan Show* in the ratings. Garner began to wonder why he was being paid $500 a week while Sullivan made $25,000 a week. In fact, Garner's weekly paycheck was $285, the remainder withheld as "advance against residuals." The studio had granted actors payments from reruns of television shows, but studio bookkeeping rendered such payments invisible. Garner was further incensed because Jack Warner paid him $285 a week to appear in two features, *Up Periscope* and *Cash McCall*.

The indignities mounted. Hugh Benson called Garner to tell him he was booked to appear on *The Pat Boone Show* on ABC. "Great! What do I get—seventy-five hundred?" Garner asked. He had previously been offered the show for that amount. Benson explained that all the studio's television cowboys were appearing on the show for nothing and that Garner had already been commited to appear. "Then uncommit me," said Garner.

Bill Orr arrived at the *Maverick* set to reason with the star. Garner remained firm. "Go ahead and fire me," he suggested. Next, a phone call came from Steven Trilling, Jack Warner's assistant. He warned that Warner Bros. might have to sue him. "Anybody sues me, I'm not about to work for them," Garner replied.

Finally, a call from Ben Kalmenson, who was the only executive at Warner Bros. whom Garner respected. Garner issued his terms for doing the show: he would never again be booked without his permission; he would receive half of future fees; he would receive $2,500 for the Boone show plus a new Corvette, free of taxes. Kalmenson agreed. The other six actors were paid a flat $500.

Garner realized the quality of *Maverick* had started to deteriorate as the studio cut budgets after the first season. He endured another year, and then encountered something serendipitous: a writers' strike.

Hugh Benson told Garner he was being laid off, possibly for eight weeks because the studio had no *Maverick* scripts. "It's the force majeure clause in your contract," Benson explained. That didn't sound right to Garner. Maybe the series had been forced to halt, but why couldn't the studio put him to work in another feature? He consulted Martin Gang, the lawyer who had liberated Olivia de Havilland, and filed suit to break his contract.

The *Maverick* costar, Jack Kelly, vowed to join Garner in his crusade. But then Jack Warner stepped in. He offered to sweeten Kelly's contract and pay him fifty-two weeks a year instead of the usual forty and also to give him a feature film each year. Kelly acquiesced, so Warner was assured of the continuance of a valuable series. Another contract player, Roger Moore, filled the gap left by Garner, portraying the Mavericks' English cousin.

Garner would not be dissuaded from the lawsuit. Warner dispatched the customary telegrams to producers, warning them not to hire Garner. The actor worked eight weeks in summer stock and earned more than he had in a year at Warner Bros.

Jack Warner felt so strongly about the Garner issue that he agreed, much to the delight of Martin Gang, to testify in court. Warner's performance was abysmal, and James Garner won his freedom. Ever afterward, Warner Bros. lawyers settled contract disputes out of court rather than allow Jack Warner to be subpoenaed to appear as a witness.

Jack Warner could not understand how Garner and other television stars on whom he had bestowed immediate fame could be so ungrateful. Bill Orr noted that of the scores of photographs of the studio's personalities on the walls of J.L.'s office, not one was a television star.

Jack Warner still hated television.

Chapter 14

The Prince in His Sixties

JACK WARNER GAVE NO INKLING of decline as he reached his mid-sixties. His reign over the Burbank studio remained absolute, and his will implacable. He continued his skirmishes with actors and their agents, whom he considered venal and rapacious. With Harry more withdrawn from the operation of the company, Jack's decisions went unquestioned, though he always listened to the opinions of Ben Kalmenson.

Warner's final word in any argument remained the same: "Whose name is on the water tower?" An adventuresome writer once responded, "Yeah, but it took somebody to paint it." The writer was soon working at another studio.

His power remained unchallenged, and he sometimes appeared to exercise it unmercifully. One day Warner summoned his producers and executives to a meeting to discuss the studio's yearly production quota. Toward the end of his rundown of films, Warner commented, "And we'll make the usual number of Randolph Scott westerns at seven hundred and fifty thousand apiece. We can always count on rentals of a million and a quarter."

At the end of his report, Warner asked, "Now, have you guys

got any ideas?" A newly arrived production executive raised an eager hand.

"Could I make a suggestion?" the young man said. "Why not spend a million dollars on the Scott westerns? With improved quality, maybe they could bring back two million."

"Kid, you're fired," Warner replied sternly. "I'll tell you why you were fired. Those westerns are a dying market. The public is getting all the shitkickers they need on our TV shows. Now if you had said, 'Why don't we make the Randy Scott westerns for half a million,' I would have made you my assistant."

Studio workers could almost set their clocks by Warner's daily routine. Starting at eight o'clock at home, he spoke on the phone to Kalmenson and other New York executives. At nine he called his secretary, Bill Schaefer, dictating notes on dailies he had seen the night before. Schaefer reported on any news about Warner Bros. in the Los Angeles *Times, Daily Variety* or *Hollywood Reporter* and detailed the day's appointments and important correspondence.

Warner drove his Cadillac or Rolls Royce to the studio, arriving promptly at noon and parking in the semicircular driveway in front of the administration building on Warner Boulevard. He took a flower from the car and on arriving in his second-floor office placed the flower in a small vase in front of the portrait of his parents. At one o'clock he arrived at the executive dining room.

This was his court, where he presided like a Plantagenet ruler, except that he was the clown. The jokes and wisecracks flowed unceasingly, with the sycophants responding with laughter, the more independent listeners forcing smiles. Warner sat at the head of a U-shaped table, and the chairs on each side remained unoccupied; no one wanted to present a close target. The colonel was apt to deride those producers who had gone over budget or whose films had died ingloriously at the box office.

About thirty of the high-ranking executives and producers were privileged to patronize the dining room. Except for the jeopardy of facing the boss's scorn, they enjoyed a good arrangement; for twenty dollars a week apiece, they were served a gourmet meal prepared by chefs Warner had imported from France. No alcohol was allowed. Actors and directors ate in the dining room only by invitation, though top-rank stars who were working on the lot, like Gary Cooper and Cary Grant, were welcome.

Normal studio business was prohibited during lunch. If Warner had any business to conduct, he went to an adjoining trophy room where he could make phone calls and sign papers in private. After lunch, he often strolled around the lot, poking his head into stages to inspect new sets and exchange banter with directors and actors. He enjoyed walking in the sun with his collar unfastened; he thought the tanned, healthy look made him seem younger. Indeed he seemed ageless, his slight paunch controlled by tennis, his round, smiling face accented by the narrow burlesque straight man's mustache.

A session in the barbershop followed. He exchanged quips with passersby and those who dropped in, but discussed no studio business while he enjoyed the ministrations of Don Johnson, his barber. Then to the office for a few hours of answering telephone calls, listening to the grievances of actors and directors, conferring with producers and heads of departments, making deals with agents, all with a steady barrage of repartee.

Occasionally the Warner temper would be ignited by the misdeed of another studio head, an agent or someone else outside the studio. He would unleash a string of expletives and then dictate a scathing letter to Bill Schaefer. The secretary would wisely set the letter aside. Usually on the following day, the boss would say, "You know that letter I dictated yesterday? Have you sent it yet? No? Well, I've been thinking it over. Better not."

Warner sought any reason not to go home at night. Department heads dreaded the six o'clock call from the boss. As they prepared to join their families at the end of the workday, they would be summoned to J.L.'s office, to be engaged in lengthy conversations, not necessarily about studio matters. Warner often asked them to join him for dinner at a restaurant in nearby Toluca Lake; it was an unrefusable invitation.

Rushes of a film in production provided evening recreation, with or without the presence or permission of the director. As a new generation of directors came into the industry, they insisted on more independence. That meant seeing their rushes first and preparing their own rough cuts. Warner refused to observe such restrictions. He ran the rushes and made the editors swear they would not reveal his subterfuge to the directors.

"Warner was a coward, a real coward," says Robert Wise. When Wise was directing *Three Secrets*, Warner forced the editor to show him rushes before Wise had seen them. Warner made suggestions for changes, and warned the editor, "Don't say they came from me; you suggest them and make him do them." The editor confessed to Wise, who did not confront Warner, lest the editor be fired. Says Wise: "Warner didn't have the guts to ask me to make the changes."

After filming *Helen of Troy* in Italy, Wise was preparing a new film for MGM while final editing was being done. When Wise viewed the cut of *Helen of Troy* with Warner, the director said, "That's not the way I left it."

"We didn't do a thing," Warner claimed. "We didn't touch it; not a thing is missing."

"Goddamn it, Jack, I know my own film. I know it goddamn well," exploded Wise, himself a former editor. "If you want to make changes, you can throw me off the lot, don't let me in. It's your picture, I don't own it. But don't tell me I don't know what the hell is going on in my own film." *Helen of Troy* was restored to Wise's satisfaction.

Warner prided himself in his ability to edit, as did Harry Cohn, Darryl Zanuck and other studio heads. Indeed his firm hand on the editing of films contributed to the zippy pace of Warner Bros. films of the 1930s.

"Why have the guy drive up to the house?" Warner would say during rushes. "It's a time-waster. Show him at the front door."

He had an unlimited supply of tips to speed up the action. For a western: "Speed up the horses on the charge." A war film: "That whole battle can come out and you won't lose a thing."

Filmmakers heard the Warner comment again and again: "We're supposed to be making *moving* pictures. Make 'em move, not just sit there." He especially detested meaningless shots of people walking to get somewhere. "Too much shoe leather! Too much shoe leather!" he ranted.

Previews had been a Warner ritual from the 1920s. The studio's top executives and the producer and director of the film gathered at six for drinks—the only time alcohol was served—and dinner in the executive dining room. A row of limousines waited outside. J.L. always occupied the lead car of the caravan, and he always sat in the front seat next to the driver.

The previews were held at outlying towns: Santa Barbara, Riverside, Huntington Park, Pasadena. Warner sat on the aisle where he worked the fader, regulating the sound volume. Next to him was Bill Schaefer, then the editor. Schaefer made notes in the dark.

The postpreview conference was held in the theater manager's office. The pattern was the same: the cost-conscious business people urging, "Ship it! Ship it!"; the creative people saying, "Let's make some changes." Warner listened to them and made his own decision. He had an uncanny memory for film. Sometimes he would ask what happened to a scene he had viewed months before. Told that it had been removed, he commanded, "Put it back."

The old order of Hollywood society was changing. Jack and Ann Warner no longer hosted the grand parties attended by the movie greats. They still entertained, but on a more modest scale. Usually they invited guests for dinner and a new movie in the home theater. There was an A list and a B list, depending on the guest's importance. Also a C list for people who were invited for the movie only.

Ann Warner appeared less often at these occasions. Her once svelte beauty was fading to stoutness, and she rarely descended from her quarters to receive Jack's guests. Often she removed herself to the Palm Springs house or the apartment at the Pierre Hotel in

New York. He remained his jovial self, making no excuse for her absence.

Jack had fallen into a pattern that continued for the rest of his life. He had a series of "girlfriends"; they were not actresses and often not particular beauties. To Jack's companions, the women seemed like hookers. He consorted with them openly, sometimes taking them to his Palm Springs house where they functioned more or less as his hostess. He made no explanations. But then, no one asked.

Warner had a poor memory for names. Throughout her tenure at Warners, he referred to Olivia de Havilland as "Oliva." Mel Shavelson and Jack Rose were a producer-writer team whom Warner always saw together, so he simply greeted them with "Hello, boys." One day Warner saw Rose approaching alone on a studio sidewalk. Warner seemed momentarily panicked; then he greeted Rose with a cheery "Hello, boys."

As a comic gesture Warner sometimes invented names. Hugh Benson was an important executive at Warner Bros. for years, but his boss always introduced him as "Monroe Dockfeather." To visiting senators, diplomats, and governors, he always said, "This is Monroe Dockfeather." Benson knew better than to ask that he be recognized under his real name.

Warner loved comics. Whenever he went on the *Sayonara* set, he ignored Josh Logan and Marlon Brando and went directly to Red Buttons. "Two Jews and an Arab got on a streetcar," Warner began, and he and Buttons exchanged jokes for several moments.

Alan King met Jack Warner at a party given by Mervyn and Kitty LeRoy. A little-known comedian, King performed with his friend Tony Martin for the party guests. Jack Warner arrived and watched the show and then took over with his own songs and jokes. It grew late, and Warner said to King, whom he had just met, "C'mon, there's a party in Bel Air, we can do some shtick there."

They drove up and down the Bel Air hills in Warner's Bentley convertible, and King asked, "Mr. Warner, do you know where the party is?"

"No, but we can find it because of all the cars," Warner said with assurance. They never did find the party, but they enjoyed telling jokes and singing Jolson songs loudly in the night air.

A couple of weeks later, Jack Warner, Steve Trilling and an entourage paid a state visit to the set of a Tab Hunter movie, *The Girl He Left Behind*. There were eighty soldiers in a barracks scene, and Warner spotted one. "Alan, how are you?" he exclaimed while bystanders gazed in awe. "What are you doing here?"

"I work for you, Mr. Warner; I'm under contract," King said.

Veteran comedians heaped scorn on Jack Warner's attempts to invade their realm. At stag dinners Milton Berle assailed Warner with such lines as: "I saw Jack Warner in vaudeville in 1915 and he was so bad that I wouldn't even steal from him. . . . He was so low on the bill that dogs pissed on his billing. . . . That's a lovely suit you have on, Jack. You don't throw anything away, do you?"

Berle notes that Warner's idea of humor was to talk in a Dutch accent and make flapping noises with his cheeks and lips. His favorite comics were Smith and Dale, and he liked to repeat the punch lines of their routines, such as, "Take off the coat, my boy."

"Jack, people don't know the connection; to them it's a non sequitur," Berle pointed out.

"Yeah, but I like to say it," Warner answered. "I like to make myself laugh."

Warner in his sixties remained one of the most prodigious gamblers, not only in Hollywood but in the western world. He disliked Las Vegas because of its tawdry atmosphere. He adored the casinos of the Riviera, where he could play the gentleman's games of baccarat and chemin de fer surrounded by world beauties in silk gowns and dashing playboys in tuxedos.

Legends of enormous losses and winnings attached themselves to Jack Warner. Finding his boss in an unguarded mood, Richard Lederer once asked him, "Is it true, chief, that you once dropped two hundred and fifty thousand dollars at the tables in Monte Carlo and then ordered champagne for everyone?"

Warner nodded smilingly. "Yeah, I was playing with King Farouk," he said. "After I lost the dough, I said to myself, 'I'm a Jew, and I'll show that fucking Egyptian that I'm better than he is.' So

I ordered champagne all round. What the hell, I could afford to lose that money."

In August 1957, Warner won at a Riviera gambling table, spectacularly. He was playing no-limit baccarat at the Palm Beach Casino in Cannes, along with Darryl Zanuck and two others. The banker of the game was a shadowy Greek who figured to take the Hollywood millionaires. Instead, they took him. After almost a million dollars in losses, the Greek shut down the game. Figuring he was on a roll, Warner drove to the Monte Carlo casino to continue gambling. He lost all his night's earnings.

Whenever Jack Warner returned to the United States after his Riviera holiday, he was never bothered by the delays of going through customs, as ordinary tourists were. "Come right through, Mr. Warner," the customs officers said affably. Such treatment resulted from Jack's friendship with J. Edgar Hoover, who had been grateful for Warner Bros. espousal of the FBI in such films as *G Men*, *Confessions of a Nazi Spy*, *The FBI Story* and the television series, *The FBI*.

In the motion picture milieu, Jack Warner feared no man. His confidence could melt when he was confronted with powerful figures from other spheres of influence. Being a prominent supporter of Republican candidates, Warner was sometimes visited by party activists. Justin Dart, Holmes Tuttle, Henry Salvatori and other backers of Richard Nixon came to lunch at the studio to seek Warner's contribution for a Nixon campaign.

These were leaders of the Los Angeles Establishment which had scorned the Warners and other Jewish movie people when they invaded the city. Now they sought Warner's help. Instead of vindication, Jack felt inferiority. His swagger was gone; he seemed the Youngstown butcher boy amid the rich power brokers. And he donated liberally to the Nixon campaign.

Warner was in awe of Richard Nixon himself. That was demonstrated when *A Fine Madness* was being edited at the studio. It was a Seven Arts production for Warner Bros., and the filmmakers spent an uncommon amount of time preparing a final cut. This rankled Jack Warner, and he sent repeated memos instructing the producer, Jerome Hellman, and the director, Irvin Kershner, to conclude their work. Finally Warner decreed: "That's it! The picture is finished!"

Hellman and Kershner argued that they needed more time, but Warner was adamant. One day Bill Schaefer announced, "Mr. Nixon is calling." Having returned to private life, Richard Nixon was associated with a New York law firm, one of whose clients was connected with *A Fine Madness*. Warner agreed to grant the filmmakers more time to edit their film.

Was Jack Warner a good Jew? In terms of attending temple and observing the High Holidays, no. But he was a fierce defender of Israel and a staunch contributor to its needs. When Israel was embroiled in the Six Day War, Warner summoned the studio's workers to a meeting on a sound stage. He implored all of them, Jew and gentile, to contribute in Israel's time of need.

More than once, Warner summoned Hollywood's Jewish officialdom to Angelo Drive. Many of them came resentfully, having never been entertained socially by Jack Warner. He cited Israel's constant peril from hostile neighbors and implored, cajoled and arm-twisted his listeners into contributions. On one occasion he rashly declared, "Whoever gives the highest amount, I'll double it." To his astonishment, Herb Alpert, leader of the Tijuana Brass and cofounder of A&M Records, offered $250,000. Warner gulped and committed himself to a half-million.

Some of Jack Warner's detractors argue that there was a dark side to the man. They cite the case of Mort Blumenstock.

His career with Warner Bros. dated back to the First National merger. He rose fast in the New York office, becoming national head of publicity and advertising in 1945. Like many hard-driving executives, Blumenstock drank too much. One night in Westchester County he was involved in a fatal automobile crash. A large amount of Warner Bros. money was required to get him off with a light jail sentence.

Blumenstock's usefulness in New York had ended, and he was sent to the studio, and, according to some of Blumenstock's friends, Jack Warner's purgatory. They tell of Warner's constant punishment of Blumenstock, giving him menial jobs, requiring that he remain at his desk from six to eight in the evening in case Warner needed him. Then he could go home. Blumenstock was at dinner with his family one night when the message came: "The chief wants you to see a picture with him." But when Blumenstock drove from Beverly Hills to Burbank, Warner said, "To hell with it, I'll see the picture tomorrow."

After having established his family in California, Blumenstock was abruptly transferred back to New York. The harassment by Jack Warner continued, and Blumenstock resigned in 1956 after twenty-eight years with Warner Bros. He died of a heart attack three months later.

No one had served Warner Bros. with more distinction than Henry Blanke. Since arriving with Ernst Lubitsch in the 1920s, he had been associated with the studio's most prestigious films. A producer from 1933, his films included the Muni biographies, *The Adventures of Robin Hood, Jezebel, The Maltese Falcon, The Treasure of the Sierra Madre, The Fountainhead, The Nun's Story.*

In 1945, Blanke had been rewarded with a fifteen-year, no-option contract that gave him $5,000 a week and tax benefits. With the studio in a slump in the mid-fifties, Blanke's contract bothered Jack Warner. "I want you to change it," Warner told the producer. "Why should I?" Blanke replied. "You gave it to me. I wouldn't dream of changing it."

Warner began a campaign of humiliation. He removed Blanke's secretary, his spacious office, his Oscars. He gave Blanke cheap pictures to prepare and then removed his name from the credits. Finally in 1961, the weary Blanke resigned, sacrificing four and a half years in vacation credit.

"I think that Warner derived pleasure in such things," says Gottfried Reinhardt, a friend of Blanke's. "Harry Cohn was a son of a bitch, but he did it for business; he was not a sadist. [Louis B.] Mayer could be a monster, but he was not mean for the sake of meanness. Jack was."

Warner's defenders claimed that "his word is as good as his bond." Others who dealt with him disagreed.

Daniel Taradash was a hot writer after winning an Academy Award for *From Here to Eternity*. He and Julian Blaustein, a successful producer at Fox, formed their own company and bought film rights to James Gould Cozzens' novel, *Guard of Honor*. They offered it to Harry Cohn, who declined. Always eager to prove Cohn wrong, Jack Warner accepted the project. But when he discovered that the novel concerned a black soldier's plight in the south, he reneged.

Gottfried Reinhardt had reached an agreement with Warner Bros. in 1955 to coproduce a new version of *Rosalinda* in London with Joan Fontaine and Van Johnson. Suddenly the deal was canceled. Reinhardt was desperate; he was faced with paying off those he had committed to the production. He placed a call to Jack Warner at Cap d'Antibes. "Come on down," Warner said genially.

Jack had finished a session with his tennis coach when Reinhardt arrived at the Villa Aujourd'hui. "What can I do for you?" Warner asked.

"I'm getting a good fucking from your company," said the producer.

"Good! Because we're getting a good fucking from everybody," Warner laughed. Gottfried explained his plight and invoked the memory of his father Max. When Warner agreed to reinstate the contract, Reinhardt suggested, "Why don't you call right now?" "No, I'll send a wire; it's cheaper," Warner said, and he did.

Reinhardt flew back to London in a jubilant state. Only later did he learn that Warner had sent a second telegram: "Forget my wire."

The tales of Jack Warner's ruthlessness are legion. Was there another, softer side to the man? Ann Warner claimed so in a note to Dean Jennings during the research for *My First Hundred Years in Hollywood*. She said of her husband:

"He is extremely sensitive, but there are few who know that because he covers it with a cloak. He is a deeply religious man, and he has a great sense of obligation. . . . I have never known him to hold a grudge. It takes continual harassment before he believes there is more evil than good in a man. . . . He expects nothing and asks for nothing, and he can be affected to the point of tears by personal thoughtfulness. . . . It is too bad that so few people understand him, or his self-consciousness, or the fact that he is naturally a happy man."

If few people understood Jack Warner, that appeared to be the way he wanted it. He had thousands of acquaintances and scores of friends, but none could claim truthfully to be close to him. All were kept at a distance by his unceasing japery.

"He was an enigma; he didn't want anyone to figure him out," says Max Bercutt. "If you toadied up to him, you were dead. He wanted nobody near him. That was true of all the studio heads— Cohn, Mayer, Zanuck. Each was afraid people wanted something out of him. And they did."

Bugs Bunny, Porky Pig, Daffy Duck, Elmer Fudd, Wile E. Coyote, Road Runner and Pepe Le Pew may have been stars to cartoon lovers, but they were always stepchildren at Warner Bros. Jack Warner paid them no heed; he considered cartoons no more than an extraneous service provided to exhibitors who wanted a full program for their customers.

Warner Bros. issued the first *Looney Tune* in 1930, contracting with entrepreneur Leon Schlesinger, a humorless man who was the image of Porky Pig. Schlesinger sold his studio to Warner Bros. in 1944. To head the cartoon operation, Jack Warner appointed publicity director Eddie Seltzer, following, says animator Chuck Jones, "a diligent search of the studio to find out who hated laughter most."

Despite the supervision of a boss who knew nothing about cartoons, Jones, Tex Avery, Bob Clampett, Friz Freling, Frank Tashlin and other animators created six-minute masterpieces that convulsed audiences then and are treasured today. In 1953, Jack and Harry paid minor attention to the cartoon makers by entertaining a few of them at lunch in the executive dining room.

"I don't even know where the hell the cartoon studio is," confessed Jack. (It occupied a ramshackle building on the Sunset lot.)

"The only thing I know is that we make Mickey Mouse," added

Harry. The cartoonists assured him they would continue taking good care of Mickey, and they returned to their drawing boards with heavy hearts.

A few years later, Jack Warner sold all of the 400 cartoons made before 1948 for $3,000 apiece. They have since earned millions, but not for Warner Bros.

Merv Griffin was a fresh-faced, outgoing young man who sang with the Freddy Martin orchestra, a favorite of the movie crowd during Martin's long tenure at the Cocoanut Grove. A hit record brought Griffin to prominence and the attention of the Warner Bros. talent department. Jack Warner looked at Griffin's screen test and muttered, "Hire him."

In 1952 Griffin was cast opposite Kathryn Grayson in *So This Is Love*, a romanticized biography of the singer-actress Grace Moore. After six months at the studio, Griffin still had not met the boss. One day he received a call from Richard Gully, Jack Warner's social secretary, a Britisher with connections among the socialites of America and Europe.

"The colonel would like you to come to dinner," Gulley announced in tones that hinted of Mayfair. "You will be better off if your lady friend is titled. She should dress in black or white. Very little jewelry. The skirt should be twelve inches above the floor."

"You mean," Griffin replied incredulously, "I've got to find a titled lady and tell her all that?"

"Yes, that's the way Mr. Warner wants it."

Happily, Griffin was acquainted with a Manville heiress who had been married to a European count. They arrived at the Warner house and joined a glittering throng, few of whom Griffin recognized.

"Griff!" He heard a hearty voice, turned and saw the formidable figure of Jack Warner coming toward him. "Jack Warner," he announced. Griffin introduced the countess, and Warner replied, "That's okay, but you're a little outranked here, countess. This is Princess Aly Khan." He introduced the stunning Rita Hayworth.

Warner grabbed Griffin by the arm and led him across the room. "Get a load of this, kid," said Warner, indicating a row of splendidly gowned women seated against the wall. He rattled off their titles: the queen mother this, the princess that, the duchess whatever. All this royalty, deposed or not, dining at the home of Jack L. Warner, late of Youngstown, Ohio.

The dinner befitted the royal guests. The food was superlative, served by omnipresent butlers who kept the wine glasses filled with the finest vintages. When the meal was over, Warner gave a toast to his visitors and recited a poem he had composed for the occasion.

"And now," he announced, "the men can stay here and have their cigars, and the ladies can go take a piss."

Warner was pleased with the affable, quick-witted Griffin and took an interest in the young man's personal life, though not his career. Merv recalls that after hearing of a Griffin date, Warner telephoned, "Griff, don't you ever see that broad again. Hooker! Hooker!" "Yes, colonel," Merv replied dutifully.

Griffin became a regular for Sunday night at Jack Warner's. He brought Barbara Warner to the intimate dinners attended by Warner and his European-born mistress—Ann was spending her time at the Arizona ranch—Bill and Joy Orr, Robert and Ursula Taylor, Michael Wilding and Elizabeth Taylor, Richard Gully and a lady friend. When dinner was over, they joined a large party in the den. Most of the guests were familiar names, and stars like Judy Garland, Doris Day and Gordon MacRae would be called on to perform.

Merv Griffin had his own Sunday parties during times when Jack Warner wasn't entertaining or was at Cap d'Antibes. His guests included many of those who attended the Warner parties, but also younger figures of Hollywood such as Tony Curtis and Janet Leigh, Aldo Ray and Jeff Donnell. Griffin played the piano while his guests entertained. One Saturday he was surprised to receive a phone call from Jack Warner.

"Having a dinner tomorrow?" Warner asked brusquely.

"Yes, colonel."

"Everybody I know is going to it. How many times have you come to my house to dinner?"

"Many, many times."

"So why the hell wasn't I invited to your house, goddammit?"

"Well, of course I'd like you to come. I just didn't think you'd want to."

"What time is the party?"

"We'll have dinner at four o'clock."

"I'll be there."

Warner arrived on time and mingled jovially with the astonished guests. He watched the young entertainers perform; then he announced that it was his turn. While Merv played "Tea for Two" on the piano, Jack performed a tap dance while whistling in Jolson style. He beamed at the wild applause.

Among the guests at Griffin's party was his uncle Elmer. Warner inquired, "What does your fat uncle do?" Merv explained that his uncle was in the real estate business and had been a tennis champion. When Warner doubted that such a fat old man could have played tennis, Griffin replied, "He could whip you and Solly Biano any day of the week." Warner scornfully accepted the challenge: "Next Sunday. You got a match."

After two years under contract to Warner Bros., Griffin had appeared in only three movies. The company had started making films in CinemaScope, which meant that musicals and comedies would be reduced. Griffin had received lucrative offers in Las Vegas and elsewhere, and he hated movies. He wanted out of his contract.

Elmer, who was wise in the ways of Hollywood, listened to his nephew's plight. "What score do you want?" Elmer asked. "If you like, I will give you six-love, and you will be out of that studio."

On the day of the match, Elmer again asked for instructions. "Six-love," Merv reiterated. "I want out."

Warner entered the court with supreme confidence. His attitude changed as Uncle Elmer smashed balls out of his and Biano's reach. "For crissake, can't you hit the ball?" Warner screamed at Biano. Elmer's partner, Bill Orr, watched wide-eyed as Elmer hit one winner after another. Final score: 6-0, 6-0.

Within a few weeks Merv Griffin was dropped from the Warner Bros. contract list.

Chapter 15

Films of the Late Fifties

JACK WARNER WANTED TO STAR William Holden or Marlon Brando in *Mister Roberts* even though Henry Fonda had created the role of the gentle naval officer in the hit play. Warner told John Ford, who had been chosen to direct the film, that he preferred a younger actor. Ford replied: "Mister Roberts is Henry Fonda's part. He's right for it on the stage, and he's right for it on the screen. If he doesn't do this picture, I don't do it either."

Warner, who was afraid of the gruff, unpredictable director, acquiesced. To make Fonda seem less old, Warner cast the roles of Doc and the skipper with two actors whose ages would have disqualified them for sea duty. Both were old-time Warner Bros. stars: James Cagney and William Powell. It would be the last of Cagney's forty-four Warner Bros. films, and the last ever for Bill Powell. Jack Lemmon provided a note of youth as Ensign Pulver.

Fonda and Ford had made eight films together, but they clashed immediately on the Hawaiian location of *Mister Roberts*. Fonda believed, with some justification, that no one knew the story better than he did, and he was alarmed when the director began injecting slapstick. During one argument Ford punched Fonda in the jaw.

The USS *Reluctant* began listing badly. Director and star rarely spoke. Ford began drinking beer on Midway Island, and when the company returned to Honolulu, he climbed aboard his yacht *Araner* and drank himself senseless. Leland Hayward shut down production for five days while Ford recovered.

Jack Warner received daily reports of the *Roberts* sea battle with mounting concern. After the company returned to Burbank, Ford collapsed with a ruptured gall bladder. Warner replaced him with Mervyn LeRoy. The mix of the two old-time directors almost destroyed the magic of *Mister Roberts*, but it earned a $8.5-million profit for Warner Bros. and an Academy Award for young Lemmon.

After producing *Mister Roberts*, Leland Hayward remained at Warner Bros. to make *The Spirit of St. Louis* and *The Old Man and the Sea*. Both were celebrated books that seemed ideal film material. They were proven otherwise.

Charles Lindbergh had won a Pulitzer prize with his account of the historic trans-Atlantic flight. Converting it to the screen was another matter. Billy Wilder and his script collaborator Wendell Mayes never licked the problem of how to dramatize Lindbergh's lonely flight over the ocean in a tiny plane.

Casting Lindbergh was another problem. Warner and Hayward agreed on a rising young actor, John Kerr. But Kerr objected to Lindbergh's prewar espousal of Nazi strength and refused to portray the Lone Eagle. Meanwhile James Stewart had been campaigning to play his boyhood idol. "You're too old; Lindbergh was twenty-five when he made his flight," said Stewart's longtime friend and agent, Hayward. But Stewart, who was forty-eight, won by default.

Billy Wilder directed *The Spirit of St. Louis* with his customary skill, but the film failed to find an audience. Warner Bros. lost all of the $6-million cost, and Jack Warner said afterward, "I have never been able to figure out why it flopped." Part of the reason was the growing youthfulness of the movie audience and a new generation who didn't know Charles Lindbergh. In an era of jet travel and oncoming space flight, what was so remarkable about flying the Atlantic?

The Old Man and the Sea was an overlong short story that had helped Ernest Hemingway win the Nobel prize for literature in 1954. Hayward convinced Hemingway to write the script himself, and the author even volunteered to lead an expedition to film the landing of the shark. But no shark could be found, and he soon soured on the film project. He groused that the actor chosen to play the Cuban boy resembled a cross between a tadpole and Anita Loos. In the early rushes he thought Spencer Tracy, in the role of the peasant fisherman, looked like "a very rich, fat and old" though still competent actor. He abandoned the film, declaring it had wasted three or four months of "my one and only life."

The sea, the mechanical shark and Tracy misbehaved on the Cuban locations, and Warner sent Fred Zinnemann angry wires. The director answered patiently, asking for "greater courtesy in your future messages." It was not forthcoming, and the exasperated Zinnemann resigned from the film. He was replaced by John Sturges.

The Old Man and the Sea failed to enthrall critics or movie patrons. *Time* observed that the slender volume was "a literary property about as suited to the movie medium as *The Love Song of J. Alfred Prufrock.*"

James Dean came and went like a lightning streak across a black prairie sky. Three landmark films, and his life was snuffed out on Route 466.

Jimmy Dean had been Elia Kazan's secret. The director had watched Dean as an Arab in the play *The Immoralist* and was unimpressed. But he agreed to test the young actor for *East of Eden*. Curiously, it was a double test with Paul Newman, whom Kazan was also considering for the role of Caleb (Cain) in the biblical allegory. Newman self-admittedly was "too Ivy League." Dean was just right.

Jack Warner had taken *East of Eden* on a hunch. Kazan came to

Warner's office, laughed at his lame jokes and then described the new John Steinbeck novel he wanted to film.

"What'll it cost?" Warner asked.

"One million six," Kazan replied.

"You've got it."

When Kazan mentioned that he wanted to cast newcomers because it was a story of young people, Warner replied, "Cast who you want." Further, he granted the director's prize: the final cut.

Warner may have seen the tests made of Dean in Burbank, but he made no comment. Kazan went off to the Salinas valley for locations. When *East of Eden* returned to the Burbank studio, Dean took up residence in his dressing room, which included a kitchen and bedroom. Jack Warner prohibited stars and directors from staying overnight because the studio had no insurance to cover them. He made an exception for Kazan's young star. But as soon as *East of Eden* finished, Warner ordered his eviction. "The little bastard was bringing broads to his room," said the outraged Warner.

When Dean reported to the studio the following Monday, all his belongings were ready for him at the studio gate. Dean asked if he could visit his room, and he retrieved $3,500 in cash he had hidden in a vase.

The previews of *East of Eden* were sensational. Even Hedda Hopper, who had scorned Dean in her column as one of the new breed of slouching, sloppy actors she loathed, was impressed. She telephoned Jack Warner to request an interview. The puckish Dean arrived handsomely groomed in a charcoal suit, and he completely charmed her.

Warner quickly cast Dean in *Rebel Without a Cause*, a property the studio had owned for eight years. The film was swallowed whole by the young generation and became a symbol for the rebellion of youth.

At times Jimmy Dean seemed to be living his rebellious on-screen role. One day he and Jim Backus were walking on a studio street when they approached Jack Warner, who was talking to a pair of theater executives. Warner was giving a sales pitch about his hot new star. Dean approached him, took note of Warner's iridescent suit and muttered, "Have it cleaned and burned." He walked on.

George Stevens chose Dean to star with Elizabeth Taylor and Rock Hudson in *Giant*. Stardom had eroded Jimmy Dean's unstable nature, and his behavior on *Giant* became more and more eccentric and irresponsible. He delighted in roaring his motorcycle around the stages, performing stunts on the seat and handlebars. He learned that his Actors Studio chum, Shelley Winters, was at Warner Bros. starring in *I Died a Thousand Times*, a remake of *High Sierra*.

"C'mon, Shelley. I'll give you a ride to the commissary," Dean insisted. Winters climbed warily on the back of his motorcycle, and Dean took off for the mountain trails across the river from the studio. She was reprimanded by her director, Stuart Heisler, on her return. Jack Warner fired off an angry note: "Don't ever do that again or . . ."

Dean became almost uncontrollable on the *Giant* set. One day Stevens marched him up to Jack Warner's office like a schoolteacher leading a mischievous pupil to the principal. Stevens ranted that the actor was tardy, rude and unresponsive, and he threatened to ruin Dean's career in Hollywood.

Dean countered that Stevens treated him like a machine, ordered him to the set in the morning and didn't use him all day. He scoffed at Steven's threat to run him out of Hollywood. Jack Warner listened to the arguments with an indulgent smile, made a few wisecracks and sent the pair back to work.

Stevens continued his exasperating routine of endlessly filming scenes from every angle. Dean was immensely relieved when *Giant* finally concluded. With a full year off from his Warner Bros. contract, he sped his Porsche Spyder, which he nicknamed "Little Bastard," northward to the road races in Salinas.

"The worst movie filmed during the 1950s." That was Paul Newman's critique of *The Silver Chalice*, in which he made a sorry film debut.

Jack Warner had signed Newman to a $1,000-a-week contract in 1954 during Hollywood's raid on the Actors Studio to capture new Marlon Brandos and James Deans. Newman was horrified to find himself cast as Basil, the Greek slave silversmith, in an overripe biblical epic, *The Silver Chalice*. Not only was he burdened with lugubrious dialogue; he was required to wear a scanty tunic that exposed his knobby knees, about which he was self-conscious. A few years later he refused the title role in *Ben-Hur* with the comment, "I wore a cocktail dress once, in *The Silver Chalice*. Never again."

The reviews were as Newman feared. John McCarten in *The New Yorker*: "Paul Newman, a lad who resembles Marlon Brando, delivers his lines with the emotional fervor of a Putnam Division conductor announcing local stops."

Newman scurried back to Broadway to redeem his reputation and self-respect, playing a hoodlum holding a family hostage in *The Desperate Hours*. The actor dreaded a return to Warner Bros. Then the role of prizefighter Rocky Graziano in *Somebody Up There Likes Me* was vacated by James Dean's death. Newman was loaned to MGM, and he restored his reputation as an actor.

Jack Warner paid Newman $1,000 a week while collecting $75,000 from MGM. The practice continued as Newman was loaned out for five other films. His Warner Bros. roles during the period were undistinguished: as a gangster in *The Helen Morgan Story*; Billy the Kid in *The Left-Handed Gun*; a social climber in *The Young Philadelphians*.

Newman received $17,500 for *The Young Philadelphians*. Having gained his reputation at other studios in films like *The Long Hot Summer* and *Cat on a Hot Tin Roof*, he believed he could make better career decisions for himself than Jack Warner could. One day in 1959 he stomped into Warner's office and said, "I want out."

"It'll cost you," Warner said. The price: a half-million dollars. Although he realized it would take years to pay off the ransom, Newman readily agreed.

Years later when *The Silver Chalice* played nightly on a Los Angeles television channel, an advertisement appeared in the Los

Angeles *Times*: "Paul Newman Apologizes Every Night This Week."

A new breed of directors trained in the robust world of live television drama was being drawn to the film studios in the fifties. Sidney Lumet was one of the promising candidates. Jack Warner had been persuaded to seek out Lumet as director of *Marjorie Morningstar*, based on Herman Wouk's novel about the coming of age of a New York Jewish girl.

Lumet admired the novel and knew the milieu firsthand. He agreed to fly from New York to Los Angeles for a conference with Jack Warner.

Arriving in California at 11 a.m., Lumet was met by a limousine that glided him over the freeways to Burbank. He was escorted immediately to the office of J. L. Warner.

"Glad to see ya," Warner beamed. He told a few jokes and then got down to the business of *Marjorie Morningstar*. "I want to make it a universal picture, one that will appeal to audiences everywhere," he said.

"Does that mean that you are not going to hire any Jewish actors?" Lumet asked.

The temperature of the room dropped noticeably. The interview soon ended with no mention of lunch. Lumet was on the two o'clock plane back to New York. *Marjorie Morningstar* starred Natalie Wood and Gene Kelly.

"A Marilyn Monroe Production."

If anyone had suggested to Jack Warner before 1956 that such a credit would appear on a Warner Bros. movie, he would have replied with a shower of expletives. But in 1956 stars were scarce and dear, and they and their agents could virtually dictate terms to the studio bosses. So when Jack Warner was presented with a package of Marilyn and Laurence Olivier in *The Prince and the Showgirl*, he reluctantly accepted.

The film was disastrous from the beginning—she was an hour late to the London press conference—to the end, when she and Olivier parted loathing each other. Both were emotional wrecks; his marriage to Vivien Leigh and hers to Arthur Miller were shattering. Olivier railed at Marilyn's acting methodology and her reliance on the constant coaching by Lee Strasberg's wife Paula. Olivier cherished one of Strasberg's instructions to Marilyn: "Honey, just think of Coca-Cola and Frank Sinatra."

Jack Warner read with growing alarm the reports of filming delays because of script conflicts and Marilyn's tardiness. Finally the filming concluded, but not the disputes. Marilyn wrote Warner a letter filled with complaints: ". . . pacing in first third of the picture slowed . . . one comic point after another flattened by inferior takes . . . jump-cutting kills the points, as in the panty scene . . . Americans are not as moved by stain-glass windows as the British are and we threaten them with boredom . . . much of the movie is without music when the idea was to make a romantic movie."

Marilyn followed up with a phone call to Warner, who tried to assure her that the movie was perfect. He was wrong and she was right. Despite the provocative casting, *The Prince and the Showgirl* was a flop.

No film gave Jack Warner more headaches than *A Star Is Born*.

Judy Garland had made a much-publicized comeback at the Palace in New York after her career had hit the skids following a nervous breakdown and her firing from MGM. Garland's manager and husband, Sid Luft, came to Jack Warner with the idea of a remake of the Hollywood saga that had starred Janet Gaynor and Fredric March in 1937.

A Star Is Born was a coproduction of Warner Bros. and Luft-Garland's Transcona Enterprises, and Luft spent much time rounding up his half of the financing. Harry Warner groused: "He's the only producer I know who has his office at Santa Anita."

Jack Warner was in a constant uproar over the film's extravagances. Judy was not well when filming started, and she fell into the same pattern of late appearances that had led to her downfall at MGM. At times her behavior seemed to border on dementia. She borrowed expensive dresses to attend parties and premieres and returned them in tatters. When she wanted to own a white gown created for the Academy Award sequence, she staged a scene in front of Jack Warner: "Look at this thing! How can you expect me to wear this? It makes me look like the great white whale!" Warner resignedly ordered a new gown, and Judy took home the white one.

George Cukor finally completed *A Star Is Born* and presented Jack Warner with a three-hour cut. Warner was impressed with the film, and it previewed well. But Ben Kalmenson kept telling him: "The theaters can't make money on two runs a day. You gotta cut the picture so they can get three runs out of it."

As usual, Warner bowed to Kalmenson's judgment. While Cukor was on a safari in Africa, Warner ordered an editor to remove thirty minutes. Then Luft insisted on adding a lengthy musical number, "Born in a Trunk." Additional cuts had to be made.

Jack Warner adored premieres, and he instructed his publicity chief, Bill Hendricks, to stage one for *A Star Is Born* that would set new records for glamor and excitement. Warner sent personal telegrams of invitation to all the big names in Hollywood, and most of them accepted. To his dismay, James Mason did not.

Warner dispatched another wire to Mason with the veiled threat: "There's an old adage: One must put something back if they want to continue taking something out. . . . So why not get on the team and have a good time with us all?" Mason, who detested "that premiere nonsense," again politely declined.

Groucho Marx at first declined, but after Jack Warner's urging, he wrote: "I received your wire and contents barely noted. Seriously, folks, if you are as eager for me to go to *A Star Is Born*'s opening—I almost said Judy Garland's opening—as you profess to be, I will make a deal with you: You either pick me up with your car and chauffeur or send a car for me, and I will cancel my Wednesday night [television] performance. . . ."

The brilliance of the Pantages Theater premiere outshone *A Star Is Born* itself. The cleverness of Cukor's direction and Moss Hart's script was clouded by the overproduced musical numbers and the loss of key scenes. Many critics preferred the 1937 William Wellman version. Bloated costs precluded any profit, and Garland's movie comeback failed.

Warner scorned Sid Luft in his autobiography as "one of the original guys who promised his parents he'd never work a day in his life—and he kept his promise." He recited his version of Luft's transgressions, the most serious concerning a horse bet. Luft filed a million-dollar law suit, claiming the book libeled him. Warner Bros. publicity chief, Max Bercutt, advised settling the suit, realizing that his boss would lose the jury on the witness stand. An agreement was reached out of court to pay Luft $75,000.

Transcona was only one of the independent companies which Jack Warner tolerated at his studio because Warner Bros. had virtually emptied its contract list of actors, writers, directors and producers. Others included Jack Webb's Mark VII, Doris Day's Arwin, Charles K. Feldman's Group Productions and John Wayne's Batjac.

Wayne, who had appeared in program westerns at Warner Bros. in the early thirties, produced and starred in seven films at the studio in the mid-fifties. Then he took Batjac to other studios.

One day Wayne and his son Michael had some business to transact at Warner Bros. They encountered Jack Warner on a studio street, and he greeted them warmly.

"You really oughta bring Batjac back to Warner Brothers, Duke," said Warner. "You should be here, where you can be fucked by friends."

Chapter 16

The House Divided

"MY HEART IS BROKEN," declared Harry Warner. He was devastated in March of 1956 by Jack's insistence on selling all of Warner Bros.' pre-1949 films to Elliot Hyman, who headed United Artists Television.

"This is our heritage, what we worked all our lives to create, and now it is gone," Harry lamented. He was grieved as much by the loss as by the purchase price: $21 million. Twentieth Century-Fox had sold its library for $30 million, Paramount for $50 million.

Jack would not be dissuaded. For the past few years the company's profits had ranged from two to four million dollars, despite his renewed efforts to economize. Warner Bros. needed an infusion of cash to remain in competition with the other studios. Ben Kalmenson had advised him that selling the backlog would be the quickest way to restore financial balance.

Harry fulminated against his youngest brother, but Jack was unhearing. He no longer feared Harry, who now was seventy-five years old, bony and cadaverous, a caricature of the canny trader who had guided Warner Bros. into greatness. He was no match for Jack, a robust sixty-four-year-old, still swinging a tennis racket and bedding the younger women he found so amusing. Harry thought

Jack had done a terrible thing by selling the old films. He didn't know that Jack had something even more devastating in store for him.

The Warners had considered selling the company before. In 1954 an old pal from Jack's early San Francisco days, Louis Lurie, who had become a theater chain owner and financier, made an offer for a buyout. But Lurie could not assemble the financing, and the deal fell through. In 1956 one of Jack's eastern buddies, a Boston banker named Serge Semenenko, headed a group of investors who offered to pay the Warner brothers $22 million for their 800,000 shares. All three brothers would remain as members of the board, but a new administration would run the company.

Feeling the burden of his years, Harry Warner agreed to sell. Albert, who was seventy-three years old, was eager to relinquish his duties as vice president and treasurer. After forty years of being caught in the cross fire between his two brothers, he welcomed the tranquility of Miami Beach, where he owned a grand home.

The sale by the founders of Warner Bros. was announced in July of 1956, surprising the film world. What happened next was astonishing. Jack Warner bought back his shares and announced he was staying with the company as its largest stockholder. And he would occupy the position that had always been held by Harry: president of Warner Bros.

Harry Warner was thunderstruck. The perfidy of his brother staggered him, and he vowed never to speak to Jack again. Ill health soon overtook him, and there were reports he had suffered a stroke and had been paralyzed. Still, he and Rea gathered their family in August 1957 for a celebration of their golden wedding anniversary.

"What the hell, I'll go out and join the party," said Jack. As soon as Harry saw Jack arriving outside, he retired upstairs. Jack entered to a restrained greeting by his grim-faced relatives. He made light of the situation and ordered a drink. Only when he had left the house did Harry return to the party.

Harry Warner died on July 27, 1958, of a cerebral occlusion. The funeral was held at the Wilshire Boulevard Temple in Los Angeles, and among the mourners were Edward G. Robinson,

James Stewart and Michael Curtiz. Rabbi Edgar Magnin delivered the eulogy, calling Harry "a plain, simple man who loved above all else being a farmer" (apparently a reference to Harry's ranch). Harry's widow issued the malediction: "Harry didn't die; Jack killed him."

Missing at the funeral service was Jack Warner. He had departed for his annual vacation at Cap d'Antibes. Visitors at the villa were surprised that he exhibited no mournfulness over the passing of his late brother. "I didn't give a shit about Harry," he said, "but hey, looka this." He waved a letter on White House stationery. "It's a letter of condolence from President Eisenhower. Ain't that something?"

Jack had bought the Villa Aujourd'hui in 1949, and it provided retreat from the abrasions of the Burbank studio. Warner enjoyed telling visitors that the place had been occupied by German and American generals during the war. Built in 1939, the villa had twenty-three rooms but did not seem palatial. It stood behind a long wall that faced the street. On the other side of the property was 450 feet of private beach, with a view out of a Matisse painting. An American widow had sold the villa to Warner for $160,000.

Warner hosted small lunches and dinners on the terrace so that he could show off the view to his guests. For his birthday celebration the party was larger. One year he decided to invite all of Warner Bros.' European managers. He instructed Joe Hyams, a marketing executive who was visiting him, to issue the invitations. "I gotta get more silverware," Warner said. "Come with me."

Warner drove his station wagon to the Monte Carlo casino, steering to the service entrance. The manager greeted Warner warmly. "What can I do for you, Monsieur Warner?" he asked.

"I need dinner service for fifty," Warner said. The manager disappeared inside, and his assistants carried out hampers filled with the casino's gold place settings. While Warner directed the loading of the station wagon, Hyams asked the manager, "Would you like me to sign for it?"

"Oh, no, monsieur," the manager replied. "Considering what Monsieur Warner has left in the casino over the years, we do not need a receipt."

On the night of August 5, 1958, three days after his sixty-sixth birthday, Jack Warner spent an enjoyable evening at the baccarat table of the Palm Beach Casino in Cannes. Fortune was on his side, and his fellow players marveled at the streak of good cards. He was not playing for high stakes, and after six hours at the table he quit with $4,000 in his favor.

Warner climbed into his little 1947 Alfa-Romeo roadster for the drive back to the Villa Aujourd'hui. As he was passing Aly Khan's villa, the Alfa-Romeo suddenly swerved across the highway and into the path of a coal truck. The head-on collision reduced the sports car to a tangle of metal, and it burst into flame. Because of a loose door on the driver's side, Warner had been thrown forty feet by the impact. He lay beside the highway, blood-soaked and unconscious.

Motorists stopped and picked up the injured man and drove him to the Cannes hospital. Doctors took x-rays of his head and could find nothing wrong. But he was in a deep coma, and his vital signs were poor. At the suggestion of a young intern, the doctors decided to reduce his body temperature with ice, in an attempt to forestall further damage.

Barbara Warner, Ann and Jack's daughter, was the only family member at Cap d'Antibes. She telephoned Bill Orr in Los Angeles at 5 a.m. and asked him to tell Ann. Ann and Joy left immediately for France. Because of pressing studio business, Bill could not leave for a couple of days.

JACK WARNER NEAR DEATH IN CAR CRASH

Newspapers across America headlined the news. Sources in Cannes were quoted as saying that Warner could not recover from his injuries. Papers and wire services began preparing obituaries, and some of them were printed. Jack read them later and found them dull.

An alarmed Jack Jr. joined the rest of the family in France.

What happened after his arrival has been the subject of rumor and conjecture. Jack was questioned by reporters, and his remarks were interpreted as indicating his father was dying. This would later infuriate Jack Sr. Also he would be subjected to Ann's wrath because Jack Jr. had had not paid proper respect to her. All accounts agree that Jack Jr.'s visit to the hospital marked the end of the tenuous relationship between father and son.

The ice treatment worked. Jack struggled out of the coma and began groping for one-liners. When Bill Orr arrived from Burbank and entered the hospital room, his father-in-law blinked open his eyes and muttered, "Heart of gold and teeth to match." It was an old line of Orr's that Jack enjoyed repeating.

Another visitor was Jack's longtime pal Darryl Zanuck. "See what you get, you old bastard," cracked Zanuck. "This is your retribution for not attending Harry's funeral."

Warner spent four months in France, and Ann remained with him throughout his recovery; it was the longest time they had spent together in years. When Warner returned to Los Angeles, he joked with reporters: "I forgot to duck—and bang! I thought I had the right of way, and eighteen seconds later I knew I didn't." He added seriously: "I'm glad to be home. I feel great. The good Lord has been good to me. This is where I belong."

After a few weeks in Palm Springs, he returned to Burbank with no apparent loss of his power to run a big studio. One of the first things he did was fire his son.

Warner had been fully aware that Jack Jr. remained steadfastly loyal to his mother. Hence Warner was uncomfortable in his son's presence and did not include him in the inner studio circle. A few years after the divorce from Irma, Warner picked up the newspaper and was horrified to read that she was suing him for nonpayment of alimony. He summoned Jack Jr. and demanded, "Did you know this was going to break?" When Jack Jr. admitted he did, his father ranted, "Why the hell didn't you tell me? I have the money to pay. I don't want publicity like that."

The distance between them grew. The hospital incident provided the break. Warner was particularly angry because Jack Jr.

had told reporters that his father was not expected to live. Warner resented the suggestion he might not survive to continue his leadership of Warner Bros.

In late December 1958, Jack Jr. picked up the trade papers and read the news that he had been released from his position as Warner Bros. vice president in charge of commercial and industrial films. He consulted his lawyer, who advised him to report for work regardless. The press had been informed, and young Warner's arrival at the studio and his refusal of entry by guards was duly recorded.

"I went out to the studio this morning just like a normal business day and was denied admittance to my office," Jack Jr. told reporters. "I have practically grown up in this studio. I have worked here almost all my life, except for five years during World War II."

His days at Warner Bros. were ended forever. Except for one brief encounter late in Jack Warner's life, he never spoke to his son again. Nor would Warner entertain any of his son's attempts at reconciliation. One year a Father's Day card from young Jack arrived at 1801 Angelo Drive while Warner was conferring with his assistant, Robert Solo. Warner tore the card apart in a fury, muttering profanely against his only son.

Jack Warner had long grumbled that the Academy had given the Thalberg Award twice to Hal Wallis and three times to Darryl Zanuck, but had never bestowed the honor to the man who hired them both. Perhaps because of Jack's near-rendezvous with death, the Board of Governors remedied that omission, and on April 6, 1949, Warner received the Thalberg at the thirty-first Academy Awards ceremony. To everyone's relief, his acceptance speech was humble and brief.

Errol Flynn died on October 14, 1959, clutching his last nymphet.

Jack Warner was truly grieved. He had not felt the same when Humphrey Bogart died in 1957, because he and Bogie had long harbored a mutual antipathy. Flynn had done terrible things while under contract to Warner Bros., yet Warner admired his insouciance, his unquenchable gallantry. Jack always called him The Baron. Errol's name for the boss was Sporting Blood.

When newspapers had printed reports that Warner would dispose of his interest in Warner Bros., Flynn had telegraphed: "Don't sell. Who would I have to fight with? The Baron."

Flynn had returned to the studio in 1957 to play his old friend John Barrymore in *Too Much, Too Soon*, based on his daughter Diana's confessional about her own dissolute life. Flynn was perfectly cast for the role of the boozy, ruined Great Profile. Jack had not been able to bear watching the rushes of his once vibrant star, now a bloated wreck at forty-eight.

Jack Warner delivered the eulogy at The Baron's funeral. When he saw Jerry Giesler, the crafty lawyer who had sprung Flynn from the rape charge, Jack commented, "I wish you could get him out of this one, Jerry."

Jack Warner had a curious relationship with Darryl Zanuck. As titans of two of Hollywood's most powerful studios, they combatted each other in fierce, everyday competition. When Zanuck stepped down as production chief of Twentieth Century Fox to pursue independent production and the beauties of France, his abandoned wife Virginia found sympathetic support from Jack Warner. Yet on the playing fields of the Riviera, Jack and Darryl acted like reunited old high school buddies. They assessed the nubile French girls, exchanged the latest gossip from Hollywood, gloated over the woes of their mutual enemies and played side by side in endless gambling matches.

"Mr. Zanuck calling from Paris," Bill Schaefer announced.

Warner lifted the telephone immediately and heard Darryl's angry voice. Jack could always tell how angry Darryl was by the range of his high-pitched Nebraska voice.

"I'm goddamn mad at those idiots at Fox," Zanuck railed, and he poured out his grievances.

He had left his son Richard in charge of his independent production operation in Hollywood, and Richard had made a creditable film, *Compulsion*. Now the Zanucks had planned a film based on the best-seller *The Chapman Report*, which capitalized on the celebrated sex survey, the Kinsey Report. But the new Fox regime had refused the project on the grounds that it might offend moviegoers and inflame censors both in the United States and abroad.

"Are you interested?" Zanuck asked.

"Hell, yes," Warner replied.

"Good. Give Dick a call."

Dick Zanuck was summoned to the Warner office. Warner looked up from the theater grosses he was perusing and greeted the young man warmly. "Tell me, who's going to be in this thing?" he asked.

Zanuck explained that George Cukor had been assigned as director but no casting had yet been done. "Would you like to read the script?" he asked.

"Don't need to. I know it's in good hands. Go ahead with it. The studio is at your disposal."

When Zanuck told Cukor of the deal, the director despaired, "Oh, no, not Warners; they're so cheap!" He advised Zanuck: "I know Jack Warner, and I know you've got to strike while the iron is hot. Ask for everything you want on the first day. The second day is too late; they cool off quickly." Zanuck heeded the advice. All his requests were granted.

The Chapman Report was cast with Efrem Zimbalist Jr. as the sex researcher and Jane Fonda, Shelley Winters, Glynis Johns and Claire Bloom as subjects of his inquiries. Richard Zanuck had no problems from Warner Bros. and surprisingly few from the Production Code, despite the theme of nymphomania.

When Dick Zanuck prepared to show a rough cut, Warner asked, "Is this a one-piss or a two-piss picture?"

"What do you mean?" Zanuck asked.

"What's the length of the picture? I always have to take a leak during a picture. If it's too long, I have to take two leaks."

"I don't think it's too long," Zanuck said. "I would consider it a one-piss picture."

Warner enjoyed the film, made a few minor suggestions and ordered a preview in San Francisco, where a more sophisticated audience might be more receptive to the frank discussion of sexual matters.

The Chapman Report suffered a disastrous preview at the Warfield Theater in San Francisco. The audience seemed to be an unlikely mixture of prudes and hooligans, half of them sitting in shocked silence, the others yelling epithets at the screen.

Near the end of the screening, a fat old woman rose from her seat and hobbled up the aisle, a cane in one hand and a half-finished soft drink in the other. She stared at Jack Warner sitting in his usual aisle seat, and her puffy eyes flickered with recognition. "This picture is disgusting!" she exclaimed, hurling the soft drink in his face.

She continued up the aisle as the shaken Warner wiped his face and suit with a handkerchief. Ten minutes before the film ended, he leaned over and whispered to Dick Zanuck: "Kid, I'm going down to the men's room and lock myself in a stall until the audience gets out of the house. If I were you, I'd do the same."

After the audience had left, Warner joined Zanuck, Cukor and studio officials in the theater manager's office. He seemed unaffected by the incident, and he congratulated the filmmakers. "It just needs a little fixing and it'll work," said Warner.

Subsequent previews drew better receptions, and *The Chapman Report* was a moderate success. It attracted no challenge from the Catholic Legion of Decency, which had been consulted on the script beforehand. Thanks to his friend Jack Warner, Darryl Zanuck was able to thumb his nose at his successors at Twentieth Century Fox.

"Who wants to see those two old broads on the screen?"

Jack Warner's reaction was the same as other studio heads when Robert Aldrich proposed a teaming of Bette Davis and Joan Crawford in a gothic tale, *Whatever Happened to Baby Jane?* Aldrich was told the project might be considered with younger stars. He rejected the idea, insisting that the film required mature actresses for credibility.

It had been Joan Crawford's idea from the start. Aldrich had directed her in *Autumn Leaves* in 1956, and she had told him, "Why don't you find something for Bette Davis and me to do together?" Aldrich agreed that it would be showmanly to combine the two legendary stars, and he developed *Whatever Happened to Baby Jane?*

Anticipating resistance to the casting of two middle-aged stars, Aldrich budgeted the film at a rock-bottom price, $850,000. Crawford agreed to work for $40,000 and ten percent of the producer's gross, Davis for $60,000 and five percent. Finding no major-studio interest at any price, Aldrich took the package to Eliot Hyman of Seven Arts, the entrepreneur who had bought the Warner Bros. backlog. Hyman made a deal with Jack Warner to release *Baby Jane*.

Unashamed that he had rejected *Baby Jane* as a Warner Bros. production, Jack Warner gave a welcoming lunch for Davis and Crawford. The Hollywood press was invited to witness the reunion.

"Oh, I've had my differences with Papa Jack," Davis told the crowd. "But he is the man who gave me my start in pictures, and I will be forever grateful to him."

"I can't exactly call you my father, Mr. Warner," Crawford said, "because I give that credit to the late Louis B. Mayer. But you are my second father." Jack Warner beamed.

Despite expectations of friction between the two high-powered actresses, filming of *Baby Jane* proceeded smoothly and within Aldrich's frugal budget. Only later did their differences surface. Bette delighted in telling interviewers that film moguls had remarked, "We wouldn't give you a dime for those two old broads." Joan sent a note to Bette: "Please do not refer to me that way again."

"Those two old broads" proved their box-office magic; *Baby Jane* turned a profit after eleven days in release. The Davis career was reinvigorated, Crawford's was not. Bette remained at Warner Bros. to play a double role of a woman who murders her twin in *Dead*

Ringer. The director was Paul Henreid, her cigarette sharer of *Now*, *Voyager*.

Jack Warner hated drunks, both on and off the screen. The peccadillos of John Barrymore, Errol Flynn and other actors contributed to a fierce displeasure with those who imbibed too freely. Warner could countenance movie drunks if they were of the pixilated variety like Frank McHugh and Hugh Herbert. But he abhorred serious dramas about alcoholism.

In the early 1950s, Bill Orr had tried to interest Jack in *The Country Girl* as a film prospect. The play was a Broadway hit, with Paul Kelly making a comeback as the alcoholic star. With some foreboding, Warner agreed to attend the play with Orr.

"Jesus Christ, who wants to see that old drunk?" Warner muttered during the first act. "Paul Kelly? We used him in bit parts." He wanted to leave, but Orr persuaded him to remain for the second act. Warner's opinion of the play didn't change.

"I think we should buy it," Orr argued. "With Bogart as the actor, Kirk Douglas as the director, and Jane Wyman as the wife, I guarantee you one or two Academy nominations. It'll be easy to make: all indoors, with lots of good drama."

Warner invoked the water tower, but Orr persisted. "All right, goddamn it, I'll make 'em an offer," Warner snapped. His offer was a laughable $25,000. Paramount had a bargain at $75,000 and cast *The Country Girl* with Bing Crosby, Grace Kelly and William Holden. The film was one of the successes of 1954 and won an Oscar for Kelly.

By 1963 Bill Orr was in charge of all Warner Bros. production, feature and television. Orr had been impressed with a television drama, *Days of Wine and Roses*, and had asked Abe Lastfogel of the William Morris Agency for a kinescope. Although he could make the decision himself, Orr sent the kinescope to Jack Warner with the message that the studio should buy the film rights.

"Bill, I didn't send you down there to buy pictures about drunks," Warner grumbled.

"Colonel, that TV show has won all kinds of awards," Orr countered.

"I don't care. It's dark and gloomy, and it's about a young drunk."

"That's a kinescope, and the quality is never good. It's a fine, fine story."

"Well, I didn't give you that job to buy pictures about drunks."

It was an impasse. Orr was so resolute that he decided on the perilous course of outfoxing his father-in-law. He called Ben Kalmenson in New York and told him the situation. "We can have Jack Lemmon and Lee Remick as stars and Blake Edwards to direct," Orr explained. "Sounds good, let me handle it," said Kalmenson.

Warner called Orr the following day: "We're buying a script from William Morris."

"What's the title?" Orr asked.

"*Days of Wine and Roses*."

"That's the same story I sent you on kinescope."

"No, no, this is an entirely different story."

Months later Warner attended a final-cut screening of *Days of Wine and Roses*, accompanied by a stylish-looking woman. Warner made only one exit to the bathroom. When the lights went up in the projection room, he announced: "Gotta change that ending. Too depressing. The audience will hate it."

Blake Edwards and Jack Lemmon argued that the integrity of the film would be destroyed by tacking on a happy ending for the young couple ensnared in alcoholism. Warner fended off their arguments, and then his companion spoke up: "I think they're right and you're wrong."

Warner whirled around and snarled, "What the hell do you know about it?"

The woman gave a complete, intelligent analysis of why the unhappy ending was the only valid way to complete the film. Warner listened in astonishment, and then hustled her out of the room. He never again mentioned another ending for *Days of Wine and Roses*.

*   *   *

Richard Nixon had long been the darling of Jack Warner. Warner applauded Nixon's Red-hunting, his conservatism, his opportunism, and he donated lavishly to all of Nixon's political campaigns. When Nixon ran for the presidency in 1960, Warner paid for full-page ads in *The New York Times*, Los Angeles *Times* and other newspapers to proclaim why Nixon should be elected.

During the presidential campaign, Warner called a meeting of all the studio's executives and department heads, except those who were openly Democratic. Warner delivered an oration about the importance of electing Richard Nixon as President of the United States. "Now when you leave here," he instructed, "I want you to hand Bill Schaefer your contributions to the Nixon campaign. The *minimum* is two hundred dollars."

Warner did not mourn the Nixon loss of the election for long. When he read that the newly elected President Kennedy was coming to Los Angeles for a fund-raiser at the Palladium, Warner summoned his publicity chief, Max Bercutt. "I wanna go to that affair," Warner said.

"Jesus Christ, colonel, those ads you took!" Bercutt replied.

"That's all right, I wanna meet him. Get me a table."

"But how, after you campaigned against him?"

"That's your job."

Bercutt called Pierre Salinger, Kennedy's press secretary, whom he had known when Salinger was a reporter on the San Francisco *Chronicle*. "You got a funny boss," Salinger laughed, and he arranged for Warner's table.

Warner and his party were positioned to the right of the Palladium stage, where Kennedy would make his entrance. As soon as "Hail to the Chief" started playing, Bercutt rose and approached the presidential party. Secret Service men started to grab him, but Salinger intervened. "Jack Warner would like to meet you, Mr. President," said Bercutt.

"He's the guy who took those ads," Salinger explained.

"Let's meet him," said Kennedy. He smiled knowingly as the beaming Warner shook his hand.

A few weeks later Warner received a call in his office. "Jack, this is Joe Kennedy."

Warner recognized the pinched, Boston accent. He and Joseph P. Kennedy had sat together at many producers' meetings when Kennedy owned RKO. Kennedy explained why he was calling. His son Jack, who had just been elected President, was the subject of a book about his World War II exploits, *PT 109*. Jack felt an obligation to the author, Robert Donovan, who had done extensive research for his book. Would Warner be interested in buying the book for a movie?

"Hell, yes," Warner replied. "You got a deal."

President Kennedy specified that the contract would include payments to survivors of the sinking of the patrol torpedo boat. He also reserved the right to approve the script and the actor portraying him. To oversee the film, he appointed Salinger and George Stevens, Jr., director of motion pictures for the U.S. Information Agency.

Warner appointed his old pal Bryan Foy to produce *PT 109*. That was his first mistake. Brynie had been a personal favorite of Warner's since the 1920s, as much for his raffish humor as for his contributions to the studio. Foy was a whiz at exploitation pictures—he had made Warner Bros.' first all-talkie and first 3-D movie—and no one outside of Poverty Row could pinch a production penny more tightly. He also seemed qualified for *PT 109* because the Foys and the Kennedys had been friendly during the vaudeville heyday of Eddie Foy, Sr.

But Brynie was totally wrong for *PT 109*. As a depiction of a living president, the film required a certain amount of class, of which Brynie had none. To him, it was just another exploitation movie to cash in on a headline figure. And Kennedy's liberalism was anathema to Foy, who was rightist and bigoted.

Jack Kennedy had seen Warren Beatty in his first film, *Splendor in the Grass*, and announced, "That's the guy. He's the one who should play me."

Young Beatty, a devoted democrat, was honored to be the President's choice, but his doubts about accepting the role were confirmed by a disastrous meeting with Bryan Foy. "Don't worry, I'll talk him into it," Warner assured. He summoned Beatty and his agent, Abe Lastfogel, to a meeting. Warner expounded on all the reasons why Beatty should accept *PT 109*, invoking patriotism as well as some implied threats.

Beatty remained firm: "I won't play a living president."

"The President wants you," said Warner.

"I don't care."

Peter Fonda, Cliff Robertson and other young actors were tested for the role, and the footage was sent to the White House. Kennedy chose Robertson. The casting of the director also presented problems. Warner suggested Raoul Walsh, a veteran of action movies. He sent the White House a print of Walsh's latest film, *Marines, Let's Go*, a brawling movie about Korean War fighters on leave in Japan.

George Stevens, Jr., arrived at the White House for a screening of *Marines, Let's Go* with Pierre Salinger. The pair walked from the West Wing through the mansion and to the East Wing, where the projection room was located. "I haven't seen a movie in three months; I'm really looking forward to this," said Salinger, who had spent the day on the telephone answering questions about the latest crisis with Khrushchev.

Stevens did not have the same anticipation. He had already seen *Marines, Let's Go* and had found it to be a tasteless movie filled with macho dialogue and phony fisticuffs. It looked no better on second viewing. The movie-starved Salinger seemed to enjoy it, laughing when a Japanese went sliding down the bartop when slugged in a saloon brawl.

As the two men watched the movie unfold, a door at the right of the screen was opened by a liveried footman, and a slouched figure entered the darkened room and sat in a rocking chair in the middle of the first row. He nodded to Stevens and said, "Hello, Pierre." Then he turned his attention to the screen.

After ten minutes, Jack Kennedy said curtly, "Pierre, stop the movie." Salinger signaled the projectionist to halt. The President rose from the rocking chair and said, "Tell Jack Warner to go fuck himself."

Jack Warner came to Washington to help solve the question of the director. He brought along Brynie Foy, and they lunched with Salinger and Stevens at a restaurant called The Bistro. Salinger emphasized the President's wish that *PT 109* be made with dignity, and he asked for Stevens' opinion about a director. Stevens remarked on the need for a director of quality, and he mentioned such names as John Huston and Fred Zinnemann.

Brynie fumed as Stevens delivered an analysis, and he finally interrupted: "Kid, I don't think you should be trying to tell us how to make an exploitation picture."

Warner gave no evidence of chagrin at having his producer refer to a movie about the President of the United States as an "exploitation picture." Warner finally found a director who was acceptable to both the studio and the White House: Lewis Milestone, who had directed such war movies as *All Quiet on the Western Front*, *A Walk in the Sun* and *The Halls of Montezuma*.

The *PT 109* company left for locations in the Florida keys, where friction between Foy and Milestone began immediately. They were a continent apart politically as well as artistically. Milestone was sensitive, intellectual and radical; Foy was a fast-talking blusterer and a reactionary. "Keep it moving, keep it moving," Foy instructed, but the director, a forty-year veteran of dealing with studio authority, would not be hurried.

Milestone's mistake was to tell reporters: "It's not a very good script, but we're going to make a good film out of it." That was just the thing to inflame Jack Warner, who was already being cannonaded by Foy's complaints. Milestone was fired.

The *PT 109* cast and crew, who were devoted to Milestone, were thunderstruck. Mutterings of a mutiny arose: "We gotta stand up for Milly." Cliff Robertson, who was equally fond of the director, calmed his fellow workers: "Hey, guys, I feel terrible about this, too. But we can't go on strike. We all have contracts."

Robertson telephoned Pierre Salinger at the White House to

report the company's confidence in Milestone. Salinger called Warner, who said the decision was irreversible. Milestone was unsuited for an action picture and was filming too slowly, Warner claimed.

Les Martinson was told to report to Colonel Warner's office. Martinson had established himself as an astute director of Warner Bros. television films; his only experience with features came when he replaced a faltering director.

"Kid," said Warner, "we're having a little problem on *PT 109*." He explained that Milestone had fallen behind the schedule, and he stressed the importance of the film.

"Do you think you can handle it, kid?" Warner asked.

Martinson, who was astonished that he would be chosen out of all the directors available in Hollywood, responded affirmatively. He saw Milestone's footage on Friday and on Monday he directed his first shot on Munson Island. The filming went as smoothly as the weather and Brynie Foy would allow. Some of Foy's battles with Martinson equaled those he had had with Milestone.

One final scene remained, Martinson's favorite. Kennedy was to trudge through the water to deliver a coconut to a pair of natives. A message arrived from Burbank: "Finish shooting today and return to studio." Martinson tried to appeal the summons, but he could reach no one in authority at the studio. The company packed up and flew to California.

The initial four-hour cut was reduced to two hours and twenty-two minutes. Even that was a bit long for Jack Warner. "Well, kid," he told Martinson after the screening, "you made one helluva three-piss picture."

Warner took a print to the White House, and President Kennedy expressed his approval of the picture. Critics and audiences did not. Released in March 1963, *PT 109* was lambasted as the same old Warner Bros. hokum, and the company lost five million dollars.

PT 109 was withdrawn from release on November 22, 1963.

Chapter 17

The Last Tycoon

LOUIS B. MAYER AND HARRY COHN were dead, Darryl Zanuck languished in the fleshpots of Europe and Sam Goldwyn had made his last film. Only Jack Warner remained on his throne as founder-ruler of a movie empire. And rule he did.

Newly hired publicists were instructed that all press releases began in one of two ways: "Jack L. Warner announced today . . ." or, "It was announced today by Jack L. Warner . . ." After Bill Hendricks became publicity director, he remained active in the Marine Corps Reserve's Toys for Tots campaign which he had founded. When a small story about Hendricks' efforts appeared in the Los Angeles *Daily News*, he received word that J.L.W. was displeased; press agents were not supposed to get publicity. Hendricks persuaded a friend on the *Daily News* to carry a story about Jack Warner's contributions to Toys for Tots, accompanied by a photo of Warner in a Santa Claus suit. Jack Warner was placated.

Years later, when Hendricks became head of the cartoon department, he was praised by the New York office for the quality of the cartoons. He showed the wire to Warner and suggested that he either get a raise or producer credit on the shorts. "Take the credit," Warner advised. "If you don't get credit, boy, you didn't do it."

Hendricks always lingered in the executive dining room and accompanied the boss back to his office; Warner did not like to walk on the lot alone lest he be accosted and importuned. One day as they reached the security gate, the guard slammed down the phone and said, "Mr. Warner, the studio is on fire!" Warner and Hendricks rushed through the casting and wardrobe departments, a shortcut to the back lot. When they emerged, they could see the New York tenement street engulfed in flames.

The gate to the back lot was locked, but a guard came along to open it. As Warner rushed toward the fire, he noticed a worker sitting on the ground. "I think I'm having a heart attack," he said. Remembering the 1934 fire that killed the fire chief, Warner hailed a fire truck and told the driver: "Take this guy to First Aid right away, then get the hell back here."

Warner watched helplessly as the studio and Burbank fire departments tried to stop the fire, which was racing through the dry timbers supporting the outdoor sets. A television camera crew arrived, and Warner posed watching the blaze. Then he told Hendricks, "Get these guys outa here; you know we don't allow TV cameras on the lot." The publicity chief allowed the crew to shoot the collapse of the tenement street; then he evicted them.

Warner remained calm throughout the ordeal. Nor did he mourn the loss of sets that had been used hundreds of times. They were insured. They could be rebuilt. Warner Bros. kept going.

As the sole remaining mogul in power, Jack Warner continued receiving awards and honors, all of which he cherished. On January 24, 1960, the Screen Producers Guild saluted him with its Milestone Award at a Beverly Hilton Hotel banquet. It was a dazzling affair, attended by the great names of Hollywood. But Jack Warner's big night was spoiled by a single word uttered by an actress.

Jack Benny served as master of ceremonies, and he made great sport out of *The Horn Blows at Midnight*: "I knew something was wrong when they previewed the picture at a drive-in theater in Palm Springs . . . in the middle of the July . . . at noon." Among the first speakers Benny introduced was Eva Marie Saint, whose name befitted her willowy, virginal appearance. She was to present an award to a college filmmaker. Benny launched into an uncharacteristic, flowery introduction of the actress.

As the applause died down, Miss Saint glided to the microphone, glanced at Benny and said, "All I can say after that is 'Oh, shit.' "

The silence of the twelve hundred listeners was deafening. That word. And from Eva Marie Saint. Nothing racier than a "hell" or "damn" had ever been heard at an industry gathering. The evening never recovered its gaiety. Afterward Miss Saint said she had used the word as a satire of pomposity. No one got the joke, least of all Jack Warner, whose night of honors had been tarnished.

Warner's antipathy toward agents grew in direct ratio to the agents' mounting power as the big-studio era faded. With Cohn, Mayer and other studio bosses gone, Warner appointed himself the last crusader against the incursion of the agencies. His principal target remained the all-powerful MCA. He ranted against the demands of Jules Stein, Lew Wasserman and their underlings, and his intransigence led to the loss of promising deals that were offered to more receptive studios.

When a young television actor, Charlton Heston, was brought to Hollywood, MCA negotiated a nonexclusive contract with Hal Wallis. Warner was furious that a potential star had been snapped up by his longtime rival. He issued an order barring MCA agents from the studio.

After Heston had become a star, Warner Bros. sought him for a combat movie, *Darby's Rangers*. MCA made the deal, and Heston prepared for the role, conferring with experts at the Pentagon, discussing the film with the director, William Wellman, and being fitted for uniforms. Then Jack Warner scrutinized the contract. It stipulated that Heston would receive ten percent of the gross—ten cents of every dollar collected by the company.

"Never!" Warner exploded. MCA argued that a deal had been made. Warner refused to sign it. The studio instructed Heston to report for the start of production. MCA said he couldn't go. Heston didn't report, and the studio declared him in breach of contract. MCA said Warner Bros. had broken the contract.

Law suits were filed, and depositions were taken. Heston was questioned by the Warner Bros. lawyers, and he described the events in full. "You did okay, Chuck," his attorney said afterward, "but there are really some questions you can answer with a simple yes or no."

Next it was Jack Warner's turn. Prodded by MCA's attorneys, he recited his objections to the contract the agency had negotiated. In answer to one question he blurted, "Aw, those fucking actors deserve anything bad that happens to them anyway."

"Thank you, Mr. Warner," the MCA attorney smiled. "That's all we need from you."

Heston received a substantial settlement. The leading role in *Darby's Rangers* was given to a contract player, James Garner, who starred for the first time.

He first saw her across a room crowded with the better-known names and faces of Hollywood. She was seated alone at the dinner table, a curious mixture of fragile beauty and worldly wisdom. He strolled toward her, and she immediately felt the powerful presence of Jack L. Warner.

"Hi, kid. Why don't you sneak out with me?" he muttered with a wide grin.

Why not? she contemplated. Her escort at LaRue's, the Sunset Strip restaurant owned by *Hollywood Reporter* publisher Billy Wilkerson, was Cornelius Vanderbilt, Jr. But Vanderbilt was rebounding from a messy divorce and was drinking heavily. Now he stood at the bar, exchanging ribald stories with his cronies.

"Okay, I'll go with you," she said. Jack took her arm and led her swiftly through the tables to the restaurant's back door. They glided out Sunset Boulevard in his Rolls Royce and ended up in bed at the Angelo Drive mansion.

Her name was Jackie Park, and she was experienced in the Hollywood demimonde. Her life had been the stuff of trashy novels: born in Philadelphia without a father; raised in Hell's Kitchen by a promiscuous mother; worked as a dancer in Manhattan night spots; recruited by a madame as the plaything of a millionaire; sent to Hollywood for the kinky pleasures of Edmund Goulding, the director. She tried to be an actress, but mostly she worked nighttime for well-known figures. Among them was Cary Grant, who was experimenting with the mind-expanding capabilities of LSD. He introduced Jackie to the drug and to his psychiatrist, Mortimer Hartman, with whom she had a brief, disastrous marriage. She was still suffering from the trauma of the LSD treatments when she met Jack Warner.

A year passed after the first encounter of Warner and Jackie. Then in 1961 she learned that he had parted with his latest mistress. Jackie telephoned him. Warner hired Hollywood private eye Fred Otash to investigate her background. Satisfied that Jackie was neither a professional hooker, an ex-convict or a communist, Warner began a four-year alliance.

At first he tried to model her in the image of Ann Warner. With her hair darkened, pulled back and knotted, Jackie bore a startling resemblance to Jack's wife. He delighted in introducing her as Countess Gomez. After a year, he changed her appearance. Now he told people she was Lady Scarborough (she had told him Scarborough was a family name).

"But last year you were Countess Gomez," a photographer complained.

"I divorced Count Gomez and married Lord Scarborough," she replied airily.

Warner made a business arrangement: she was paid $350 a week, no extras. He expected her to be available at all times, and he thwarted her ambitions to act in films and write scripts. In the beginning she acquiesced. She was dazzled by this powerful man and amused by his endless stream of wisecracks.

Jackie was also amazed by the cheapness of this multimillionaire. His underwear was torn, he patched the soap in his bathroom, he had his double-breasted suits altered to single-breasted when the style changed. When he paid her allowance, he wetted his finger to count the bills (once he shortchanged her). He was a notoriously poor tipper. For a full Chinese dinner he would leave $1.50 tip. To Bill Schaefer and other loyal assistants, Warner handed out Christmas bonuses of $25. Jackie convinced him to raise it to $200.

When they flew to the Riviera, Warner occupied the first-class compartment; Jackie and one of his aides sat in the tourist section. She was embarrassed by his parsimony in the casinos. After hours of gambling at the tables, he left without a tip to anyone. Jackie followed behind, doling out francs to waiting hands.

Ann Warner was ever-present in their relationship. Jackie dined with Warner three or four times a week, usually at Alphonse's in Toluca Lake, because he didn't want to go home to face Ann. He feared her, as he feared no one else. He trembled when he faced telephoning her from the south of France. Her unexpectedness kept him constantly on edge. One weekend he planned a weekend with Jackie at the Palm Springs house. He telephoned her Friday night: "Unpack your bags. Ann decided to go at the last minute."

Jackie Park savored the residual power that resulted from her position as Jack Warner's mistress. William Dozier, John Farrow, Jack Webb and others asked her to intercede with Warner on their behalf, and sometimes she was able to. "I shake every morning when I shave," Webb told her. "I never know what that man will do or say."

Jackie noted how Warner used his position as a man of power to indulge in childishly outrageous behavior. At a reception before a *Photoplay* magazine awards dinner, he studied the ample behind of one of the lavishly gowned guests. He gave it a continental pinch. Zsa Zsa Gabor whirled around, prepared for combat. But when she recognized that the offender was the boss of Warner Bros., she merely smiled as if he had been a naughty boy.

When Warner flew to London for a command performance of *My Fair Lady*, Jackie accompanied him. At the theater, they sat together with royalty, who gazed with curiosity at the beauty he introduced as Lady Scarborough. At the reception afterward, Warner basked in the plaudits for the movie. He shook the hand of Princess Margaret and introduced Jackie: "This is Lady Scarborough. Heart of gold and snatch to match." The Princess smiled indulgently, perhaps not believing what she had heard.

The one place Warner did not take Jackie was the White House. In Washington to confer with Jack Kennedy on *PT 109*, he told Jackie, "I have too much respect for the presidency to take my mistress to the White House." He was outraged when he returned to the hotel. "For God's sake!" he exclaimed. "He had a broad for himself, and one for me!"

By 1965, the liaison had lasted four years, a longer span than any of the Warner mistresses. His attempts at humor amused Jackie, but she also saw another side of Jack Warner: the indifference to his children, the cruelty to underlings, his cheapness. Except for $100 for her birthday, he gave her no gifts. He paid her studio money under the pretense that she was writing scripts—"That makes it look good," he explained. But when she submitted scripts she had written, he refused to read them.

One night he took her to dinner at their favorite Alphonse's and professed his love. The next day she was summoned to the house of a Warner aide and handed a check for $5,000—severance pay. Jackie drove in fury to the Burbank studio. The gate man told her, "Mr. Warner doesn't want to see you." "That's what you think!" she replied, and she barreled her car through the gate. She was immediately surrounded by studio police and firemen, but word arrived from Warner's office: "She can come up."

"If you don't want to see me anymore, sit down and tell me face to face," she ranted. "This is not the twenties. I'm not some gun moll you can discard like yesterday's newspaper." He explained that Ann, who was always aware of his mistresses, had decided that Jackie had stayed long enough. He placated Jackie and acceded to her demand for "the most expensive screen test this studio has ever made." Not for herself, as it turned out, but for a close friend.

Warner and Jackie continued their relationship, but it was never the same. She had a secret affair with Greg Bautzer, the Hollywood lawyer and man-about-town, and he was seeing other women. Warner took Jackie to Cap d'Antibes, where they were constantly at odds. "If you don't like it, get out," he told her angrily. "I've bought you a ticket back to New York." She tried suicide with brandy and pills but was revived. Back in Hollywood, she received word from Jack Warner: "Get out of town." Realizing that it was more than an idle threat, she did.

Jack Warner never enjoyed looking backward. Reminiscing was for old fossils; he preferred to consider the present and the future. Yet he prided himself (perhaps too highly) as a storyteller, and he was pleased when people told him: "You should write a book."

Bill Hendricks had that in mind when he induced the boss to recite his history. Every evening at six o'clock the publicity director reported to Warner's office and listened to him spin tales like a Burbank Scheherazade. How he and Sam had blown their nest egg from *Dante's Inferno* in a crap game. How the brothers used an insurance policy ruse to avoid usury laws when taking loans out at forty percent interest. How they had to grind out two-reelers fast to repay the loans.

When Jack Webb came to Warner Bros. to head the television department, he wielded considerable influence on Warner. Webb urged him to collaborate on an autobiography with Dean Jennings, an able writer for the *Saturday Evening Post*. Jennings moved into a studio office for a five-month assignment. He stayed for a year and a half.

Published in 1964, *My First Hundred Years in Hollywood* was pure Jack Warner: anecdotal, gag-ridden, selectively historical. More space was given to his fanatically loyal masseur, Abdul Maljan, than to most of his stars. His devotion to Sam was conveyed touchingly, but his long antagonism with Harry went unreported. Notable omissions: Irma, Jack Jr., Hal Wallis. Large portions of Warner Bros. history were ignored in favor of jokes, including the ethnic slur about Madame Chiang Kai-shek. Jennings deftly captured the Warner voice, but the autobiography drowned in an outpouring of wisecracks.

Now in his seventies, Warner retained his old-time vigor. On his tours of the lot he zipped along at a Harry Truman pace. Whether on Angelo Drive, at Cap d'Antibes or in Palm Springs, he played tennis every weekend. His appetites for French food, Jack Daniels and pliant women were undiminished. Ann Warner was never seen in public, and there were rumors that she had put on much weight. She remained upstairs in her quarters at the main house or spent her time at her La Jolla house or the Arizona ranch. That left Jack free to enjoy the company and pleasures of a wide array of women. None was a celebrity. Some were beauties; others seemed common.

That the companions were more than decoration for an aging mogul was indicated by a woman with whom he shared the Villa Aujourd'hui one summer. She had left her husband, a physician, and she accompanied Warner on his nightly forays into the casinos. One night Warner was busy gambling with an old Hollywood friend, Cubby Broccoli, producer of the James Bond films. The doctor's wife sat at the bar with Broccoli's assistant, Michael Wilson.

"I'll bet you're wondering why a woman of thirty-five is hanging around a guy in his seventies," she said tipsily.

"No, not at all," said the embarrassed young man.

"Well, I'll tell you," she persisted. "That man in his seventies is more sexually alive and proficient than any man in his thirties I've ever known."

Warner's energy amazed and exhausted his associates, even those who were thirty and forty years younger. He was especially exuberant on his trips to New York, where he acted "like a kid out of school," an executive recalls. Once Warner arrived in Manhattan with the mission of seeing a Jean Kerr play, *Poor Richard*, which the studio had bought. Kerr's *Mary, Mary* with Debbie Reynolds had been a 1963 success for Warner Bros., and Warner hoped *Poor Richard*, despite lukewarm reviews, would perform as well.

The New York office arranged for house seats, and Warner invited Ben Kalmenson and Richard Lederer, the publicity-advertising chief, to dinner at a 50th Street fish restaurant that was a Jack Warner favorite. Kalmenson was in a sour mood when he entered the limousine. He considered New York his own fiefdom, and it upset him to have the company president invade the city, taking the spotlight with his bumptious airs.

Warner swept into the restaurant and wrapped his arms around the owner, greeting him with joyful shouts. Kalmenson skulked behind him as they were led to a prized table. "Ya still got those terrific oysters?" Jack asked. "Yeah? Great. I'll have a dozen of 'em. How about you, Benny?"

Two Jack Daniels later, Warner ordered the lobster dinner "with plenty of French fries. But first, bring me another dozen of those oysters." Kalmenson said sourly, "I'll have the sole, grilled and dry, nothing else."

Warner finished the meal with gustatorial zest and told the waiter, "You know what I'd like? A slice of the apple pie with some of that great cheddar cheese from Oregon."

"That does it!" Kalmenson said, throwing down his napkin. "I'm leaving. And I'm taking the car. You can get to the theater on your own."

"Poor Benny," Warner said to Lederer. "With him it's work, work, work. He doesn't know how to live."

Warner and Lederer finished their coffee a half hour before curtain time. "Let's walk to the theater," Warner proposed.

"But chief, it's eight degrees out there," Lederer protested. "I'm responsible for getting you there. Let's find a cab or a limo."

"We'll walk," Warner decreed. They set out on foot through the icy streets. En route Warner stopped at a small theater in Radio City and started talking to the cashier, a stout woman with blue hair. "How's business tonight, sweetheart?" he asked.

"Not so good, Mr. Warner," she said. They chatted for a few minutes and Warner walked on.

Warner and Lederer took their seats in the fourth row center. Three minutes after the curtain had gone up, Warner was fast asleep. The embarrassed Lederer tried to waken him by coughing, to no avail. Two minutes before the end of the first act, Warner was wide awake, and he nodded toward the stage and muttered, "I can fix it."

Warner hurried to the men's room during the intermission. When he returned, he asked Lederer, "Did you see that good-looking broad on the aisle with that agent? I forget his name. I'll think of it in a minute." The pair went over to talk to the agent and his beauteous client.

The second act kept Warner awake, and he joined in the restrained applause at the curtain. In front of the theater, Lederer hailed a cab. "You go ahead without me," said Warner. "I'm a big boy, I can take care of myself."

When Lederer last saw his boss, he was walking into the frigid night with the agent's client on his arm.

Jack Warner played hard, but he also worked hard. His day in California was the same: telephoning his office and New York in the morning, arriving at the studio at noon, presiding over the lunch gathering, attending conferences in the afternoon, and viewing rushes and previews at night. Younger producers and directors were amazed by his memory for rushes he had seen weeks before and by his grasp of cinematic style.

He paid almost as much attention to the studio's program pictures as he did to the specials. When he brought Howard W. Koch and Aubrey Schenck to the studio to make $200,000 movies, he oversaw their product. Koch showed him a Mamie Van Doren rock 'n' roll movie, *Untamed Youth*, expecting that Warner would spend the time making phone calls and walk out with no comment. Instead Warner was attentive throughout, and afterward he made fifteen editing suggestions: "Why are you in a close-up when it should be a two-shot? . . . . Cut down the car scene; it's a time-waster. . . . Get 'em to the party faster. . . ."

"What do you need to make the picture better?" Warner asked.

"Well, the ending is a cheater," Koch admitted. "We see the

husband and the sister watching Mamie perform on TV, but we don't see the number."

"How much do you need for the number?"

"Ten grand."

"Ya got it."

In the early 1960s, Mervyn LeRoy returned to Warner Bros. to direct films based on three Broadway hits Jack Warner had bought: *Gypsy*, *A Majority of One* and *Mary, Mary*. Even though LeRoy had achieved the eminence of producer-director, he still couldn't escape instruction by the studio boss on how to make a film economically.

When LeRoy fell four days behind schedule on *A Majority of One*, he received a friendly but firm letter from J. L. Warner: ". . . . stop overshooting and getting protection and protection. If we are stuck, we will go back and pick up the actual shots we need. As it is now, you make the master scene once or twice then you do the same thing from four or five angles. Stop being so meticulous. Look up the word in the dictionary. I have, and being over-meticulous is being overripe—which you are not!"

While Warner maintained ironfisted control of the studio, Ben Kalmenson ran the company's affairs in New York. His underlings puzzled over Warner's deference to Kalmenson. "Ben says we gotta have more product," Warner said. Or, "Ben says don't make any more weepers; they don't sell." Some theorized that Warner knew he neglected his obligations as chief executive officer, leaving the burden to Kalmenson. Hence Warner's guilt was transformed to acquiescence.

Like Harry Warner before him, Ben Kalmenson believed that those profligates on the coast were impoverishing the company. His economies were shortsighted, as when he insisted that the television department earn a profit on the first run of series. That meant leaner budgets and a decline in quality. Other studios and television companies offered more first-rate entertainment, and Warner Bros. series were canceled.

Kalmenson convinced Warner to fire his own son-in-law, Bill

Orr, and his partner Hugh Benson from the television department and to hire Jack Webb. (Orr stayed on at the studio and was assigned to produce *Sex and the Single Girl*.) Webb produced no miracles, and Warner Bros. television remained stagnant.

The feature film operation was satisfactory but unspectacular. The Warner Bros. films of the early 1960s lacked the adventurous spirit of those of the 1930s and 1940s. Somehow the company managed to continue showing profits; except for a small blip in 1958, Warner Bros. remained in the black from 1935 to 1964. Stockholders were content, and there appeared no reason why Jack L. Warner would not remain president of the company for life.

His kind of guy, Sinatra was. Not since Jolson did any performer entrance Jack Warner as did Frank Sinatra. With his own frustrations as a performer, Warner recognized and envied the singer's pure talent, as well as his supreme self-confidence and sheer arrogance. Even at times when Sinatra was more difficult than Bogart or Davis had ever been, Warner always sided with him.

Sinatra first came to Warner Bros. in 1954 for *Young at Heart*, a remake with music of *Four Daughters*. His costar was Doris Day in the last film of her Warner Bros. contract. It was made under her production company, which was headed by her husband, Marty Melcher. From the start, Sinatra made no secret of his antipathy toward Melcher.

Sinatra announced that he would not die at the end of the film, as had John Garfield in *Four Daughters*. No amount of persuasion could shake him. Change the ending or I walk, he declared. It was changed.

Shortly after filming started, Sinatra stalked off the set, saying he wouldn't return until the cinematographer was replaced; he took too much time to light the set, the impatient Sinatra decreed. Warner assigned another cinematographer.

Always on the hustle, Marty Melcher tried to induce Sinatra to include in the film songs that Melcher owned. Sinatra ordered him off the set and declared he would leave if Marty Melcher ever appeared at the studio. The message was conveyed to Jack Warner.

Warner issued the order: "Frank Sinatra does not want Marty Melcher around, and I want you to find the lousy bum and run him off the lot and be sure he stays off until this picture is in the can. That's it. Period. An order. Ya got it?"

Sinatra's tardiness plagued *Young at Heart* throughout the filming, but Jack Warner never complained. To him, Sinatra could do no wrong.

Frank Sinatra got in trouble in 1963 for entertaining mobster friends at his Cal-Neva resort at Lake Tahoe. On the day before he was scheduled to answer charges by the Nevada Gaming Board, Sinatra announced he would sell his interest in Cal-Neva as well as his nine percent interest in the Las Vegas Sands. The scandal cast a cloud over the singer, and he needed something to restore his reputation. Jack Warner stepped in to offer a merger of Sinatra's Reprise Records with Warner Bros. Records and a film deal at one million dollars per picture. Sinatra Enterprises moved into an even more luxurious bungalow than Marion Davies'.

Warner was delighted that the studio could boast Sinatra and his ring-a-ding-ding coterie: Dean Martin, Sammy Davis, Jr., Peter Lawford, Joey Bishop. Whenever Jack saw Davis, he broke into a tap dance. "No, you don't have it yet, colonel," Sammy commented.

Sinatra's company made six films for Warner Bros., all of them slapdash because of his insistence on speeding things along. Trouble was inevitable when Robert Aldrich, a strong-willed director related to the Rockefellers, was assigned to *Four for Texas*.

The western was partly filmed on location at Lancaster, north of the San Fernando Valley. Aldrich called for a close-up of Sinatra on top of a stagecoach, with only sky for background. "You could do this on the back lot at Warner Bros.," complained the actor. "Why are you doing this here?"

"Because we have all the equipment set up and ready," the director explained. "It would require a whole new setup to do it on the back lot."

"Yeah, but it's a waste of my time. All you see is the reins and the sky."

The argument grew hotter, and Sinatra walked away from the set, entered his helicopter and flew back to Los Angeles. Aldrich watched him with mounting anger. He turned to Howard W. Koch, who was producing the film for Sinatra's company. "You tell that son of a bitch he'll do what I tell him or he's off the picture," said Aldrich.

"Come on, Bob, you know that Frank Sinatra is not going to be fired from the picture," said Koch placatingly.

Aldrich dispatched a wire to Jack Warner declaring he would not permit such outrageous behavior by an actor. Warner tried to pacify both parties, and he negotiated an arrangement under which director and star would convey their wishes through intermediaries.

Sinatra was unrelenting. When Aldrich ordered a close-up of a completed scene, Sinatra turned to Koch and said, "Nothing doing. He's got to get it the first time."

After a few days, Aldrich complained to Koch that he lacked the camera angles to edit the film properly. Koch offered a solution: install four cameras to photograph each scene from four angles. The rest of *Four from Texas* was filmed that way.

When production was finally completed, Jack Warner told Koch, "That Aldrich is a pain in the ass. I don't want to work with him ever again. I don't even want to see him on the lot again." As Koch was going out the door, Warner added, "Until I need him." (The remark has also been attributed to Harry Cohn.)

Jack Warner had only one outburst at Sinatra. That came after speculation arose that the singer might take over Warner Bros. Warner read such a report in *The Wall Street Journal* one morning as he breakfasted in his Sherry Netherlands apartment with Jackie Park. Warner exploded, and he immediately telephoned Sinatra.

"What is this I'm reading, Frank?" Warner demanded. He recalled how he had rescued Sinatra from the Cal-Neva scandal and warned that he wouldn't stand by if Sinatra or any of his mobster acquaintances tried to muscle in on Warner Bros. "I have friends, too," he added menacingly. (Warner was on friendly terms with

Allan Smiley, the minor mob figure who was sitting on the same couch when a hit man gunned Bugsy Siegel through a Beverly Hills window.)

Sinatra protested that he had nothing to do with the rumors and would never consider replacing Warner as company head. Warner was still furious when he hung up the telephone. Never during his long princedom had there ever been a suggestion that his reign was threatened. He ordered a press release detailing the association of Frank Sinatra and Warner Bros. and emphasizing that Sinatra owned no Warner stock. The release concluded:

"This association, plus the warm friendship that exists between Mr. Sinatra and myself, has led to a certain amount of speculation that I am considering Mr. Sinatra as my successor as president of Warner Bros. Pictures—or that Mr. Sinatra desires to be my successor. There is no evidence or reasons for such speculation."

Despite the brouhaha, Warner resumed his good relations with Sinatra. Warner was in Jackie Park's apartment at Sunset Towers in December of 1963 when he heard that Frank Sinatra, Jr., had been kidnapped and was being held for ransom. Warner immediately telephoned Sinatra and told him: "Look, Frank, I've got three million dollars in cash in the safe at the studio. If you need money in a hurry, you can count on me." Sinatra thanked him but declined the offer.

A Fine Madness was the kind of movie Jack Warner dismissed as "artsy-fartsy." Based on a novel about a New York poet given to fits of violence, it had been brought to Warner Bros. by Seven Arts. Although Warner had little control over creative matters, he still held the purse strings, and he issued his customary jeremiads about economizing.

Warner was appalled when he learned that *A Fine Madness* would require ten days additional shooting beyond the regular schedule. That meant that Sean Connery, then riding the crest of the James Bond films, would receive a paycheck of $50,000 a day.

"No, goddammit, I'm not going to pay any actor fifty grand a day!" he exclaimed. He was convinced that the film would make no sense without the added scenes. He finally agreed, but insisted on five days of filming, not ten.

As soon as he completed his scenes, Connery flew back to England. When he arrived, his agent told him that Warner had decreed, "Don't pay him."

"What do you mean, 'Don't pay him'?" Connery demanded. "It's in my contract!"

"I know," said the agent, "but it's not a good idea to antagonize a big man like Jack Warner."

"Fuck him!" said Connery, his Scottish spirit inflamed. "I'm suing the bastard."

Connery learned that because his contract had been signed in Great Britain, he could sue Warner in an English court, which would not be intimidated by a powerful Hollywood mogul. Shortly before the case was scheduled for trial, Connery received a telephone call from someone he identifies as a " 'dese' and 'dose' guy." Most likely it was Ben Kalmenson.

"Look, Connery, Mr. Warner doesn't want a lot of trouble," said the voice. "I'll make you an offer. You'll get sixty thousand dollars in any currency in the world, deposited in your name."

The fact that he could make a nice profit by avoiding England's tight currency laws did not ameliorate Connery's rage.

"I don't know who you are," he growled, "but I will tell you right now that this conversation is over."

The next day Connery was notified that Warner Bros. would pay him all the money he was owed.

The actor immediately flew to the south of France for a vacation. His James Bond director, Terence Young, invited him to a party —at Jack Warner's villa. Connery warily accepted.

Warner himself swung open the door. "Jack, this is Sean Connery," announced Young.

Warner's eyes narrowed. "I know him. He's the son of a bitch who sued me." Then he flashed the Warner smile and put an arm around Connery's shoulder. "Come on in, kid. Have a drink."

*   *   *

In February 1962, Jack Warner launched the biggest crapshoot of his lifelong gambling career.

He had coveted *My Fair Lady* ever since he had seen it at the New York premiere on March 15, 1956. But William S. Paley, whose CBS owned the musical through a $400,000 investment and buy-outs of Frederick Loewe, Alan Jay Lerner and Moss Hart, shunned all offers for the film rights. For six years Warner persisted. When he visited New York in 1962, he heard that another studio had offered Paley $3.5 million for *My Fair Lady*. Jack hurried to Paley's office at CBS and offered $5.5 million.

"Jack, you got a deal," Paley smiled.

Other studio heads suspected Jack Warner had finally lost his marbles. Five and a half million was an outrageous price for a literary property. Moreover, Paley had exacted stringent terms: fifty percent of the distributor's *gross* (not net) above $20 million, plus ownership of the negative at the end of the contract.

Warner was intensely proud of his achievement. He announced that he would personally produce *My Fair Lady*, marking the first time since the early 1920s that he would receive producer's credit.

Josh Logan was his first choice for director. But when Logan insisted on filming part of *My Fair Lady* in England, Warner cooled. He planned to spend more money than ever before on a Warner Bros. picture, and he wanted it made entirely in Burbank, where he could control costs.

Warner asked George Cukor if he would like to direct *My Fair Lady*. "Yes," Cukor replied, "I think you've made a very intelligent choice."

Warner did not consider casting the musical's original stars. Rex Harrison had never been a box-office star, and Julie Andrews was strictly a Broadway name. Warner tried to induce Cary Grant to play Henry Higgins. "There's only one actor who can play the role, and that's Rex Harrison," Grant replied. "Furthermore, if he isn't in it, I won't go see your picture."

Rex Harrison was signed. Jack Warner reasoned that he needed a top film actress as Eliza Doolittle. Audrey Hepburn, who had just provided Warner Bros. with a hit in *The Nun's Story*, was the logical choice. Warner agreed to pay her a million dollars, the highest salary ever for a Warner Bros. actor.

Warner hoped for another star name as Eliza's errant father, and he sought his old enemy, Jim Cagney. Cagney admired the role of Doolittle, and at parties with close friends he delivered inspired renditions of "Get Me to the Church on Time" and "With a Little Bit of Luck." But he had retired from movies in 1961, and he told George Cukor, "I just can't summon the interest. I really can't." The original Doolittle, Stanley Holloway, was assigned the role.

Cecil Beaton came to Burbank to create the costumes. Photographer to the British royals, Beaton was charmed by Jack Warner's gaucherie, and Warner was pleased with a listener receptive to his jokes. Later Beaton wrote his impressions of Warner:

"His shining teeth stretched wide, his eyebrows high in youthful surprise, his complexion clear and tanned, his hair shining, nut-brown, he caressed the length of his silk tie with well-manicured fingers. He is an amazingly agile figure, and holds himself with such a straight spine that sometimes he almost seems to be toppling backwards. In his yachting jacket and sportive shoes, he has something about his swashbuckling style that reminds me of Douglas Fairbanks, Senior, and the great era of silent movies. . . . in spite of the aura of the vaudeville theater in which his career started, the jocular gags with twirling cigars and schoolboy jokes, one sees that for every good reason he is still the head of one of the few great film empires to survive."

Beaton was able to convince Warner to sit for a series of photographs in the Beaton style. He envisioned Warner as an eastern potentate and posed him in the surroundings of a Turkish seraglio. When he saw the result, Warner ordered all the photos destroyed.

Amazing his underlings, Warner acceded to the extravagances of Cukor, Beaton and set designer Oliver Smith without a whimper. But his patience grew thin as he saw the cost rising to $17 million, the biggest budget for any movie made in Hollywood. After Cukor had completed the Ascot sequence, he decided he needed retakes. Warner argued that they were unnecessary, but Cukor persisted. Warner settled the issue one night by ordering a bulldozer to raze the Ascot set.

Joe Hyams, who was national publicity manager, was placed in charge of the *My Fair Lady* campaign with Warner's instructions: "I want this to be a Tiffany operation. Everything you do must be one-hundred percent style and class, money no object. Just remember: it's a Tiffany product."

For the premiere in October 1964, Hyams planned the splashiest Broadway event in years, attended by all the major cast members. The benefit party afterward, chaired by Mrs. William S. Paley, the Duchess of Windsor and Mrs. Winston Guest, was sure to attract the great names of New York society. Brimming with anticipation, Jack Warner arrived the day before the premiere and took up quarters in the lavish apartment he had long maintained at the Sherry Netherlands Hotel.

Mrs. Paley had planned for Warner to escort her daughter to the premiere and the ball. On the day of the premiere, Mrs. Paley called Hyams to report that her daughter had a cold and would be unable to attend. Hyams met with Warner in the Sherry Netherlands bar in the late morning and told him the news.

"Now Mrs. Paley is worried about your having someone to sit with at the head table," said Hyams.

Warner listened to Hyams' report and glanced around the bar. Seated nearby was an attractive young woman, who appeared to Hyams to be one of the high-class hookers that were allowed to work the hotel as a convenience for guests.

"Come over here, kid," Warner told her. She ambled to his table and sat down. He introduced himself and Hyams, and she ordered a drink, wondering what the Hollywood mogul had in mind.

"What are you doing tonight?" Warner asked, though the answer was predictable. He continued: "I have a movie opening, and I need a date for the evening. Would you like to come?"

The girl kept looking for a joker in his proposal, but found none. "Do you have something nice to wear?" he asked. "Don't worry.

I'll send you over to my friend, Ceil Chapman, the designer. She'll find something for you." He turned to Hyams and gave him instructions to arrange for the gown with Ceil Chapman, hairdressing with Kenneth and whatever else was needed.

"See ya tonight," Warner said. "I'm going upstairs to take a nap."

The girl stared at Hyams and asked, "What's happening?" "You heard the man, he's serious," Hyams replied. Still dumbfounded, she left the hotel in a Warner Bros. limousine.

Before the premiere, Warner hosted a reception for the stars and the charity organizers in his Sherry Netherlands apartment. In the midst of the festivities, the girl in the bar arrived, looking like Eliza Doolittle on the occasion when she could have danced all night. The guests studied the stunning arrival, and Warner hurried over to greet her. She remained by his side as he spoke with his guests.

"Mrs. Paley, this is Lady Cavendish. . . . Duchess, I'd like you to meet Lady Cavendish. . . . Audrey, meet Lady Cavendish."

She nodded smilingly and said little. Everyone accepted her as Lady Cavendish—except Professor Higgins himself. "Who is that girl?" Rex Harrison asked Hyams. "She certainly isn't any Lady Cavendish." Hyams, terrified that the charade would be uncovered, professed ignorance.

Lady Cavendish remained at Warner's side throughout the triumphant premiere and sat with him among the society swells at the ball. As the guests were starting to leave, Warner instructed Hyams: "See that she gets home. And make sure she gets the dress back." He gave her a fatherly kiss, and Hyams escorted her to a limousine.

"What an unbelievable night!" she said as she settled in the cushiony seat. "And you know something? I had such a good time, I'm not going to charge him."

The *My Fair Lady* gamble paid off. The film was a roaring success in theaters, producing a $12-million profit. Reviews were mostly excellent, though many critics lamented that Julie Andrews had not played Eliza. Some felt Audrey Hepburn was unbelievable as the smudge-faced cockney flower girl, and they decried the fact that Marni Nixon's voice had to be dubbed for the songs. That feeling was reflected by Academy voters who failed to nominate Hepburn as best actress. Although Warner was furious and Cukor remarked "I'm sick about it," Audrey made no comment. With her inherent dignity, she agreed to substitute for the ailing Patricia Neal and present the best-actor award at the ceremonies.

Rex Harrison won the Oscar and so did George Cukor as director and *My Fair Lady* as best picture. It was the first best-picture Academy Award for a Warner Bros. film since *Casablanca* nineteen years before. This time Jack Warner didn't need to rush to the stage to beat Hal Wallis. Warner was validated as producer.

"I am indeed gratified to be here tonight," he said. "It is something we will always be proud of, and I speak for those in the back lot, the front lot, upstairs, and downstairs and everywhere."

The winner for best actress was Julie Andrews in her film debut, *Mary Poppins*. Jack Warner himself claimed he voted for her. Some observers believed that Academy voters were swayed less by her performance as the flying nanny and more by sympathy because Warner had failed to cast her as Eliza. A month earlier, Miss Andrews had added fuel to such a belief in her acceptance of a Golden Globe for *Mary Poppins*. With Warner seated in front of her, she delivered the customary thanks and concluded with only a hint of tartness, expressing her gratitude to "Jack Warner for making it all possible."

Chapter 18

Who's Afraid of
Virginia Woolf?

"JACK L. WARNER/DAT JACK L. WARNER/He don't know nothin'/But he must say somethin'/He keeps on yakkin'/ He keeps on yakkin' along."

Dean Martin sang the Sammy Cahn parody at a Friars Club Roast for Warner in April 1965. The speakers and their gag writers took delight in making sport of the guest of honor. Jack Benny remarked that Warner's first choices for the leads of *My Fair Lady* were Ozzie and Harriet Nelson. George Burns said, "I remember Jack Warner when he was gray." Frank Sinatra: "Mr. Warner and his partners have shown this town the true meaning of brotherhood: They were brothers and they were hoods." In his own speech Warner matched insult for insult, laden with non sequiturs and dangling sentences.

At age seventy-three Jack Warner seemed fully able to keep on rolling along. *My Fair Lady* recharged his vast store of energy, and he bristled with fresh plans for exciting projects. He had found a way to absorb the perilous dips in movie revenue: Warner Bros. Records. The idea had come from Rudi Fehr, who was a musicologist as well as Warner's favorite editor. Fehr argued that other companies were making millions from the music of Warner Bros. films and pointed out that MGM, Paramount, Columbia and Universal had record subsidiaries.

"We tried that with Brunswick Records and it didn't work," Warner replied.

"But you bought Brunswick when radio was taking over, and nobody wanted to buy records," Fehr reasoned. "Later people didn't want to wait to hear their favorite records on radio, so they bought them. That's what kids are doing today."

Warner waited eighteen months until he found the right manager. Warner Bros. Records amassed $2 million in losses until Warner appointed Mike Maitland to head the operation. Then it became a money-maker, and it brings in huge profits today.

The Great Race was designed as a large-scale comedy in the vein of *Around the World in 80 Days* and *It's a Mad, Mad, Mad, Mad World*. Blake Edwards had conceived a slapstick story of a vintage car race from New York to Paris. With misgivings about the cost, Warner authorized the production, with Jack Lemmon, Natalie Wood, Tony Curtis and Peter Falk as stars. Warner remained calm through the expensive European locations, including a ball in Vienna that lasted a minute and a half on the screen.

When *The Great Race* returned to Burbank and Edwards continued filming at a deliberate pace, Warner steamed. He ranted that Edwards was trying to bankrupt the studio and decried the purchase of hundreds of pies for a pie-throwing sequence of mammoth proportions. Edwards heard reports that Warner was preparing to "pull the plug" on the movie, and he arranged an audience with the boss. He explained to Warner the problems of foreign locations: weather, language, currency, inexperienced crews.

"Okay, get back to work," Warner grumbled. "But for God's sake, speed it up."

As the cost of *The Great Race* mounted toward $12 million, Warner despaired of Edwards' attempt at speed. One morning the director drove up to the guard gate and was told Mr. Warner had barred his entrance. Another director had been assigned to finish the movie.

Lemmon, Wood and Curtis went on strike. They remained loyal to Blake Edwards and would finish the film with no other director. Warner was furious, but he was forced to allow Edwards to return. Stringent conditions were imposed, and Edwards was unable to complete *The Great Race* as he had conceived it.

Warner's antagonism continued throughout postproduction. The first preview drew a hearty response from the audience, and studio executives were elated. Jack Warner wasn't.

A jubilant Jack Lemmon walked into the men's room after the screening. The lone figure at the urinals was Jack Warner. Lemmon took a position beside him and commented cheerfully, "Seemed to have gone very well, don't you think?"

"Um," Warner replied noncommittally.

"They seemed to be with it all the way, huh?"

"Mmmm," said Warner.

"I mean, it looks like it might be a hit."

Warner zipped his trousers and turned to Lemmon with a stony face. "Look—good, bad or indifferent, that fucker better make a fortune or we're all in a lot of trouble."

Released in October 1965, *The Great Race* grossed $26 million, but according to the studio bookkeeping, it never turned a profit.

Nobody knows why *Who's Afraid of Virginia Woolf?* appealed to Jack Warner as the subject of a movie. Edward Albee's corrosive study of a violent marriage was scarcely Warner's style of entertainment. Yet he had seen the play in New York and had been devastated by it. Perhaps he saw in it a mirror of his own destructive marriage to Ann.

Abe Lastfogel of the William Morris Agency had tried to sell *Virginia Woolf* to the studios as a package, with the Broadway team repeating their functions: Albee as writer, Alan Schneider to direct, and Richard Barr to produce. No takers. Jack Warner and other studio heads were unwilling to entrust a potentially expensive film to stage people.

Lastfogel next tried to interest his client Ernest Lehman in adapting the play. Lehman, a hot screenwriter on the basis of *North by Northwest*, *West Side Story* and other films, had been "indefinably disturbed" on reading *Virginia Woolf* and resisted seeing the play. When he finally did, he was so overwhelmed that he couldn't speak.

Warner bought the screen rights to *Virginia Woolf*, and Lastfogel proposed Lehman as producer and writer. Warner agreed. Lehman, who had never produced a film, was reluctant to assume both duties. But he decided *Virginia Woolf* would be an important and provocative film. He and Lastfogel met with Warner, who agreed to grant Lehman approvals of the cast, director and other particulars. "Subject to my *final* approval," Warner added.

Lehman, who had just finished writing *The Sound of Music*, established his headquarters in a bungalow recently vacated by George Cukor. Jack Warner visited him to suggest Patricia Neal as Martha and Cukor as director. "I'll let you know when I make up my mind," Lehman replied.

As he wrote the script, Lehman received phone calls and messages from agents proposing their clients for the lead roles. Burt Lancaster telephoned and asked to be considered as George. (Edward Albee had told Lehman that he preferred Bette Davis and James Mason.) Lehman was considering Elizabeth Taylor for Martha.

"What are you talking about?" Jack Warner exclaimed. "Elizabeth Taylor is too young, too beautiful, all wrong for the role."

"We'll age her." Lehman replied. "She'll be great."

"Besides, she'll want a million dollars. We gotta make this picture at a price."

"We can get Sidney Guilaroff to make some gray wigs, have her put on some weight, pad her dresses," Lehman countered. "In the play Martha is fifty-two. She doesn't *have* to be fifty-two. She could be in her forties. Things that go wrong in marriages can happen in twelve years as well as twenty."

"All right, what do you want me to say?" said Warner.

"I want you to say yes."

"All right," Warner said grimly. "Yes." Lehman still marvels that Warner could have made such a radical decision in an instant.

Elizabeth Taylor had finished interiors for *The Sandpiper* in France, and she read the script on the train to the northern California locations. Richard Burton insisted that she must do *Virginia Woolf*, arguing that it would be *her Hamlet* (he had recently completed *his*). She finally accepted the challenge. Though Jack Warner grumbled that he had wanted to hold the budget to $3 million, he agreed to pay Taylor $1.2 million for her services. She also was given costar and director approval.

Lehman prepared a list of ten potential Georges, including Jack Lemmon, Peter O'Toole and Arthur Hill, who had originated the role on Broadway. Not included was Richard Burton, because Lehman feared the expectable media exploitation of a husband and wife, especially "Liz & Dick," playing George and Martha. He met with the Burtons in their Beverly Hills Hotel bungalow and went over the list with Elizabeth as Richard looked quietly on.

"I wouldn't even go to see a picture with *him* in it," Elizabeth scoffed at one of the names. She pointed to her husband. "What about him?"

"Richard is one of the world's greatest actors," said Lehman, concealing his embarrassment, "but I think he's too strong for the role."

"Look, luv," Burton told Lehman, employing an odd metaphor for a Welshman, "if you don't get who you want, I'll always be in the bull pen, ready to come into the game."

After the Burtons returned to Europe, Lehman became convinced that Burton would make an ideal George. He took his decision to Warner, who balked, claiming the budget couldn't afford him. Lehman kept talking until finally Warner agreed—"but you gotta tell Hugh French to cooperate this time." French, agent for both Burtons, asked for $750,000 plus a percentage. Warner screamed, but acquiesced.

Lehman flew to Europe to discuss a director with the Burtons. Over champagne-drenched dinners they considered numerous candidates. One young director had announced he wanted to make *Virginia Woolf* but only if his name was above the title. "Fuck him," Richard blurted out. "If that's how much he wants to do this picture, fuck him," Elizabeth agreed. Elizabeth suggested Henri Clouzot. "Ridiculous," said Burton. "Why don't you direct it, Ernie?" said Richard. "I wouldn't do that to you or Edward Albee; I've never directed," Lehman said.

Lawrence Turman, who had already signed Mike Nichols to direct *The Graduate*, called Lehman in Paris to say that Nichols was interested in directing *Virginia Woolf*. Lehman sparked to the idea of Nichols, and so did the Burtons.

Lehman returned to California with the Burtons' list of approved directors, Nichols' name on top. Lehman marshaled his arguments for Jack Warner. Drawbacks: it was going to be an expensive film; Nichols had never directed a movie; he was known for directing comedy in the theater. Assets: he could control the Burtons; his reputation would give the picture an aura of distinction.

Again Jack Warner made a daring decision: yes.

Warner suggested Sandy Dennis for the role of the young wife. She tested well, and both Lehman and Nichols agreed to the casting. Robert Redford as the young husband was first choice of Lehman and Nichols, who had directed him on the stage in *Barefoot in the Park*. Redford decided at that stage in his career it would be suicidal to play a character who is emasculated by the three other members of the cast. George Segal, whom Nichols had directed in *The Knack*, was the final choice.

There is another aspect to the filming of *Who's Afraid of Virginia Woolf?* that, unbeknownst to any of the participants, was to prove historical. Jack L. Warner became the unwitting leader of a revolution as profound in its ramifications as the one he and his brothers had perpetrated forty years before.

By the mid-sixties the administrators of the Production Code were struggling against a tidal wave of changing morality. A new breed of filmmakers was howling for the liberty that their European brethren had long enjoyed. Still, the thirty-year-old Code was enforced like the papal codex and supported by the aging leaders of the industry.

As early as 1963, the industry censors had reviewed the *Virginia Woolf* play script and found it wanting in a hundred ways. Their objections included the entire situation of "hump the hostess," the forbidden profanities—"for crissake" and "goddamn"—as well as such Albee phrases as "monkey nipples" and "angel tits."

Ernest Lehman's screenplay was submitted to the Production Code, as were all scripts of major studios. The answer came back that Lehman's script had just as much vulgarity, profanity and sexual language as the play. But, according to procedure, no ruling would be made until the final film was submitted.

The Producers Association, which administered the Code, had been leaderless for a year and a half after the death of Eric Johnston. In the spring of 1966, the company heads decided on a successor: Jack J. Valenti, special advisor to President Johnson. Valenti met his new bosses on June 1, 1966, at the Producers Association's New York office on Fifth Avenue. Among those present were Lew Wasserman, Spyros Skouras, Barney Balaban, Arthur Krim, Abe Schneider, Darryl Zanuck and Jack Warner. Valenti especially wanted to meet the legendary Zanuck and Warner. He found Zanuck in a disgruntled mood, but Warner was expansive.

"Kid, I'm going to give you a piece of advice," said Warner with a broad grin. "You're gonna be able to handle all the problems in this job without any trouble. But I'll tell ya, the biggest fucking problem you'll have are these guys sitting around this table."

He laughed, gave Valenti a bear hug and went back to his seat with a cheerful, "Don't forget what I told you, kid."

Valenti traveled to California to present his credentials to the creative community at a meeting in the Beverly Hilton Hotel. A compact, blunt-faced man prone to florid phrases, he dedicated himself to the cause of artistic freedom and creative excellence. He added a Churchillian warning: "I did not take the job of President of the Motion Picture Association to preside over a feckless Code."

Just a few months hence, Valenti would be facing Jack Warner in a struggle that would determine just how feckless the Code would be.

The *Virginia Woolf* explosions started early.

Elizabeth Taylor discovered her contract did not stipulate that she could arrive on the set at ten o'clock in the morning instead of nine. She threatened to fire her agent, Hugh French, and he pleaded with Lehman to rectify the issue. "I'll give her what she wants, but not in writing; she'll have to accept a gentleman's agreement," said Jack Warner. "Oh, no," said Elizabeth, "I'll be damned if I'll ever expose myself to a suit for nonappearance." Her contract was changed.

Warner called Lehman and Nichols to his office for a conference on the script's language. Nichols and Lehman fought against any excisions and managed to save everything except two "Jesus Christs" and one "goddamn." At the end of the conference, Warner dropped a bombshell.

"Benny Kalmenson tells me that many exhibitors have agreed to show the picture as a road show under the condition that it is in color," he said.

Lehman and Nichols were shocked. They had fought that battle a month before, arguing that the whole picture took place at night, that Taylor's makeup and costumes would look phony in color, and that the dramatic power of the film would be dissipated by color.

"I won't do the picture in color," Nichols declared. "The critics would destroy it. The whole thing would be obscene in color."

"All right, don't worry," said Warner, backing off. "Make the tests in black and white tomorrow. Then we'll have enough ammunition to change Kalmenson's mind."

Harry Stradling, who had been hired to photograph *Virginia Woolf*, shot the black-and-white tests. After seeing them, Warner said he would like some tests in color as well. Nichols and Lehman, who thought they had won the battle, were aroused. Nichols said he saw no reason for color tests since he would not make the film in color.

"Now wait a minute, Mike, don't talk like that," Warner cautioned. "You're a professional, and I'm a professional. You know that I could *tell* you to shoot it in color. But I'm not that kind of fellow."

The argument continued for thirty minutes, with Nichols implying that the Burtons had signed on with *Virginia Woolf* with the understanding that it would be in black and white. Warner realized he was on dangerous ground. "I'm on your side, fellas," he said. "You know I want this picture to be in black and white. I have to find a way of convincing Benny."

He called Kalmenson in New York. Kalmenson's blustery voice could be heard ranting against Warner's arguments. Warner seemed embarrassed that he as president of the company could not override his underling. They talked for twenty minutes, and Kalmenson was unyielding. Lehman took the phone, but he had no better luck.

"You can talk for four thousand years and not change my mind," Kalmenson ranted. "Anyone doing a black-and-white movie nowadays is setting the business back twenty years."

Warner returned to the phone and mentioned that the Burtons had agreed to make *Virginia Woolf* in black and white; any change might upset the applecart. Kalmenson's arguments ceased. The battle had been won in absentia by Elizabeth Taylor and Richard Burton. Everyone was relieved, including Warner. He was leaving for France, and he wanted nothing to interfere with his summer vacation.

Another crisis occurred. Mike Nichols and Harry Stradling clashed over the low-key photography. "If that's the kind of picture you want, I don't want my name on it," said Stradling. "I'm too rich and too old to put up with this kind of crap." Nichols and Lehman took the matter to Jack Warner. "I knew this would happen," said Warner. "Get a new cameraman." Haskell Wexler was chosen even though Burton complained to Lehman, "He'll make my pockmarks look like craters on the moon."

Nichols rehearsed the four actors for three weeks, an unusual concession by Jack Warner. Warner departed for the Riviera on

July 21, and filming began five days later. After a month in Burbank, the company left for locations at Smith College in Massachusetts. When Warner returned from Europe, he called Lehman to a meeting at the Sherry Netherlands with Ben Kalmenson. Warner was worried about the schedule.

"If you go into overtime," he said, "then I would rather be an actor instead of president of the company, because that's where the money is." Taylor was scheduled to be paid $100,000 a week for overtime, Burton $75,000 a week.

Warner returned to Burbank and saw the first four reels of *Virginia Woolf.* He was ecstatic. He telephone his praise to Lehman, who spread the news through the company. The Burtons were so pleased that they agreed to work overtime without pay. Warner was overjoyed.

Filming resumed in Burbank. Warner's elation over the overtime pay was offset by Nichols's deliberate pace. Warner summoned Nichols and Lehman to discuss seven pages of script that had been added. Warner expounded on how the film had already gone over budget and schedule. But Taylor had insisted that the pages were needed to help explain her character, and Warner gave in.

"Can't you do less shooting and get the picture done faster?" Warner pleaded.

"I'm going as fast as I can," Nichols replied. "If you can find anyone to shoot it faster, I'll be happy to be relieved."

"No, no, forget it," said Warner, declining to call Nichols' bluff.

Warner continued fretting over Nichols' pace of filming, and a few days later he suggested that Lehman send a stern memo to the director. "I think you should send it yourself," the producer said. "I'll even write it for you, and you can sign it." Lehman prepared a strongly worded memo to himself and Nichols. Warner recoiled when he read it.

"I can't sign that—people will think I'm an ogre," Warner said. Lehman was amazed. Jack Warner concerned that he might be considered an ogre? Jack Warner, who had suspended actors by the carload, fired directors at will, double-crossed his own brother, ruled a film empire with cunning and stealth? It seemed late in life for him to be concerned with image problems. In the end, Warner sent the memo.

On December 13, 1965, Mike Nichols called "Cut!" for the last time.

Nichols: "This picture is officially over."

Lehman: "Mike, you've directed your first picture."

Nichols: "I think I'm going to cry."

Taylor: "I can't believe it's over."

Burton: "I think I'll have a drink."

A bar and buffet offered refreshment for the cast and crew, and a jukebox added to the revelry. Jack Warner appeared, and he posed for triumphant photographs with the *Virginia Woolf* principals. Amid all the hoopla, Elizabeth flashed her green eyes at Warner and said, "You know, Jack, all my producers give me presents at the end of a picture. I would just love to have a diamond brooch to go with my earrings."

Warner, who never liked to be asked for a beneficence, bristled. "Look, honey, I gave you a million dollars, and I gave your husband three-quarters of a million," he replied. "That's enough."

The matter didn't end there. In the weeks that followed, Elizabeth continued with her request. In his elation over seeing a final cut of *Virginia Woolf*, Warner agreed to buy her a diamond necklace. In a handwritten note from the *Taming of the Shrew* set in Rome, she thanked him and included the address of her favorite jeweler, David Webb. She concluded, "Don't lose it now! Much love, Elizabeth."

The *Virginia Woolf* battles weren't over.

Jack Warner imposed a rush schedule on Nichols' editing because the negative had to be out of California by March 1, after which the state imposed a tax on unreleased films. Nichols rebelled against such a stringent schedule, threatening to return to New York and give out interviews detailing what had happened. Warner relented on the tax deadline but urged speed.

Nichols proceeded with his editing, and he listened to the themes Alex North played on the piano. Nichols disapproved, and without informing Lehman, he reiterated his earlier request that North be replaced by Andre Previn. Warner recoiled at such a challenge to his authority. Both he and Lehman wanted North. Not only would a change of composer slow completion of *Virginia Woolf*, it would also add $30,000 or more to the budget, which had ballooned to $7.5 million. He ordered Nichols removed from the picture. Rudi Fehr convinced Warner to rescind the order.

Still, Warner was agitated over Nichols' actions. He, Jack Warner, continued to be president of Warner Bros. The name remained on the water tower. No director was going to tell him to replace a composer, or anything else. Mike Nichols would be allowed only two more days of editing. Warner refused to meet with Nichols. The decision was final.

On Friday, February 11, Nichols started editing at 8 a.m. in an attempt to complete his last scene. He asked Lehman to plead for permission for him to work on Saturday without pay. Lehman agreed to try.

When Warner saw Lehman approach him in the dining room, he exclaimed, "More intrigue? We oughta shelve the picture and release the intrigue." He rejected Lehman's plea on behalf of Nichols, declaring his own integrity had been threatened.

Lehman sadly informed Nichols that not only his days but his hours were numbered. That evening Nichols collected his belongings and left the studio.

Next, the censorship war.

The Production Code people reviewed *Virginia Woolf* and were appalled. Yes, it was powerful drama, but the language! Elizabeth Taylor in full close-up bawling "Screw you!" Richard Burton suggesting an evening's recreation of "hump the hostess"! As well as a plethora of language that had never been heard in an American movie. Warner Bros. was defying the very structure of the Production Code, Jack Valenti was told, and its collapse was threatened.

Valenti conferred with Louis Nizer, who had been hired as general counsel of the Producers Association, and both agreed a confrontation with Jack Warner was necessary. They flew west with firm resolve.

Warner greeted them warmly in his office, embracing Valenti with the comment, "We're fortunate to have a leader like you in our industry." He also had an affectionate welcome for "my old friend Louie Nizer."

Seated in a corner was a glum Ben Kalmenson, his stubby body poised for the offensive. Valenti and Nizer soon found themselves in a good cop-bad cop scene worthy, except for its comic aspects, of *Dragnet*. Warner played the Jack Webb role, kind and conciliatory. Kalmenson was the aggressor.

"I've got to talk to you about *Virginia Woolf*," Valenti began. "There is language in the film that we've never had on the screen before. Jack, I'm calling on you as a statesman and a founder of this business. Take this stand with me and remove all the foul language."

"I must say, Jack, if you feel this way about it," Warner said earnestly, "I want to do my duty. I consider myself as someone who cares deeply about the industry and my country."

Valenti felt a warm surge of accomplishment, believing the issue to be resolved. Then came the attack.

Kalmenson leaped to his feet and stood behind Warner.

"This is the goodamndest thing I ever heard!" he shouted at the astonished Valenti and Nizer. "What're you talking about? That fucking language, everybody uses it. You say we're not gonna have sex in this thing? You commie bastards come in here and try to tell us how to run our fucking business?"

Valenti was too shocked to speak, a rare occurrence for him. Warner looked at Kalmenson with a beatific expression, "like a choirboy gazing at a foul-mouthed motorcycle gang member," Valenti recalls.

"Benny, you shouldn't talk that way to Mr. Valenti and Mr. Nizer," Warner said calmly.

"Whadya mean I shouldn't talk that way?" Kalmenson demanded. "Goddamn it, I'm laying it on the line. We're not gonna fuck around."

The charade continued for half an hour. Whenever Valenti made a statement, Warner agreed with him, only to have Kalmenson explode in obscenities. Valenti soon realized he was being intimidated, Warner escaping with white gloves unsoiled while Kalmenson wielded the tar brush.

Finally Nizer intervened, asking Warner, "Jack, can we find some middle ground here?"

Warner to Valenti: "Do you have any middle ground? I want to be with you, but I can't ignore what Benny is saying."

Valenti: "Let's figure out how we can soften this. Would you be willing to take some words out?"

Warner said he would, but Kalmenson blustered, "Absolutely not! We won't take out one fucking word." Valenti was both furious and admiring. He felt like punching out Kalmenson, yet he had to marvel at Warner's mastery of politics, superior to anything Valenti had witnessed in Texas or Washington. He thought to himself, "So that's how the son of a bitch has run the studio and survived all these years: he's always had a Mr. Bad Guy at his side."

Finally Valenti said, "Jack, I'm not going to leave this room until we work something out. Otherwise I'm going to the press and denounce you, and especially Kalmenson. Now you can have it either way."

The solution was reached. The four men spent an hour poring over the script, bargaining one "screw" for another. Warner was allowed to keep "hump the hostess" in return for removal of a "screw" synonym. In the end two "screws" and "hump the hostess" stayed in, three "screws" and the synonym were removed. Kalmenson protested throughout, denouncing Warner for acquiescing. Valenti feels certain that after he and Nizer left the meeting, Warner probably turned to Kalmenson and smiled, "Ben, you get the Academy Award."

Afterward Valenti told Nizer: "I'm not going through that again. I'm not going to spend my life sitting in movie-set offices and saying, 'I gotta take out one "shit" and one "screw." ' This is crazy. I'm not gonna do it." And so he introduced the rating system, which would grant freedom to filmmakers while warning parents about content that might be objectionable for children.

"The guy who ought to be called the father of the rating system," says Valenti, "is Jack Warner."

Before the rating system was installed, Warner voluntarily announced that *Virginia Woolf* would be restricted to adults only; all theater contracts would prohibit sales of tickets to those under eighteen.

Virginia Woolf was a huge success, both with audiences and critics. The Academy gave it thirteen nominations. Elizabeth Taylor promised Jack Warner she would attend the ceremonies, but Burton was outraged that she would go without him. She was torn between defying her husband, who was also nominated but couldn't attend because of a film schedule, and breaking her promise to Jack Warner.

Warner pleaded with Taylor not to offend the Hollywood community nor himself by failing to appear. "Don't burn the bridges you have built," he cabled to Europe. In the end she sided with her husband. She won the Oscar; Burton didn't.

Chapter 19

Goodbye to All That

J. L. Warner sells interest in Warner Bros.

The news struck the movie world like a thunderclap. Warner Bros. without Jack Warner? Inconceivable. Yet on November 14, 1966, Warner announced plans to sell his 1.6 million shares, one-third of all Warner Bros. stock, to Seven Arts Productions for twenty dollars a share. The total sale would be $32 million. Seven Arts had been a latecomer to films. Headed by Eliot Hyman and his son Kenneth, the company had profited from sales of movies to television, and then moved into the backing of such films as *Moulin Rouge, Moby Dick, West Side Story, The World of Suzie Wong* and *Lolita*.

Warner made it clear that he was not vacating as president of Warner Bros.—yet. While the Seven Arts deal was being completed, he would continue as company president, and he was personally producing another Lerner-Loewe musical, *Camelot*. In the summer of 1967, he would become vice chairman of Warner Bros. and an independent producer for the company.

Why was he selling out? Industry observers and even those close to him pondered the question.

"It isn't fun anymore," he complained to Bill Orr. "Casting a picture is a pain in the ass nowadays; I've got to deal with all those fucking agents." He also hinted that at seventy-four, it was time to get his estate in order.

Many believed that Ben Kalmenson played Iago to Warner's Prince, wheedling him into a fatal decision. Kalmenson had much to gain. He would succeed Warner as president of Warner Bros. Some of Kalmenson's enemies believed he had connived with Seven Arts to maneuver the sellout in return for his own exalted position.

"Warner was talked into selling by Kalmenson," declares Max Bercutt, the studio's publicity chief. "Ben kept feeding him stories of how bad the picture business was going to be. If Warner had held out for a couple of years, he could have sold his shares for seventy dollars instead of twenty. I asked him if he regretted that. He said, 'What's a few million, more or less?' But I really think selling broke his heart."

Kalmenson had found an ally in his campaign for Warner to sell. Ann Warner had been urging her husband to slow down his work pace and also to get his estate in order. Without prudent planning, she argued, his wealth would be plundered by tax collectors and disgruntled relatives.

Jack Warner didn't miss a beat after announcing the sale. He continued commanding the studio, though there were signs of his eroding control. Warren Beatty brought him a project based on the violent lives of the 1930s desperadoes Bonnie Parker and Clyde Barrow. Walter MacEwen and Robert Solo, Warner's assistants, thought the script was extraordinary and urged the boss to undertake the film.

Warner was against it. He knew that both United Artists and Columbia had rejected *Bonnie and Clyde*. Beatty himself proposed producing it, and Warner was dead set against actors as producers. Besides, he was still angry with Beatty for refusing to play Jack Kennedy in *PT 109*. Warner had also sought Beatty for *Youngblood Hawke*. After repeated refusals, the actor agreed to the film and then changed his mind shortly before production started. James Franciscus played the role.

"I don't like the idea of dames shooting guns," Warner declared.

"It's a *gangster* movie," Beatty argued. "Warner Bros. was *built* on gangster movies."

"Yeah, but we didn't have dames shooting guns."

Beatty would not be resisted. He pleaded, he cajoled, he used every actor's trick to sway his audience. "For God's sake, Warren," Jack pleaded, "I've got other business to deal with." Beatty would not leave the office. He continued his pitch until Warner exclaimed, "All right, damn it. What is the picture going to cost?"

"A million and a half," said Beatty.

"Will you give me a letter in that regard?"

"Sure."

"Okay, make the damn picture. Now will you leave?"

Warner fretted throughout the location filming of *Bonnie and Clyde*. The reports from Texas were skimpy. "What the hell are they doing down there?" he demanded. The rushes came to the studio, and he hated them.

When filming extended beyond its schedule, Warner exclaimed, "That's it! Pull the plug! Let 'em finish it on the back lot." Beatty protested, but Warner remained firm. The final two weeks of *Bonnie and Clyde* were filmed in Burbank.

When Arthur Penn presented a final assembly of *Bonnie and Clyde*, Warner hated it. He continued hating the picture until it started drawing huge crowds at the theaters. He said smilingly, "*Now* I like it."

Warner never did receive the letter from Beatty about the cost of *Bonnie and Clyde*. The final figure was $2.3 million.

To Jack Warner, Audrey Hepburn was everything that an actress should be: brilliant, charming, and untroublesome. He welcomed her back to the studio for *Wait Until Dark*, produced by her husband, Mel Ferrer. The film was based on a hit play about a blind woman who is menaced by hoodlums in search of narcotics hidden by her husband in their apartment.

While Ferrer was preparing *Wait Until Dark* at the studio, Warner invited him to lunch in the executive dining room. Ferrer sat next to Francis Coppola, a fledgling director, and both were awed by Warner's exercise of his waning power and by the banality of his jokes. Warner asked Ferrer, "Hey, kid, who do you want to direct your picture?"

When Ferrer replied with the name "Terence Young," Warner grumbled, "You better come and talk to me in my office. I'm not gonna say what I think about Terence Young in front of all these people." In his office Warner flatly refused to hire Young.

"Absolutely not!" he declared. "I have a house near his in the south of France; he's always over at the casino; he's going to gamble with my money; he's going to go way over budget. Don't even talk about the schedule. I know what he did on the last few pictures: he went way over schedule. Be sensible. Be reasonable. Forget Terence Young."

Ferrer argued that before Young had directed the first two James Bond films, *Dr. No* and *From Russia with Love*, he had made stylish, suspenseful movies. "He knows the camera and he knows suspense; he'd be ideal for *Wait Until Dark*," Ferrer said. In the end his arguments prevailed.

Although the film was being made by the Ferrers' independent company, Warner still insisted on maintaining control. He clashed with the Ferrers and Young over the wardrobe and whether Audrey should wear opaque contact lenses to convey her blindness. While in New York, Warner dispatched an angry telegram to Walter MacEwen:

"Sometimes I think and believe these independent goniffs think I am still head of the Bon Ton Woolen and Underwear Company. Why is it so hard to convince people for their own good [in matters] such as wardrobe and blindness effect? Read Mel, Audrey & Terence this telegram. . . . This picture not being made on London's Carnaby Street. Again, if Audrey not photographed as being blind otherwise we destroying great picture. We insist stop this nonsense. Teletype that tests are being made today, that Terence everybody understands as we are financing huge sum because I bought play. Why must I go through this when I know they are wrong?"

The imperious studio boss underestimated the stubborn Dutch will of his favorite star. Audrey was convinced that she alone knew what looked best on her celebrated form, and she insisted on the dresses she had selected. She hated the idea of wearing contact lenses, which she considered an actressy, prosthetic device. Having researched with the blind at The Lighthouse in New York, she believed she could convey blindness by not looking directly at persons she talked to. Warner acquiesced.

Ferrer had been warned by an old Warner hand: "If you ever get a call on the set from Jack Warner, first go to your office and put your stuff into your briefcase, because that means you're off the lot." One morning on the *Wait Until Dark* stage, a white-faced assistant reported to Ferrer: "The boss is on the phone!" While everyone watched with apprehension, Ferrer listened to Warner's voice: "Listen, kid, I just wanna tell ya that I saw the rushes and everybody looks wonderful. That's all. Keep up the good work." His enthusiasm was fueled by the fact that Young was already two days ahead of schedule.

Toward the end of filming, Warner called again. "You probably read the papers, so you know I sold the studio. . . . I'm sick of it; I'm not feeling so hot; I got a great price. Aw, forget it. Just wanted to let you know I'm not the boss anymore. Finish up the show. It's your baby now. You did a great job. Don't tell that Terence Young I said so, but you picked the right guy for the job."

Even though Warner no longer exercised control, Ferrer and Young arranged a screening of the edited *Wait Until Dark* for him. Jack remained alert throughout, commenting only in the climactic scene in which the hoodlum, Alan Arkin, leaps in the dark to grab Audrey by the ankle. "Why is that such a wide shot?" Warner asked. "It seems all wrong to me."

Ferrer explained what the stage producers had learned: that if the burglar grabbed the blind woman in one leap, the audience would see only a blur. But if he jumped once, then bent his knee and jumped again, the audience screamed. Warner was dubious until he attended the preview. When the scene evoked shrieks of terror for almost a minute, Warner rose from his seat, glanced to

Ferrer at the other end of the row and flashed him an emphatic okay sign.

Josh Logan was not going to make the same mistake that cost him *My Fair Lady*. When Warner spoke to him about directing *Camelot*, Logan swore he would shoot the entire film on the Burbank lot if Warner so decreed. They reached an agreement and started to discuss casting. Despite his humiliation at the hands of Julie Andrews, Warner suggested her to repeat her Broadway role as Guinevere.

"No," Logan replied. "She was never right for Guinevere. Get a great actress, a beautiful one, a girl who can sing, a ravishing bitch." He also rejected Warner's suggestion for Richard Burton to play the King Arthur role he had created on the stage. Those were the first two mistakes on *Camelot*.

Logan went to England to cast the film, and he chose Vanessa Redgrave for Guinevere and Richard Harris for King Arthur. For Lancelot, he selected a little-known Italian actor, Franco Nero. None of the trio was a singer.

Alan Jay Lerner wrote the script, and a young Australian, John Truscott, created the costumes and scenic design. Still weighted with his studio duties, Warner brought in Joel Freeman to assist him. Freeman had come to Warner Bros. as assistant to Dore Schary on *Sunrise at Campobello* and had stayed to help oversee *The Music Man*. Freeman asked if his title on *Camelot* would be producer or associate producer. Warner would allow no one else to have a producer credit. He tried to persuade Freeman to accept "Assistant to the Producer."

"Only if my name is the same size as yours," the young man said. To his surprise, Warner agreed.

After analyzing the script, Freeman told Warner that it was too long and two numbers should be eliminated. "Tell that to Alan," Warner said. Lerner agreed to the cuts; Logan did not. On his knees before Warner's desk, he pleaded to retain Lerner's original script. Warner relented.

Afterward, Freeman asked Warner: "Why give in? It'll mean a four-hour movie, and something will have to be cut?"

"Come'ere," Warner instructed. "Look out the window and what do you see?"

"A water tower."

"What does it say on the tower?"

"It says 'Warner Brothers.' "

"When it says 'Freeman Brothers,' we'll do it your way."

The start of filming was delayed because Vanessa Redgrave had a contract to appear in *The Prime of Miss Jean Brodie* on the London stage. Warner grew impatient, especially with the end of the company's fiscal year approaching. If *Camelot* didn't start before that date, Warner Bros. would lose a tax advantage. "Do we really have to wait for that tall pinko dame?" Warner asked.

That was the opening Logan had been waiting for. He said he could start—if Warner would allow him to shoot scenes in Spain of Lancelot's quest, as well as the joust between Lancelot and King Arthur. Warner reluctantly agreed. He later issued a memo ordering that all members of the *Camelot* company flying between Los Angeles and Spain should travel the polar route, not via New York—"I want people to go to and from their jobs without any stopovers."

The rain in Spain and the jumbled logistics caused delays on the location, and Jack Warner dispatched pleas for Logan to hurry along. The company finally returned to Burbank in time for Miss Redgrave's arrival. She came full of ideas. At first she wanted to wear the same costume throughout the film; she was dissuaded by Logan who pointed out the story's time span of twenty-four years. Once she translated a key song into French, saying it would be a lark to sing it to Lancelot in his native language. She was advised that neither Jack Warner nor Alan Jay Lerner would approve.

Warner was disturbed by reports of Richard Harris's high jinks on the set. There were stories of the actor's afternoon boozing, and Warner shuddered with memories of the late Errol Flynn. When Harris was summoned for a bathtub scene, he walked out of his dressing room naked with a full-scale erection. Everyone, including Redgrave, thought it was hilarious. Jack Warner did not.

After Harris fell in the shower and cut his forehead, Warner was convinced that his King Arthur was malingering. He ordered a full investigation. It was reported that Harris had attended a party at the Logans' house even though he claimed to be ill. Harris remained absent from *Camelot* for a week. He claimed that Warner had called him a lying, drunken crook, and he refused to return until Warner apologized.

It was either apologize or stall the movie indefinitely. Warner sent Harris an uncharacteristic telegram: "It is with much regret that I learned of the complications that have happened to you in the past few days. I am deeply in sympathy with you not only as a producer but as a human being. If there is anything we can do to get you back on the high road, we will do it. . . ." Harris returned to *Camelot*.

Warner plotted his revenge. As soon as there was enough footage to complete the picture, he pulled the plug. Logan pleaded that he had two more weeks to film. "Finish tonight," he was told. The company worked until early morning and then disbanded. Logan was confident he would be recalled for more shooting. He wasn't.

Logan's muddled direction and the miscasting of the leads inspired scathing reviews, and *Camelot* performed poorly as a roadshow attraction, though it improved in general release. The $14.5-million cost was not recovered. Jack Warner's dream of a melodic finish to his Warner Bros. career went unrealized.

Albert Warner died at his Miami Beach mansion on the day *Camelot* was released, November 26, 1967, having reached his eighty-fourth year. The major, as he preferred to be called, had lived all his life in the shadow of his brothers Harry and Jack. He didn't seem to mind. He was content to let them hog the spotlight, while he quietly tended to the company's financial matters with an acuity that earned him the title of Honest Abe.

While Harry raced his horses in California and Jack played the tables on the Riviera, Albert preferred to sun at Miami Beach, where he first bought a home in 1938 on what later became the site of the Eden Roc hotel. He and his second wife, Bessie—the first Bessie had died in 1922—spent every winter in Florida. Albert had no children.

Albert's service with Warner Bros. ended in 1955, when the brothers sold out their interests only to have Jack stage his flip-flop and remain as president. Unlike Harry, Albert did not rage over his younger brother's perfidy. Albert was sixty-nine years old and happy to be relieved of his role as arbiter between his two warring brothers.

Jack and Albert rarely saw each other except at corporate meetings; Albert remained a member of the Warner Bros. board. By the end of Albert's life they had nothing in common except a mutual history and blood.

When Jack Warner was told that Ronald Reagan planned to run for governor of California, he commented, "No, no. *Dennis Morgan* for governor. Ronald Reagan for best friend."

It became Jack Warner's most famous quip and almost compensated for the thousands of bum jokes he told over the years. Warner's humor was unfailing as he edged into his new status at Warner Bros. Yet there were signs of discontent behind the clownish facade. As part of his agreement with Seven Arts, he was allowed to keep his office. But the barbershop and the executive dining room, where he had also conducted his princeship, were gone.

The new owners were respectful of the founder in residence, but they rarely consulted him. Eliot Hyman had installed his son Kenneth in the job Jack Warner had held for so long. Kenneth was thirty-nine years old, a handsome man who had enjoyed the high-life pleasures of Europe, where he had supervised Seven Arts films. He was everything that Jack Warner wasn't: college educated, sophisticated, elegantly mannered.

Kenneth Hyman launched a series of films that reflected his

tastes, which inclined toward the European and the esoteric. Most of them were failures, and some were never released. But Warner Bros.—Seven Arts continued to profit, largely because of the films Jack Warner had overseen or set in motion: *Bonnie and Clyde, Cool Hand Luke, Wait Until Dark, Reflections in a Golden Eye, Hotel, Up the Down Staircase, Bullitt.*

Warner was eager to fulfill his contract as independent producer for Warner Bros.—Seven Arts. He became interested in a historical novel, *The Frontiersman*, based on the life of George Rogers Clark, the Revolutionary War leader who fought the Indians to gain the Illinois and Kentucky territories for the colonies. The company paid $300,000 for the book, and Warner hired a veteran screen-writer. When Warner presented a script, Kenneth Hyman found reasons not to film it. "The Seven Arts people had thrown Jack a bone," said one of his associates.

Two years after buying Warner Bros., Seven Arts sold it to Kinney National Service, a conglomerate that specialized in parking lots and funeral parlors. The price was more than twice what Seven Arts had paid for the company.

"To hell with it," Jack Warner said. "I'm not going to stay around here any longer." He told Bill Schaefer to start packing.

Warner decided to remove everything, including the films in his private vault. Many of them were family movies of Ann playing tennis, Barbara swimming in the pool, children's parties and the like. Warner watched them in the projection room with no hint of emotion. "Out! Out! Burn 'em!" he instructed Schaefer. When the secretary protested, Warner said, "I don't want 'em. Nobody's interested." He seemed to be tossing a large part of his personal life into the studio incinerator.

On Warner's last day at the studio, Schaefer and his assistant Tom Murphy were busy removing all the photographs and awards from the walls of the office and the trophy room next to the former executive dining room. The photos offered a rich slice of Warner Bros. history: Jack and Zanuck with their new star, Rin-Tin-Tin; Charlie Chaplin and Doug Fairbanks gagging it up with Barrymore on the set of *Beau Brummel*; Jack and Jolson on the set of *The Jazz Singer*; Jack and his father Albert with Einstein; Jack and Ann at a movie premiere with Irving Thalberg and Norma Shearer; Jack in poses with Kennedy, Mountbatten, Montgomery, J. Edgar Hoover, Franklin Roosevelt; Jack with his *My Fair Lady* stars.

Schaefer and Murphy piled everything into the backs of their cars and delivered it to Angelo Drive. On that last day in October 1969, Warner made no last tour of the lot, bade no farewells. At six o'clock he drove his Bentley out the Olive Avenue gate for the last time and headed over Dark Canyon to the Cahuenga Pass, leaving it all behind him.

"My God, dress extras!" said Governor Ronald Reagan, gazing over the guests in their gowns and tuxedos. "This must be costing you a fortune."

For the first time, it was a party at Warner Bros. studio that didn't cost Jack Warner anything. The gala was being given by the new studio boss, Ted Ashley, ironically, a former agent. Ashley believed that the founder's departure should be marked with a tribute.

On the evening of November 22, 1969, they returned to the studio, the famous figures who had worked for and fought with Jack Warner over the years: Jane Wyman, Joan Blondell, Pat O'Brien, Ruby Keeler, Busby Berkeley, Barbara Stanwyck, Dennis Morgan, Anita Louise, Loretta Young, Miriam Hopkins, Lew Ayres, Claire Trevor, Joseph Cotten, Warren Beatty, Tony Curtis and more. Only Jimmy Cagney turned down an invitation to attend.

This night was not a roast, though there were gentle jabs at the Warner idiosyncracies. When a telegram from President Nixon was read by the emcee, Frank Sinatra, Warner cracked, "He forgot to say 'collect.' "

"Did you say 'collect'?" Sinatra asked. "Well, one thing, Jack, you're consistent. You ain't never gonna change."

The thousand guests gathered first on Stage 7, which was still decorated as King Arthur's great hall. *Camelot* had been finished a year earlier, but the set had remained standing because there was no great need for stages at Warner Bros.

The banquet was held on Stage 1, bedecked with chandeliers and velvet draperies with all the old-time skill of the Warner Bros. prop and scenery departments. All the other studio heads were present, as well as the power agents. Even Hal Wallis appeared. Forgetting past differences, Bette Davis and Edward G. Robinson honored their old boss with kind words. Also paying tribute were Rosalind Russell, Mervyn LeRoy, Efrem Zimbalist, Jr., and Jack Valenti.

The film clips, from *Don Juan* to *My Fair Lady*, brought sighs of recognition, especially Berkeley's "By a Waterfall," the Davis-Henreid cigarette exchange, the Bogart-Bergman farewell, John Garfield's essay on "the fates," Harlow and Cagney in a clinch, Walter Huston's joyful jig, Errol Flynn swinging into battle as Captain Blood.

Jack Warner made his response with notable restraint. "Having served a long apprenticeship climaxing with this dinner," he said smilingly, "I feel qualified to go into business for myself."

Warner set up shop in Century City. It was a smart new address in Los Angeles, a burgeoning cluster of silvery towers rising from what had been the lagoons and pastures of the Twentieth Century Fox back lot. Jack Warner muttered, "That goddamn William Fox. He was a dumb bastard, but he was lucky enough to put his studio in the high-rent district. We had to choose Burbank!"

Warner rented a suite of offices on the seventh floor of 1900 Avenue of the Stars. So he wouldn't have to walk down the hall to the men's room, he had his own bathroom installed.

Bill Schaefer occupied a desk in the big reception room, where the Warner Bros. stars gazed down from the walls at visitors. Warner's private office was far smaller than the one in Burbank, but it was just as intimidating with its displays of awards and trophies:

the Oscars for *The Life of Emile Zola, Casablanca* and *My Fair Lady*; the special Oscar for *The Jazz Singer*; the Thalberg award; the Commander of the Order of the British Empire medal bestowed by Queen Elizabeth in 1960; an 1800 B.C. Canaanite bronze spearhead from Moshe Dayan and a 900 B.C. iron vase from Golda Meir, both for his support of Israel; photographs of all the U.S. presidents from Franklin Roosevelt on.

Warner arrived at the office every morning at 11:30. The staff consisted of Schaefer and his assistant, Tom Murphy, an accountant and a bookkeeper. Soon another member was added: Don Johnson, the studio barber. A barbershop was set up next to the bathroom, and Johnson took care of Warner and any visitors who dropped in. A manicurist also came every day.

For his first project away from the studio, Warner made a curious choice. He decided to produce a stage musical based on the life of Jimmy Walker, the flamboyant, larcenous mayor of New York during prohibition, despite the fact that Bob Hope had already played Walker in a movie, *Beau James*. Warner hired the film's director and cowriter, Mel Shavelson, to write the book for *Jimmy* although he had never worked in the theater before. The songs were done by Bill and Patty Jacobs, a married couple who had written music for industrial shows.

Warner sought Gene Kelly and other top names to play Jimmy Walker without success. He chose Frank Gorshin, the impressionist. Shavelson had designed *Jimmy* to be an all-media show, using screens to depict New York harbor, Times Square and other sights. Warner invested a quarter-million dollars in computerized slide and movie projectors. At the dress rehearsal in Philadelphia, nothing worked. The entire system was junked.

Opening night in Philadelphia was calamitous. Critics pronounced *Jimmy* a misguided piece of claptrap, and audiences agreed. Mel Shavelson sent the distress signal to Warner in California: "Jack, you gotta close this turkey. You'll get killed in New York, and it'll fold anyway. Get out while you can. It's not a show, it's a vacuum cleaner: everybody's in it for what they can take out of your pockets."

"Stop worrying about my money," Warner said grandly. "It's only a mill."

"I'm not worried about your money, I'm worried about me. You gotta close the show."

For the first time since Shavelson had known him, Warner sounded serious. "If I close the show," he said, "who'll have dinner with me?"

Jimmy staggered into the Winter Garden in New York, and it was bludgeoned by the critics, who seemed eager to savage a movie mogul who dared to invade the theater. The show ran for three months, largely because Warner papered the house. In the end *Jimmy* had cost him a "mill" and a half, an expensive way to learn that he should stick to movies.

Why Jack Warner was attracted to *Dirty Little Billy* remains a puzzle. It certainly wasn't like any western he or anyone else had made before. Perhaps that was its appeal to him. "You gotta do pictures that are different," he preached.

Warner's New York attorney, Arnold Grant, had instigated the project, getting Warner together with Mary Wells, the celebrity partner of the go-go advertising firm of Wells, Rich and Greene. The company wanted to enter the film business, and Wells proposed a fifty-fifty partnership to finance a script picturing Billy the Kid as a dim-witted delinquent. Two ad men, Charles Moss and Stan Dragoti, had written it. Dragoti, who had been acclaimed as a gifted maker of television commercials, would direct.

Dragoti was awed by the prospect of meeting the legendary Jack Warner, especially after he studied the outer-office portraits of the stars Warner had employed. Warner put him immediately at ease. He had a funny story for each of the portraits.

"You worried about directing your first feature?" he asked.

"Well, yes, Mr. Warner," Dragoti answered. "My pictures have been thirty seconds, one minute, two minutes tops."

"It's nothing, kid. I got an instinct for directors. That's why I gave Mike Nichols his start. John Huston, too. And lots of other guys like Delmer Daves and Don Siegel. You'll do okay."

Warner participated in all aspects of the production. He liked the anti-genre aspect of *Dirty Little Billy*, and when he found a prosaic section of the script, he asked Dragoti: "D'ya need that, kid? It's kinda hokey-pokey on-the-nose, don't you think?" Warner seemed pleased with the casting of Michael J. Pollard, a short, homely, quirky actor, to play Billy. A New York casting director submitted other offbeat types, prompting Warner to ask, "Who are they—relatives?"

"No, no," Dragoti replied. "I just want to get a different look in the faces."

"Well, I'm glad they're not relatives," said Warner. "A friend will fuck you once; a relative will fuck you twice."

Warner was amused that Dragoti chose to audition actors on videotape rather than rely on memory. When the director was in a quandary over two actors for the second lead, Warner looked at the tapes. "There's the one," Warner said after both tapes had unreeled. "The other guy is acting the role. This guy *is* the role."

Several times Warner invited Dragoti and his wife, Cheryl Tiegs, to Angelo Drive to view *Shane*, *High Noon* and other classic westerns. The host was always in good form. Ann Warner never appeared. But sometimes at the start of a screening, a figure would enter the darkened theater and disappear before the final credits.

Set designers built a frontier Kansas town at the Old Tucson western location in Arizona, and Dragoti worked from old photographs to achieve a ramshackle look. Jack Warner was there the first day of shooting to bolster his nervous director: "I know I'm asking you to go pitch against the Yankees, but I know you can do it." The first scene was an intricate camera move in a barroom that took three hours to complete. Warner waited outside, and he voiced no complaint that the picture was already behind schedule. When Dragoti finally emerged, Warner opened a magnum of champagne.

Warner made return visits to the location, and he watched over assembly of the film. During a run-through of the first reel, Dragoti complained, "It's not moving." Warner replied, "Don't worry, kid, ya got an hour and a half to go." Later when Dragoti inserted a knife fight to enliven the fourth reel, Warner enthused, "Shit, I'm staying around for this!"

Only once did producer and director disagree. Warner pressed Dragoti to complete his editing so that *Dirty Little Billy* could be entered in the Cannes Film Festival. Dragoti said he needed more time, and Warner continued the pressure. "I'll call New York and have them buy your share out," Dragoti threatened. Warner immediately backed down.

Columbia Pictures, which was releasing *Dirty Little Billy*, decided to show it at the San Francisco Film Festival. It was a mistake. San Francisco in 1972 was a cauldron of antiestablishment feeling. As soon as Jack Warner's name appeared on the screen, the audience booed. Catcalls and boos continued throughout the screening, and Warner and Dragoti were dismayed. But Warner appeared at a press conference the following day and dismissed the ugly reception as the work of radicals. He said he was convinced that *Dirty Little Billy* was a fine film.

Nobody else seemed to think so, especially film audiences accustomed to Duke Wayne tall in the saddle instead of Billy the Kid wallowing in mud. With a million-dollar budget, neither the ad agency nor Warner was hurt badly. *Dirty Little Billy* found a receptive audience in France and eastern Europe.

"Why don't you come along just for the fun of it?" Peter Stone suggested to Peter Hunt one day in 1971. Stone had written *1776*, the hit Broadway musical about the founding of the republic, and Hunt had directed it. Jack Warner had bought the film rights, and the announcement was being made at a press conference in the New York headquarters of Columbia Pictures, which would release *1776*.

Hunt decided to attend. At the press conference, Warner gave his customary performance of starting to read a speech, discarding it, telling lame jokes, and then asking for questions.

"Mr. Warner, who is going to direct the movie?"

Warner answered immediately: "The same guy who directed it on Broadway."

Hunt was dumbstruck. After the conference ended, he was standing in a daze before the elevators when he felt a tug at his elbow. "The colonel wants to meet you," said a Warner aide.

Jack Warner approached with his barber-bodyguard Don Johnson. The aide said, "Mr. Warner, I'd like you to meet Peter Hunt, who directed the show on Broadway."

Before Hunt had a chance to say a word, the elevator doors opened and Warner stepped inside. With a broad grin he said, "Kid, I'll see you in Hollywood." The doors closed.

It was the beginning of a year-long collaboration that flung Peter Hunt into the wondrous world of an old-time movie mogul. Jack, who had trouble with names, chose one he could remember for the rotund Hunt. It was Roscoe, after Fatty Arbuckle.

"That's a compliment," Warner explained. "Fatty was a good friend of mine, and the funniest man in pictures. He got a bum deal up there in San Francisco; the DA was trying to build his political career. I was the first guy to hire him as an actor after nobody else would." (Arbuckle had been tried three times in the 1921 party death of a starlet and finally was acquitted. He was blacklisted as an actor but found work as a director under the name of William B. Goodrich—Will B. Good. Warner starred him in six two-reel comedies shortly before Arbuckle's death at forty-five in 1933.)

What appealed to Jack Warner about *1776* was its fresh approach to the origins of the United States, using songs to delineate history. What he didn't like was the liberal perception of the founding fathers by playwright Stone. But he didn't interfere with the writing of the movie script by Stone. When he conferred with Stone and Hunt on production matters, Warner worked from a script marked with paper clips.

"Is this necessary?" he asked, citing a paper-clipped reference. When Stone and "Roscoe" put forth their arguments, Warner did not rebut. He seemed unwilling to engage in confrontation. "He who fights and runs away lives to fight another day," he explained to his two young collaborators.

The film was cast in New York, since most of the original cast would repeat their roles in the film. They included William Daniels, Ken Howard, Donald Madden, Blythe Danner and Howard da Silva. Warner voiced no opposition to da Silva, who had been exiled from films during the blacklist period.

Hunt had wanted to film *1776* in Independence Hall, but Warner insisted that it had to be made in Hollywood. Hunt came to California to prepare the production, and he was treated to Jack Warner's unique hospitality. Often the two men dined in Warner's baronial dining hall, seated at a card table under a single light. The adjoining rooms were dark, testimony to Jack's lifelong habit of saving electricity. Warner often ate his dinner with a transistor radio to his ear, listening to the Dodger baseball game. Occasionally he put the radio down, and they discussed *1776*. When the glaze of boredom descended over Warner's eyes, he returned the radio to his ear.

When Hunt admired the Dali painting of Ann, Warner told the story behind it. Warner had brought Dali to Los Angeles, all expenses paid, to create the portrait. The artist found the arrangement so comfortable that he kept tearing up his sketches and starting over. Warner finally issued an ultimatum: finish or get out. The contrite Dali presented not only a portrait of Ann, but one of Jack as well.

Dali had placed Jack beside a dog that was taller than he was. "That was bad enough, but I knew something else was wrong with the picture," Warner recalled. "Finally I found it. The son of a bitch had painted me with six fingers. That's when I put the picture away."

During his evenings on Angelo Drive, Peter Hunt never met Ann Warner. One night Hunt and his wife were being entertained by Jack. The telephone rang, and Jack's face became serious. He hung up the receiver and asked Mrs. Hunt if she would stand out in the driveway. She did so, sensing that she was being inspected by two unseen eyes. Later that evening, Ann had a pleasant conversation with Mrs. Hunt—on the telephone.

After a day's work in the Century City office, Hunt sometimes drove Jack to Angelo Drive. One evening they were motoring up the long driveway when Warner exclaimed, "Duck down! Duck down!" Hunt couldn't imagine what for. Then he saw a golf cart trundling down the driveway, bearing a gardener and a lovely, dark-haired, slightly overweight older woman. Hunt stopped the car, introduced himself to Ann Warner, and drove on. "God, am I going to catch hell for this!" Warner groaned.

1776 was scheduled to be filmed at the studio of Warner's old enemy, Harry Cohn. It was an eerie time to be at the Columbia studio, which was virtually empty. Columbia Pictures was moving into the Warner Bros. studio, which the two companies would co-own and operate as the Burbank studios. Thus, after all those years, the Warner name would no longer appear on the water tower. Did that concern him? He gave no evidence that it did. He considered the merger of facilities a shrewd scheme to minimize overhead. But in truth, he cared little about what happened to the Burbank lot. Bill Schaefer was accustomed to reporting to the boss on happenings at the new Warner Bros. Finally, Warner said, "Don't show me those things, Bill. I'm not interested."

Jack Warner was assigned a sizable office that had been occupied by William Wyler during *Funny Girl*. Because Wyler was almost deaf but refused to wear a hearing aid, the office was equipped with mikes and speakers to amplify conversations. As soon as Warner saw the wires, he ordered them all removed. "Maybe we wired offices at Warner Brothers, but we weren't so open about it," he said.

During a production meeting in the office, Warner began pacing, and his foot felt a ridge on the carpet that indicated a wire underneath. "The meeting's over," he announced abruptly. He would not resume until the offending wire was yanked out.

The decades of habit could not be erased, and Jack Warner considered the near-empty studio to be his very own. He strode the streets with immense assurance, issuing orders here and there.

He had a habit of bursting onto the *1776* set every day, often when Hunt was directing a key scene. His badinage with the cast and crew occupied several minutes, and then he left.

The company was falling behind schedule, and Hunt realized that Warner's visits were partly to blame. He positioned a hulking guard outside the door to bar all visitors, especially Jack Warner, from entering while the red light was flashing. Warner made his customary visit the same day, ruining a complicated take. When the director asked what had happened, the guard told him, "I worked for that man for forty years. I'm not about to tell him he can't go on a stage."

Every Monday night after filming, Warner had a production meeting in his office with Hunt and the production manager, Emmett Emerson. Warner placed a bottle of Jack Daniels on his desk, and the meeting proceeded until the bottle was empty. The boss became impatient because he had no real problems to deal with. "Goddamn it, I'm the producer, and I'm supposed to produce," he complained. "There must be something wrong."

Emerson said timidly, "Well, one of the actors was complaining about the air-conditioning in his dressing room."

"Fire him!" Warner ordered.

"We can't fire him," Hunt said. "He's the delegate from New York. We can't have New York not signing the Declaration."

"I said fire him. I know how to fix it. I did it once when I had to take over a picture from a souse of a director. I explained it with a title."

"But we don't have titles in talking pictures," protested Hunt. The argument continued until Hunt and Emerson persuaded Warner to punish the actor by removing a few of his privileges.

When it came time to preview *1776*, Hunt favored San Francisco. Warner said no. "Why not?" the director asked. Warner replied, "Because there are too many Jews and too many gentiles." Like many Warner statements, it made no sense. But Hunt had learned to search for the instinctive meaning behind Warner's non sequiturs. He seemed to be saying: "San Francisco has too many experts." Phoenix was chosen, and the audience reacted enthusiastically. Warner and the Columbia executives were ecstatic, and Peter Hunt went off to Paris on a belated honeymoon.

When the director returned, he was devastated to find that Jack Warner had reedited *1776*. All the liberal references, so carefully paper-clipped in Warner's script, had been excised. Even more destructively, Warner had lifted out a fifteen-minute middle portion that included two musical numbers: the antiwar "Mama, Look Sharp" and "Cool Conservative Men," which attacked the colonial moneymen who feared revolution would harm their investments.

Hunt protested, but Warner merely smiled and repeated his earlier warning: "He who fights and runs away lives to fight another day."

A film editor explained to Hunt what had happened. Warner had taken the preview cut of *1776* to the White House for a viewing by his friend Richard Nixon. It was Nixon who suggested the song eliminations, pointing out that "Mama, Look Sharp" could be interpreted as an anti-Vietnam War preachment, and "Cool Conservative Men" opposed all he and Warner believed in.

It was Nixon's revenge, Hunt realized. When *1776* was reigning as a Broadway hit, the company was invited to stage it at the White House—on condition that the two offending songs be eliminated. The company objected, and White House officials, fearing embarrassment by the press, dropped the proviso. Hunt was seated next to Nixon at the East Room performance, and at the finish of "Cool Conservative Men" the president rose and shouted "bravo!" Hunt considered it a brilliant political move to defuse any possible controversy.

1776 fulfilled all the hopes of Jack Warner and Columbia Pictures in its first engagement. Opening at the Radio City Music Hall in November 1972, the film played to record crowds through the holiday season. Then it was launched through the rest of the country, and it flopped.

What went wrong? It shouldn't have been surprising that a nation faced with its first defeat in war and a corrupt presidency failed to spark to a cheery exercise in prerepublic civics. Just as importantly, musical tastes of young Americans had shifted to rock, and the era of the burst-into-song musical had ended.

Warner did not outwardly despair over the twin failures of *Dirty Little Billy* and *1776*. The irrepressible grin remained, and he talked with Peter Hunt about a new project. This time he would return to his roots. "I'll show 'em how a gangster picture should be made," he vowed.

Chapter 20

Shuffle Off to Buffalo

"I THINK THIS IS THE BIG EIGHT-O," Jack Warner whispered to his son-in-law Bill Orr. "But don't say anything."

It was August 2, 1972, and Warner was having his customary birthday celebration at Cap d'Antibes. Executives of a film company in which Warner Bros. owned a quarter share had made the pilgrimage from England to present him with rare ceramic statues of Arthur and Guinevere, honoring *Camelot* as well as the birthday. Warner was expansive as ever, making jokes and recalling past triumphs with the Englishmen. Bill Orr was surprised that Jack had hinted at his presumed age (he could never be sure). Jack rarely mentioned age, his own or anyone's. His only comment would be, "I'm ten years younger than the major." Actually he was eight years younger.

Orr recalled the time when Warner received the news in the executive dining room that Joe Schenck had died. "How old was he?" Warner asked. "Eighty-two," he was told. "Tsk, tsk," said Warner straight-faced, "a young man."

Jack Warner at eighty seemed to have been time-warped for thirty-five years. His face was unlined and tanned from hours on the tennis court. His thinning hair and the mustache were brown, with help from his barber Don Johnson. His mind remained alert, and if he had trouble with names, that was nothing new. He could always manage by calling people "kid" or "the little woman."

He made small concessions to age. He no longer drove himself in one of the two Bentleys or the Lincoln Continental from Angelo Drive to Avenue of the Stars. Don Johnson usually picked him up, and Bill Schaefer drove him home. Although Warner tried to conceal the fact, his eyesight was worsening. He consulted an optometrist regularly, and each time he returned with a half-dozen glasses in a new prescription. Instead of reading the trade papers, he asked Bill Schaefer what was in them. If he heard something of interest, he said, "Read it to me."

Without the Warner Bros. publicity department to help promote *Dirty Little Billy* and *1776*, Warner assumed some of the responsibility himself. He began giving press interviews, something he had avoided during his long years as studio boss.

"They told me not to crack too many jokes because I might end up sounding like some sort of buffoon," he confided to Wayne Warga of the Los Angeles *Times*.

"I like public speaking, as any number of people are sorry they know, but I seldom give interviews. I just don't take everything seriously. You can be serious to a degree, but then you've got to laugh."

On December 14, 1972, Warner gave his only television interview, appearing on *The Merv Griffin Show* with his one-time contract player. The pair had a rousing time reminiscing about Griffin's brief movie career and dinner parties on Angelo Drive. Warner told stories about Flynn, Bogart, Davis, Jolson and others and related how he and his brothers started in movies and made them talk.

"I don't want to be called a pioneer, like the Forty-niners coming over Chanute Pass or one of those places," said Warner. "Pioneer in films, yes."

He interlarded his replies with puns and jokes, most of which misfired.

Griffin: Do you like actors?

Warner: Yes, isn't the world a stage? Aren't we all players? The answer is yes and no.

Griffin: Yes, we really are. But do you like them?

Warner: Certainly. I'm a ham at heart myself. I go to bed with some mustard and rye bread at times.

Griffin: Do you?

Warner: Oh, yes, oh, yes. I'm struggling here, but it's not bad. I like my own stuff. . . .

The interview continued in a lighthearted vein until Griffin asked about the new permissiveness of film content. That ignited a Queegian outburst:

"Oh, that is uncalled for to a great degree. Sometimes yes, most of the time no. If this sounds like a rather pious fellow, well I am. I am a great believer in God (applause)—and I believe in my country and the American flag. . . .

"I went to a certain show; they had a flag made on the suit of a guy, and they were shooting water on him all the time, he finally ended in the aisle of the theater. I won't mention the name, you probably know what it was. Desecrating the flag is what it was, walking on it, stepping on it. These are all pinko communists in the show. These are not Americans. These are not the Americans we know. I know that. I don't know you people and many of you never saw me, but actually there are two kinds of Americans: people who are for this country, who wave the flag, and those who turn it upside down. . . ."

The tirade continued for several minutes and ended with hearty applause from the studio audience. Jack Warner did no more television interviews.

Late in 1973, Bill Schaefer began to see disturbing changes in the boss he had served for forty years. When Warner arrived for work in the morning, he seemed disoriented, as if he had entered an office that was foreign to him. By noontime he seemed in sync again, barking jokes over the telephone and dictating correspondence. Old studio hands like Walter MacEwen, Max Bercutt and

Rudi Fehr sometimes dropped in, and Jack took them to lunch around the corner at Señor Pico's, a popular Mexican restaurant.

One day Warner and Bill Schaefer were lunching at Señor Pico's when Bill spotted a familiar face across the room. "You know who's over there?" Bill asked, knowing that the boss couldn't see that far. "It's Jack Jr. Don't you think you ought to speak to him?"

Warner thought for a moment and then said, "Ask him to come over and have lunch with us."

It had been fourteen years since father and son had spoken to each other. Their conversation was friendly but impersonal, and they parted with no promises to see each other again. They never did.

Don Johnson, the barber, also noticed changes in Warner. When he called at the Angelo Drive house in the morning, Don often had to waken the boss. "Are we in New York? Where are we?" Warner asked dazedly. On the short drive to Century City, Warner said, "You're not taking me to the office. Where are you going?" The barber explained gently that they were not going to Burbank but to the new office. Don had to steer the boss to the office on the seventh floor. Often when Warner came out of his own office on his way to the barber room, he turned the wrong way.

"When are we going to tell Mrs. Warner?" Johnson asked Schaefer.

"Don, I hate to tell her this kind of thing," Bill said concernedly. "I'm hoping she'll notice herself."

By the time Warner had spent a few hours at the office and had had his shave and vibrator massage by Don, he seemed rejuvenated. He went home cheerful and oriented.

Finally on February 12, 1974, Bill Schaefer telephoned Ann Warner. "How long has this been going on?" she demanded.

"Two or three months."

"Why didn't you tell me before?"

"I hated to. I thought you would see what was happening."

Jack Warner never returned to the office. Ann took him to the Scripps Clinic, and he remained at her house in La Jolla for a few months. By the time he returned to Angelo Drive he was

enfeebled and blind, the result of a stroke. Ann encouraged him
to walk around the pool and take therapy, but his condition grew
worse.

Bill Schaefer came to the house to report that things were fine
at the office. Warner asked no questions. He wasn't interested. A
few old friends and members of his family visited, but his capacity
to speak diminished. Finally his voice was gone. One studio veteran
came to the house and was shocked to see the once tanned face now
white and lifeless. He seemed unaware of his visitor's attempt to
report the latest gossip. Warner reached out a bony hand and struggled to move his mouth. "Help me," he croaked.

Death claimed him slowly. Ann shut off nearly all visitors outside the family and devoted all her time to Jack's care. This was a
curious parallel to Virginia and Darryl Zanuck. After the years of
public philandering with European beauties, Darryl came home to
his wife, who nursed him through his long, fatal illness. Ann was
doing the same for Jack.

At Christmas one year, Ann invited an old friend to the house.
She was Jean Howard, once the wife of Charlie Feldman, now a
noted photographer. Many times she had been a guest at the gala
parties on Angelo Drive. Now she found a different scene. Bill Orr
and Joy were there, though they had separated. Barbara came with
her husband, Cy Howard. Jack Warner, dressed in red pajamas for
Christmas, sat in a wheelchair oblivious of the visitors. The eyes
were lifeless, the hands palsied. The face was a mocking caricature
of the buoyant, wisecracking prince Jean Howard had known.

On August 13, 1978, Warner became too ill to be cared for at
home. He was admitted to Cedars-Sinai Hospital, and he died of
an edema on September 9. He was eighty-six, more or less.

Ann Warner called Max Bercutt, Jack's last publicity chief at
Warner Bros. "I do not want a big funeral," she declared. "I want
it to be entirely private, just the family and a few others. No
publicity."

"But Mrs. Warner," Bercutt protested. "The colonel was a giant
of the industry. His passing should be observed, like Harry Cohn's
and Louie Mayer's. He deserves a proper tribute."

"I said I wanted no big funeral," she repeated. "Now do you want to help me or don't you?"

Bercutt started to say no but then relented. "All right, tell me what you want me to do."

She dictated about twenty names of people to be called. Ann, who had not been seen in public for twenty-five years, emphasized that there would be no photographs.

The funeral would be at Edgar Magnin's Wilshire Temple, where Jack Warner had been a member for fifty years though he never attended services. Among those invited were Barbara Warner and Cy Howard, Bill and Joy Orr, Bill Schaefer and his wife, Don Johnson and others from the office, Richard Gully, and members of the household staff.

Rabbi Magnin, who had scant regard for Jack Warner, looked at the small gathering in the huge temple and suggested transferring the service to a chapel upstairs. That meant that the casket had to be moved. It wouldn't fit in the elevator, so the pallbearers had to carry it up the steps. Many of them were middle-aged or elderly, and they struggled with their heavy burden on the marble stairs. At one point, they seemed to lose control, and the casket jolted backward. Max Bercutt, who was heaving at the end of the casket, thought he would either be killed by a heart attack or crushed, at long last, by Jack Warner. Finally the pallbearers made one great effort, and they reached the top of the stairs. It was a scene Jack Warner would have enjoyed.

Jack Warner's estate was estimated for legal purposes at more than $15 million, but it was likely more than double that. The will granted Ann all the property, his belongings and memorabilia, and a yearly income of five percent of the estate. Warner had wanted to leave his son nothing, but he had been persuaded that such a gesture would inevitably lead to a challenge to the will. Jack Jr. got $200,000. Bill Schaefer received $15,000, small change after forty-five years of devoted service. A former valet was left the same amount.

The obituaries had been replete with phrases like "last of the

Hollywood empire builders" and "last of the motion picture pioneers," which he was. He was also called "last of the studio moguls," a word he disliked. "Moguls? Don't like the word," he once told an interviewer. "It reminds me of some bad Turkish cigarettes I used to smoke."

The obit writers recited the familiar history: the four brothers who left the family butcher shop for nickelodeons; the breakthrough with *My Four Years in Germany*; the revolution of sound; the gangster movies, the Busby Berkeley musicals, the Muni biographies; *Casablanca* and the war movies; the great stars: Cagney, Davis, Flynn, Bogart and more; television, *Virginia Woolf, My Fair Lady*.

The essence of the man was missing in the articles. That was captured a few months after Warner's death when his friends and foes met for what became more of a revel than a requiem. It was called "The Colonel: An Affectionate Remembrance of Jack L. Warner," and it was organized by the Friends of the Libraries at the University of Southern California.

Laughter rang through the university's Town and Gown hall as speaker after speaker recalled the absurdities of working at Warner Bros. as well as some of the glories. Bill Orr told the story about Madame Chiang Kai-shek and Jack Warner's laundry, and he related the colonel's favorite toast at dinner parties: "I'd like to deliver this first toast to my best friend, that prince of good fellows—Jack L. Warner."

The portly William Conrad told of meeting Jack Warner after being hired to produce low-budget pictures. Warner's comment: "Good God, we're not paying you by the pound, are we?" Mervyn LeRoy gave an example of Warner's repartee. When asked, "What's new, Jack?" he would reply, "New York, New Mexico, New Hampshire and pneu-monia."

Harry Warren recalled his exchange with Warner on their first meeting in 1931: "Are you that songwriter from New York?" "Yes, sir. Who are you?" "Mr. Warner." "Which one?" "You'll find out." Julius Epstein gazed at the smiling portrait of Jack Warner over the stage, and commented, "This is exactly the look he had when he fired you."

Pat Buttram remembered speaking at a banquet with Warner and deploring x-rated movies: "If Errol Flynn could see the pictures they make today, he'd turn over in his grave." To which Warner commented: "Come to think of it, that would be a more natural position for Errol."

The jocose memories continued into the night. Bill Schaefer, still loyal to the only boss he ever knew. Irving Rapper telling Michael Curtiz stories. Harry Warren, Saul Chaplin, Sammy Cahn, Sammy Fain, speaking of the songs they wrote for Warner Bros. Olivia de Havilland describing her historic battle with Jack Warner. Debbie Reynolds relating how he fired her because she worked part-time at J.C. Penny's instead of attending a studio luncheon that paid her nothing.

The laughter ended at midnight, and the emcee, Hal Kanter, advised the film students in the room to "overlook those current studio and network executives, who are for the most part lawyers and agents and accountants and assorted masters of hype, to study the work and lives of such showmen as J.L. who built this industry."

The last word came from another Warner Bros. star, Porky Pig, in the guise of Mel Blanc: "A-bee-a-bee-a-bee—that's all, folks."

Bibliography

Jack L. Warner's autobiography, *My First Hundred Years in Hollywood*, was invaluable for tracing the early history of the Warner family and their motion picture enterprise. Also of immense value was a series of 1938 *Youngstown Vindicator* articles by Esther Hamilton, who had thoroughly researched the Warners' early years. Rudy Behlmer's *Inside Warner Bros. (1935–1951)* proved a rich source of interstudio communications. Here is the complete list of book sources:

Arliss, George, *My Ten Years in the Studios*, Little, Brown, Boston, 1940.

Bacall, Lauren, *Lauren Bacall by Myself*, Knopf, New York, 1979.

Baker, Carlos, *Ernest Hemingway: A Life Story*, Scribner's, New York, 1969.

Barnes, Djuna, *Interviews*, Sun and Moon Press, Washington, D.C., undated.

Barnouw, Erik, *The Image Empire*, Oxford University Press, New York, 1970.

Beaton, Cecil, *Cecil Beaton's Fair Lady*, Holt, Rinehart and Winston, New York, 1964.

Behlmer, Rudy, *Inside Warner Bros. (1935–1951)*, Viking, New York, 1985.

———, ed., *Memo from David O. Selznick*, Viking, New York, 1970.

Berg, A. Scott, *Goldwyn*, Knopf, New York, 1989.

Bergman, Ingrid, and Alan Burgess, *My Story*, Delacorte, New York, 1980.

Blotner, Joseph, *Selected Letters of William Faulkner*, Random House, New York, 1977.

Bragg, Melvyn, *Richard Burton, A Life*, Little, Brown, Boston, 1988.

Burke, John, *Rogue's Progress, The Fabulous Adventures of Wilson Mizner*, Putnam, New York, 1975.

Cagney, James, *Cagney by Cagney*, Doubleday, Garden City, N.Y., 1976.

Capra, Frank, *The Name Above the Title*, Macmillan, New York, 1971.

Ceplar, Larry, and Steven Englund, *The Inquisition in Hollywood*, Anchor/Doubleday, Garden City, N.Y., 1980.

The Colonel: An Affectionate Remembrance of Jack L. Warner, Friends of the USC Libraries, 1980.

Crowther, Bosley, *Hollywood Rajah, The Life and Times of Louis B. Mayer*, Holt, New York, 1960.

——, *The Lion's Share*, Dutton, New York, 1957.

Davis, Bette, *The Lonely Life*, Putnam, New York, 1962.

——, with Michael Herskowitz, *This 'N That*, Putnam, New York, 1987.

Edwards, Anne, *Early Reagan, The Rise to Power*, Morrow, New York, 1987.

Eells, George, *The Life that Late He Led, A Biography of Cole Porter*, Putnam, New York, 1967.

Fairbanks, Douglas, Jr., *The Salad Days*, Doubleday, New York, 1988.

Fein, Irving, *Jack Benny*, Putnam, New York, 1976.

Ferris, Paul, *Richard Burton*, Coward, McCann and Geoghegan, New York, 1980.

Finch, Christopher, *Rainbow: The Stormy Life of Judy Garland*, Random House, New York, 1975.

Flynn, Errol, *My Wicked, Wicked Ways*, Putnam, New York, 1959.

Ford, Dan, *Pappy: The Life of John Ford*, Prentice-Hall, Englewood Cliffs, N.J., 1979.

Fowler, Gene, *Good Night, Sweet Prince, The Life and Times of John Barrymore*, Viking, New York, 1943.

Freedland, Michael, *The Warner Brothers*, St. Martin's, New York, 1983.

Gabler, Neal, *An Empire of Their Own: How the Jews Invented Hollywood*, Crown, New York, 1988.

Gehman, Richard, *Bogart, An Intimate Biography*, Gold Medal Books, New York, 1965.

Goodman, Ezra, *The Fifty-year Decline and Fall of Hollywood*, Simon and Schuster, New York, 1961.

Green, Fitzhugh, *The Film Finds Its Tongue*, Putnam, New York, 1929.

Gregg, E. S., *The Shadow of Sound*, Vantage Press, New York, 1967.

Gussow, Mel, *"Don't Say Yes Until I Finish Talking," A Biography of Darryl F. Zanuck*, Doubleday, Garden City, N.Y., 1971.

Henreid, Paul, *Ladies Man, an Autobiography*, St. Martin's, New York, 1984.

Herndon, Venable, *James Dean: A Short Life*, Doubleday, Garden City, N.Y., 1974.

Hirschhorn, Clive, *The Warner Bros. Story*, Crown, New York, 1979.

Hotchner, A. E., *Doris Day: Her Own Story*, Morrow, New York, 1976.

Huston, John, *An Open Book*, Knopf, New York, 1980.

Johnston, Alva, *The Legendary Mizners*, Farrar, Straus and Young, New York, 1953.

Jones, Chuck, *Chuck Amuck*, Farrar Straus Giroux, New York, 1989.

Katz, Ephraim, *The Film Encyclopedia*, Putnam, New York, 1979.

Kazan, Elia, *A Life*, Knopf, New York, 1988.

Kotsilibas-Davis, James, *The Barrymores*, Crown, New York, 1981.

Lambert, Gavin, *On Cukor*, Putnam, New York, 1972.

Lasky, Jesse, with Don Weldon, *I Blow My Horn*, Doubleday, Garden City, N.Y., 1957.

Lawrence, Jerome, *Actor: The Life and Times of Paul Muni*, Putnam, New York, 1974.

Bibliography

LeRoy, Mervyn, as told to Dick Kleiner, *Mervyn LeRoy: Take One*, Hawthorne, New York, 1976.

Logan, Josh, *Movie Stars, Real People, and Me*, Delacorte, New York, 1978.

Macgowan, Kenneth, *Behind the Screen*, Delacorte, New York, 1965.

Madsen, Axel, *William Wyler*, Crowell, New York, 1977.

Marx, Arthur, *Goldwyn, A Biography of the Man Behind the Myth*, Norton, New York, 1978.

McBride, Joseph, *Focus on Howard Hawks*, Prentice-Hall, Englewood Cliffs, N.J., 1971.

Meyer, William R. *Warner Brothers Directors*, Arlington House, New Rochelle, N.Y., 1978.

Navasky, Victor S., *Naming Names*, Viking, New York, 1980.

Neal, Patricia, *As I Am*, Simon and Schuster, New York, 1988.

Negulesco, Jean, *Things I Did and Things I Think I Did*, Linden Press—Simon and Schuster, New York, 1984.

Offen, Ron, *Cagney*, Henry Regnery, Chicago, 1972.

Paley, William, *As It Happened*, Doubleday, Garden City, N.Y., 1977.

Reagan, Ronald, with Richard Hubler, *Where's the Rest of Me? The Ronald Reagan Story*, Duell, Sloan and Pearce, New York, 1965.

Reinhardt, Gottfried, *The Genius, A Memoir of Max Reinhardt*, Knopf, New York, 1979.

Salinger, Pierre, *With Kennedy*, Doubleday, Garden City, N.Y., 1966.

Schary, Dore, *Heyday*, Little, Brown, Boston, 1979.

Sennett, Ted, *Warner Bros. Presents*, Arlington House, New Rochelle, N.Y., 1971.

Spoto, Donald, *The Dark Side of Genius: The Life of Alfred Hitchcock*, Little, Brown, Boston, 1983.

Stine, Whitney, *Mother Goddam, The Story of the Career of Bette Davis*, Hawthorne, New York, 1974.

Thomas, Tony, *Harry Warren and the Hollywood Musical*, Citadel, Secaucus, N.J., 1975.

Vidor, King, *King Vidor, A Directors Guild of America Oral History*, Directors Guild of America and Scarecrow Press, Metuchen, N.Y., 1988.

Walker, Alexander, *Vivien, The Life of Vivien Leigh*, Weidenfeld and Nicholson, New York, 1987.

Walsh, Raoul, *Each Man in His Time*, Farrar, Straus and Giroux, New York, 1974.

The Warner Bros. Golden Anniversary Book, Dell, New York, 1973.

Warner, Jack, with Dean Jennings, *My First Hundred Years in Hollywood*, Random House, New York, 1964.

Warren, Doug, with James Cagney, *James Cagney: The Authorized Biography*, St. Martin's, New York, 1983.

Weinberg, Herman G., *The Lubitsch Touch*, Dutton, New York, 1968.

Wiley, Mason, and Damien Bona, *Inside Oscar, The Unofficial History of the Academy Awards*, Ballantine, New York, 1987.

Yablonsky, Lewis, *George Raft*, McGraw-Hill, New York, 1974.

Zolotow, Maurice, *Billy Wilder in Hollywood*, Putnam, New York, 1977.

Index

Index

Index

Index

Index

Warner, Harry (*Cont.*):
Warner Bros. Pictures, 40; and Darryl Zanuck, 45, 88
Warner, Henry (brother), 10–11
Warner, Irma Solomons (first wife), 29–30, 33, 41–42, 69, 103, 169; end of her marriage to Warner, 94, 95, 102, 229; omission of, from Warner's autobiography, 249
Warner, Jack L.: his affair with Marilyn Miller, 69–71, 94; his aid to Israel, 208; and George Arliss, 76–77; automobile accident of, 228–229; awards to, 129, 157, 193, 230, 243–244, 290–291; and Lauren Bacall, 150; beginning of dynasty of, 20–32 *passim*; and Busby Berkeley, 86; birth and early life of, 9, 11, 13–17; and Humphrey Bogart, 109–110, 126, 144; bomb threat received by, 130; break between Jack Jr. and, 229–230; and James Cagney, 80–81, 104–106, 144, 177–178; and cartoons, 211–212; Century City office of, 290–291, 297; characterized, 4–7, 68–69, 141; cheapness of, 247, 248; and CinemaScope, 191; and Sean Connery, 257–258; contracts not renewed by, 172–176; and Joan Crawford, 150–152; and Michael Curtiz, 127, 128; dark side of, 208–210; and Marion Davies, 96–97; and Bette Davis, 82, 106–109, 143–144, 175–176; and James Dean, 217–219; death of, 305–306; deaths of his brothers, 62, 73, 120, 226–227, 286–287; his double-cross of his brothers, 226; education of, 16; end of his first marriage, 94, 95; entertaining on Angelo Drive by, 161–162; his entry into show business, 17–18; estate of, 306; feud between Harry Cohn and, 159–161; film backlog sold by, 225–226; and films with social consciousness, 83; and Flint's murder, 72; and Errol Flynn, 111–112, 144, 152–154, 172–173; his foothold in Hollywood, 33–51 *passim*; and Bryan Foy, 64–65; and Kay Francis, 101–102; French villa of, 128, 227–228; Clark Gable rejected by, 78, 79; gambling debt of, 159; and James Garner, 196–199; "girlfriends" of, 205, 245–249, 250; and *Gone with the Wind*, 121–123; and Merv Griffin, 212–214, 302–303; and Olivia de Havilland, 122–123, 144–145; and Paul Henreid, 133–134; and Alfred Hitchcock, 187–188; humor of, 68, 156–159, 205–206, 287, 307–308; interest in Warner Bros. sold by, 279–280; and Al Jolson, 68; and Ben Kalmenson, 184, 253; and Jack Kennedy, 237–241; last day at Warner Bros. of, 3–4, 288–289; as lieutenant colonel, 130–131; his love of gambling, 206–207, 228; marriages of, 29–30, 102; and MCA, 244–245; and mistress Jackie Park, 245–249; and Wilson Mizner, 91, 92; and Marilyn Monroe, 221–222; *My First Hundred Years in Hollywood*, 77, 210, 249–250; and Paul Newman, 219–220; obituaries of, 306–307; Bill Orr recruited by, 169–170; overview of career of, 4; and Ann Page, 94–95 (*see also* Warner, Ann); and Pathe rooster, 166–167; patriotic short subjects of, 129–132; and Gregory Peck, 188–189; penny-pinching ways of, 112–113;

Warner, Jack L. (*Cont.*):
physical decline of, 303–305; portrait of, in his sixties, 200–211; portrait of, in his seventies, 242–244, 250–253, 264, 280; portrait of, at eighty, 301–302; post-mortem revel for, 307–308; and postwar slump, 171–172; his presidency of Warner Bros., 226, 254, 279; as propagandist, 94, 129–132; and George Raft, 123–125, 126; and Ronald Reagan, 117, 118, 119, 178–180; and Wolfgang Reinhardt, 100; his relationship with writers, 154–155; and Rin-Tin-Tin, 42, 43, 44; and Richard Rodgers, 84–85; and Franklin Roosevelt, 93–94, 146; and scandal involving his wife, 136–138; scandals dealt with by, 113–114; and Frank Sinatra, 254–257; sole screen appearance of, 31, 37; sovereignty of, 67, split between Wallis and, 141–143, 148; stock sold by, 160; and strike at Warner Bros., 163–164; and talking motion pictures, 55–57, 64–65; and television, 190, 192–199; tennis enjoyed by, 134–136; and three-dimensional movies, 190–191; tribute to, 289–290; his troubles with actors, 104–120 *passim*, 143–145; and Warner Bros. Pictures, 40; Washington fiasco of, 164–165; and John Wayne, 224; wealth of, 112; and Loretta Young, 83–84; and Darryl Zanuck, 44, 45, 64, 88, 231–232, 233
FILMS: *Bonnie and Clyde*, 280–281; *Camelot*, 279, 284–286; *Casablanca*, 139–143; *The Chapman Report*, 232–233; *Confessions of a Nazi Spy*, 129–130; *Dirty Little Billy*, 292–294, 300; *42nd Street*, 85; *The Great Race*, 265–266; *The Jazz Singer*, 59–62; *Jimmy* (stage musical), 291–292; *Johnny Belinda*, 167–169; *Little Caesar*, 77–78; *The Maltese Falcon*, 126–127; *A Midsummer Night's Dream*, 98, 99; *Mildred Pierce*, 151–152; *Mission to Moscow*, 146–147, 164; *Mister Roberts*, 215–216; *My Fair Lady*, 247–248, 259–263, 264; *My Four Years in Germany*, 35–36, 129; *Now, Voyager*, 134; *The Old Man and the Sea*, 216, 217; *The Prince and the Showgirl*, 221–222; *PT 109*, 238–241, 248; *1776*, 294–300; *The Silver Chalice*, 219–221; *The Spirit of St. Louis*, 216; *A Star Is Born*, 222–224; *A Streetcar Named Desire*, 185–187; *Wait Until Dark*, 281–284; *Whatever Happened to Baby Jane?*, 233–234; *Who's Afraid of Virginia Woolf?*, 266–278; *Yankee Doodle Dandy*, 132–133
Warner, Jack M. (Junior, son), 30, 41, 69, 102, 103, 306; break between Warner and, 229–230; his father's automobile accident, 228–229; last meeting between Warner and, 304; omission of, from Warner's autobiography, 249; his relations with his father, 169, 229
Warner, Lewis (nephew), 66, 72
Warner, Lina Basquette (Mrs. Sam), 48–49, 54, 56, 60–61, 73–74
Warner, Lita Basquette (niece), 49, 73–74
Warner, Milton (brother), 12, 120
Warner, Pearl Eichelbaum (mother), 9, 56, 57, 94; death of, 102–103; family of, 10–17; golden anniversary of, 49; marriage of, 10; her sons' marriages, 30, 41–42, 48